WITNESS
TO THE TRUTH

Lessons learned by a veteran journalist
through four decades of watching the church

LOUIS MOORE

HANNIBAL BOOKS
www.hannibalbooks.com

"For this I have been born, and for this I have come into the world, to bear witness to the truth. Everyone who is of the truth hears my voice" (John 18:37).

Published by
Hannibal Books
PO Box 461592
Garland, TX 75046-1592
Copyright Louis Moore 2008
All Rights Reserved
Printed in the United States of America
by Lightning Source, La Vergne, TN
Cover design by Greg Crull
Family photo on page 345 by Luke Edmonson, Edmonson Photography
Unless otherwise indicated, all Scripture taken from the Holy Bible,
New International Version, copyright 1973, 1978, 1984
by International Bible Society
ISBN 978-1-934749-20-3
Library of Congress Control Number 2008928113

TO ORDER ADDITIONAL COPIES, SEE PAGE 351

What Others Are Saying About This Book:

Louis Moore's account of his career as a journalist, his own faith journey, and his detailed memories of historic religious events weave an entertaining and masterful read. *Witness to the Truth* gives readers a candid, ringside seat to the political wrangling inside the Southern Baptist Convention over the past three decades.

Debra L. Mason, Executive Director
Religion Newswriters Association

Louis Moore, who is known as the nation's dean of religion writers, presents a fresh, personal perspective on some of the most significant events in religious history during the past 40 years. I felt fortunate to work with Louis during some of the crucial times he describes. Followers of religious history, journalism students, and the average newspaper reader will all gain insights from what Louis shares.

Tommy Miller
Roger Tatarian Chair in Journalism, California State University, Fresno, CA
Former managing editor, *Houston Chronicle*
Recipient, one of Poynter Institute of Journalism's 15 outstanding journalism
        professors in the U.S.

These life experiences offer spiritual insights into the church world you will find nowhere else. This rare book by my friend and Christian leader Louis Moore reveals inside operations of the church world as few have ever had opportunity to view it. *Witness to the Truth* is choice information for all church leaders and concerned Christians.

Milburn Wilson, Ph.D.
Director, LifeBuilders Center for Biblical Discipleship and Counseling
Sunnyvale First Baptist Church, Sunnyvale, TX

Louis Moore is a living witness to the innerworkings of many faiths and especially to the diverse elements among Southern Baptists. Extremely eloquent and very courageous in truthful revelations of his observations, Louis writes in a captivating, storyteller manner. Read this book so you will have the benefit of this reporter's objective viewpoint of ecumenism and his life as a Southern Baptist.

Alice Dykeman, United Methodist layperson
Founder, Religious Communications Council, Dallas-Fort Worth Chapter
Dallas, TX

Dedicated to

my granddaughter—

Caroline Grace Moore—

standard-bearer into the next generation.

May you always walk in the truth.

Acknowledgments

Two women in my life badgered the daylights out of me until this book was done. My wife, **Kay Moore**, and my daughter, **Katie Welch**, insisted that my experiences over the years were more than just "Dad-yarns" and might actually blaze trails for others. "Yes, dear(s)" is a response I do well, so here's the project you envisioned for me. Thanks, you two, for believing in me and helping me with always-perfect hindsight. Readers can thank Kay for the storyteller's touch added to my cerebral recountings; Katie is the brains behind the book's design.

Thanks to my son, **Matthew Moore,** whose career in today's (vastly different) version of the communications industry is an enjoyment to behold. I appreciate his modeling Christian integrity in an era far more challenging than the one I was dealt. For this has he been born.

To our in-law children, **Marcie Moore** and **Casey Welch**— boundless thanks for loving our offspring and helping them fulfill their own ministry callings in their lives.
God blessed us with you.

To our four loved ones—**Grace Moore, Mable Wheeler, H. Buford Wheeler** (now in His presence) and **Frances Oyler** (at 101, our present inspiration)—thanks for being the impetus for our return, for good, to Texas in 2000. In an extraordinarily rewarding career pilgrimage, God truly saved
the best for me until last.

Contents

Foreword   11

Prologue
View from the Skybox   15

Chapter 1
That Nothing Be Wasted   22

Chapter 2
Union Card   31

Chapter 3
Ecclesiastical Dog-Eat-Dog   42

Chapter 4
Smoking Pistol   55

Chapter 5
A Good Assumption   64

Chapter 6
Household Word   75

Chapter 7
Wrong (or Right?)-Way Corrigans   81

Chapter 8
Go to Your Brother   87

Chapter 9
Nowhere to Go but Up   97

Chapter 10
An Episcopal Priest!   107

Chapter 11
Of Plans and Popes   115

Chapter 12
The President Next Door   128

Chapter 13
Never a Straight Line   136

Chapter 14
Helping the Cause   151

Chapter 15
  Woo, Pig! Sooie!   163
Chapter 16
  I Just Marvel   180
Chapter 17
  For the Pharaoh Who Knew Not Joseph   195
Chapter 18
  Learning Curve   204
Chapter 19
  Leaving the Lights Off   217
Chapter 20
  The Big Flush   239
Chapter 21
  The Alma Mater Matter   257
Chapter 22
  World Apart   271
Chapter 23
  When the Wind Blows   286
Chapter 24
  Better Than Sacrifice   297
Chapter 25
  Reborn Again!   311
Chapter 26
  Sing On!   328

Where Are They Now?   334
Photo Album   339
Index   346
Guide for Student Journalists   350

Foreword

As every elementary-school science student knows, Galileo is credited with developing the technology that gave us the modern telescope. But the gifted Italian's skills really lay as a physicist, mathematician, and astronomer rather than as an inventor. His extraordinary scientific genius is what got him in trouble with the Catholic Church. In 1632 he published *Dialogue Concerning the Two Chief World Systems,* a book that put forth in systematic fashion proof that the Earth moved. This contradicted hundreds of years of Catholic Church teaching that the Earth was absolutely static and that all the other observable objects, including the sun, moved around the Earth.

For this heresy, Galileo was brought before the infamous Inquisition. He was forced to renounce the idea that the Earth moved. Rather than prison he was subjected to house arrest for the rest of his life. That meant that one of the most gifted scientific minds in history would never teach again. In renouncing his work, Galileo was forced to make a humiliating confession while he was on his knees before the Inquisition. Historians have never confirmed this, but tradition has always held that, as he was rising from his knees, he muttered under his breath, "And yet it moves," referring to the motion of the Earth. It's one of those stories that, if it's not true, it should be.

Galileo died in 1642. In 1992, 350 years after his death, Pope John Paul II acknowledged regret for the actions of the Inquisition and said that the information on which Galileo's conviction had been based was, in fact, false. The truth emerged, finally.

Unfortunately, the truth frequently gets hidden in religion-related matters. This intriguing work, *Witness to the Truth: Lessons learned by a veteran journalist through four decades of watching the church,* by Louis Moore contains many such examples. But an overarching and consistent truth is also contained here. The truth is simply this: Despite all the crazy, mean-spirited, arrogant, wrong-headed and ungodly things people have done and continue to do in the name of the church, a living and caring God continues to be involved in the world.

I tell the Galileo story here not to pick on the Catholic Church. Plenty of modern history exists to pick on; Louis does so here. But Louis also notes that Pope John Paul II was one of the most charismatic, important, and beloved leaders in religious history. His message of God's unfailing love and grace will continue to empower the Catholic Church believers of all faiths for many years hence.

Louis is unusually qualified to focus his considerable reportorial skills on the dramatic changes he has observed in the church during the last 40 years. His training and experience from both journalism and the seminary provide a broadened perspective on the complexity of the issues. His training as a journalist makes him an astute observer of people and their motives as well as of events big and small. His seminary training affords him a theological background to understand the currents that have reshaped so much of the religious landscape in the post-World War II era.

His work here is not intended as an exhaustive history of any specific faith or denomination, even though he does have and shares numerous insights on the upheaval in the Southern Baptist Convention that began in the late 1970s. This is rather a reminiscence of a skilled observer who had firsthand and inside knowledge of so many events that affected the spiritual lives of so many. Readers will pay particular attention to his analysis of the "passive-aggressive history" of Baptists and how they dealt with the rise of the fundamentalist movement. It is often not a pretty picture on either side of the dispute. And he reveals fascinating detail on how the word *fundamentalist* became attached early on to the conservative movement among the Baptists.

Other denominational conflicts are noted here, including those of the Lutheran Church-Missouri Synod, the movement for and the ultimate failure of ecumenism in the United States, the liberation theology in Latin America, squabbles among the

United Methodists and the Episcopalians, and of course the issue involving Baptists and Louis' alma mater, Baylor University. In so many instances over so many years, the only constant is the failure of human beings thinking they were carrying out God's will.

This is also the personal journey of a man of great faith who happened to be called a journalist. In this book, Louis Moore doesn't speak fully of the changes he helped effect on religious journalism. So I will. He recounts here how he became religion editor of the *Houston Chronicle*, so I won't belabor the point. He was fortunate to be in a position of prominence at a time when Houston was defining itself as an international city with a wonderful mix of virtually every significant religion in the world. He was also fortunate to work in secular media in a time when newspapers were willing to commit significant resources to cover events and trends that mattered, rather than the sound-bite mentality that has affected so many news organizations today.

Louis was not the first religion editor at a major newspaper. But until the 1970s, religion writing mostly involved the major scandal, the significant event that attracted large crowds or major policy or doctrine changes—Vatican Council II being but one example. What Louis did was to take the day-to-day spiritual life that was so important to so many millions of people of so many faiths and give it voice in the mainstream media. He reported what happened beyond the pulpit changes, the fundraising to build new facilities, or the ecumenical breakfasts that involved all religious leaders in the community. He reported on what faith really meant to people and how they internalized that belief to face the challenges of the 20th century and beyond. And he did so in a fair, comprehensive, and elegant style. His impact on religion reporting cannot be overestimated.

The book has constant references to a remarkable woman, Kay Moore. She has been Louis' partner for this lifelong journey. She is a woman of extraordinary talent, independence, and faith. She has made her own impact on journalism and on the lives of all who have known her.

I have had the pleasure of knowing them both for more than 30 years—first as a friend, then as an editor, and now, with all of us in second careers, as a friend again. Louis and Kay continue to have a positive effect on journalism and faith through a successful book-publishing company. The fact that Louis understood his calling so clearly at such an early age is remarkable. And he was fortunate to find Kay to share the joys and the occasional heartache of life as we know it.

Indeed, as Louis notes in the following pages, many of those of the narrow mind, religiously speaking, will be surprised to meet others of different faiths in heaven. In his 40 years on the religion beat, Louis has had the chance to know many of those of the narrow mind. And so do we all.

Tony Pederson
Professor and Belo Distinguished Chair in Journalism
Southern Methodist University, Dallas, TX
Former editor, *Houston Chronicle*

Prologue

View from the Skybox

Bending over the counter of the small kitchenette, the middle-aged homemaker carefully spread a layer of grape jelly to cover the crusty bread slices that soon would be sandwiches for her husband and some of his friends in the next room.

Adjacent to her, leaning over several sheets of waxed paper, two other women presided over the peanut-butter side of the sandwich-making assembly line.

This might have been a typical noontime scene in any home in America, except that the woman wielding the jelly-spreader was Nancy Pressler, wife of Texas State District Court Judge H. Paul Pressler III, who was in the beginning stages of dramatically transforming the Southern Baptist Convention. The friends who gathered around Pressler and awaited their sandwiches represented names that were soon to become the most powerful forces in the SBC—the nation's largest Protestant denomination—and who would be Pressler's operatives in the SBC's legendary conservative turnaround.

The kitchenette the women were using was stationed in a "skybox" high above the basketball arena of the Houston Summit, then the home court for the Houston Rockets professional team. Though everything about this particular scene bespoke of Houston's elite watching a major playoff game below, the subject *du jour* had nothing whatsoever to do with the sport of basketball. Instead, all eyes were fixed on the 1979 annual SBC session meeting about 100 feet below the elegant viewing area.

As this scene unfolded in front of me, I marveled that I

was there—actually *there!*—witnessing firsthand what would become one of the most important developments in 20th-century Christianity—the transformation of the Southern Baptist Convention from a little-known (outside of the South) church group with a distinctively Southern Democratic style into one of the most powerful conservative political and social forces in the United States of America.

I had no crystal ball to tell me the exact details of the future or the full implications of what I was seeing. I only knew, deep down inside of myself, that I (as the lone reporter in the room) managed that day to have a ringside seat to something truly cataclysmic.

This was the same feeling I had experienced four months earlier at an airport in Mexico City when I stood on the tarmac and observed a highly youthful and vibrant Pope John Paul II descend the stairway from his just-landed airplane. Reaching the bottom, the pontiff quickly bent all the way to the ground, with his face brushing the asphalt surface under his feet. He stooped so far over that the huge collar atop his long, flowing robe literally cascaded down around and covered his entire head.

Standing only about 10 feet away (with only a handful of other reporters who happened to be that close to the scene), for a brief moment I thought the pope had slipped and fallen in what would surely be a highly embarrassing public spectacle on a Mexico City runway. My mind raced back to about 12 hours earlier when a modest earthquake had shaken the entire Mexico City basin and prompted many to see a connection between the trembling ground and the expected arrival of the Holy Father from Rome.

Now the poor fellow has tripped, I thought. *This will confirm in many people's minds the belief that Pope John Paul II should never be traveling on this side of the globe.*

But I soon realized that his deep, dramatic waistbend was totally deliberate, as the pontiff stooped to give a history-making kiss to the ground upon which he stepped. It was a symbolic way of saying to Mexico (his first trip as pope outside Italy) that he loved the country and its people voluminously and was humbled by being on its soil. This was a gesture I would watch *PJP2* (as I grew to call him to myself) repeat again and again as he established a reputation as a modern, globe-trotting pope and made countless goodwill visits to bring the Church to the world.

For the rest of 1979, I looked back on these mind-bending events of February and June with a tremendous sense of awe and amazement. I could hardly believe that the little boy who had grown up on the wrong side of the river in Oklahoma City and daydreamed of someday being able to write about what religious life was really like all across the globe was actually an eyewitness to the beginning of two such monumental religious events of the 20th century.

These two earthshaking happenings were but a tip of the iceberg, however, to the many events I would personally witness that shaped the modern church during my journalistic career that now has spanned more than four decades.

As I examine my life as a secular reporter and editor, columnist, denominational journalist, book author, publisher, and ongoing observer of American happenings in religion, I am astounded that, again and again, I have managed to turn up on the cutting edge of so many important religious developments that have shaped the modern church.

For example:

• In 1972 I was present in the living room of a small bungalow in the Montrose area of Houston as a group of Muslim men designated the house as the first mosque in Texas—a house that would go on to help launch the spread of Islam into everyday American life.

• In 1973 I was on the meeting floor in Louisville, KY, when the Episcopal General Convention in its triennial session altered its definition of *marriage*, a decision that became the launching pad for numerous social issues Episcopalians and other Christians face today.

• In 1982 my wife, Kay, and I found ourselves as early trailblazers in the emerging two-paycheck marriage lifestyle, which drew great ecclesiastical ire because churches stood to lose their great source of volunteer labor as women poured back into the outside employment workforce in droves. The resulting book we wrote, *When You Both Go to Work: How the Two-Paycheck Family Can Stay Active in the Church,* landed us on the Jim and Tammy Bakker *PTL* television show at the height of the televangelists' popularity and just on the brink of the Bakkers' scandal-rocked fall from the ministry.

• In 1985, I managed to be in Moscow and Leningrad visiting in the homes of Jewish "Refuseniks" who were being held against their will just as Mikhail Gorbachev ascended to power. I participated in clandestine meetings with Refusenik leadership on the eve of the Soviet Union's fall and as the stage was being set for these persecuted ones to gain freedom to leave for their motherland.

• In 1989, in accepting a job as a denominational journalist, I found myself in the first wave of "new-regime" employees after the SBC's denominational schism began to make major inroads among the rank and file. Thus, on the scene in Nashville, at the heartthrob of SBC life, I became an inside observer to the crumbling of a former religious establishment that had held sway for decades and the emergence of a new religious order that was beginning to take root.

• In 1999 I visited China at the very moment in which the Chinese government was cracking down on unregistered "house churches," including those that were enabled by clandestine American missionaries fronting as regular business people in that country.

• In 2006, I happened to be serving a term as a fill-in trustee on a denomination board just as a fresh and mind-blowing move unfolded in Southern Baptist life—a move to endorse glossolalia (speaking in tongues and ecstatic utterances), a practice that would have horrified and thoroughly offended Southern Baptists of previous generations.

And these are merely a few of the times that, for one reason or another, I looked up and saw that, once again, I stood on the precipice of contemporary religious history.

Not for one minute do I believe all these experiences happened to me because I was some sort of super-journalist or someone whose work performance merited special treatment. In most cases I was simply doing the job I'd been assigned.

Nor would I leave the impression that all my experiences have been professionally and personally rewarding. While many represent the true zeniths of my career, in other cases the age-old desire to "shoot the messenger" prevailed. Oftentimes, since I was covering cutting-edge, controversial events, readers' angst would be directed at me for reporting on a squabble rather than directed at the issues themselves.

Separating myself as an objective bystander has been simpler in some instances than in others—especially those in which my economic livelihood and that of my family was at stake. The perspective of history, hindsight, and maturity always causes one to view things more philosophically and be more charitable to his protagonists than at the period in which the fur was flying.

But for whatever His reasons and in His providence, God saw fit to place me in "the right place at the right time"—contemporary religious history in the making—usually with my journalist/observer's notepad in hand in some sort of capacity. I've seen more than my fair share of what God (and His competing gods) have been doing over the past half-century, both in the United States and around the world.

What I've seen and observed of religious life in the U.S. and elsewhere is something I feel compelled to summarize for my readers here. I see it as being a good steward of the experiences God has bequeathed me.

In doing so, I don't intend to write religious history as a collection of footnotes from other people or a laborious tome of dates, times, and precise details bundled into some kind of religious textbook. I will leave those tasks to others.

My goal is to share the feelings, the sights, the sounds, the behind-the-scenes nuances of all that these eyes have seen, these ears have heard, and this body has experienced as just an ordinary guy who happened to be in some of the most extraordinary spots at just the right moment.

Beyond just a collection of memoirs, however, I have another, more overarching goal. I want to reveal certain core truths, discerned from my unique vantage point, that I've gleaned about organized religion—truths that link together Southern Baptists, Roman Catholics, Presbyterians, charismatics, and even to some extent Jews, Mormons, and Buddhists. While their theologies and worldviews differ, so often the personalities of their leaders and their social and psychological interactions with others reflect similar traits, characteristics, motivations, and attitudes. Each of these 26 core truths corresponds to a chapter in the book. Some of them form the basis of a central theme for an entire chapter, while others may relate to one or several illustrations the chapter contains.

I believe that the person in the pew—as well as the pastor or church leader—can benefit by seeing common-denominator patterns that link the fellowship of faith—patterns that have little to do with doctrines or belief systems. I believe that the faithful will be enlightened (and even comforted) to realize that the demagogue they experience as their United Methodist bishop is really no different than the egocentric megachurch pastor in another's Baptist tradition—that a denominational bureaucrat is a denominational bureaucrat regardless of whether the Lutherans or the Presbyterians are paying his or her salary.

I hope readers will also be gladdened to see that much good work is being done in God's name by believers all over the world but also be troubled and inspired to realize how much more effort is yet needed.

I believe that when some of the hidebound arrive at heaven's portals someday and begin to spot faces among the *great cloud of witnesses* (Heb. 12:1), they may be surprised to see the Episcopalian who lived down the block or the Catholic whose church they passed on the way to theirs. I suspect that one of the most frequent comments heard in the hallways of heaven may be a surprised "Oh, really?" as a narrow-minded newcomer gives some veterans there a shocked once-over.

As I tell my story and share these insights, I do so through the eyes of one who early on claimed as his life's verse John 18:37, "*For this I have been born, and for this I have come into the world, to bear witness to the truth. Every one who is of the truth hears my voice.*" This was Jesus' claim as He stood before Pilate, but it also became my marching orders and the lens through which I focused as I attempted to share religious life with my readers over the decades.

That's again my goal as I sincerely pass on to you the truths that I've been privileged to witness.

Chapter 1

That Nothing Be Wasted

Truth No. 1: God can use any situation or circumstance at His disposal, both inside and outside the church, to fulfill His purposes on earth. In His great economy, nothing is wasted.

What makes one an incessant hound of the news?

What shapes the kind of personality that must look under every stone, every bed, and every chair cushion just for the unadulterated act of finding out what's there?

What kind of early orientation would lay the groundwork for some of the on-the-edge scrapes I would find myself in during later life?

Curiosity about the world around me has defined me from my earliest days. When I was in elementary school, my mother and teachers forever scolded me for never remaining in my seat, for always questioning others, and for generally collecting information about whatever recent interest propelled me.

If a fire, fight, car accident, or some other major incident occurred somewhere in our southwest Oklahoma City neighborhood, I wanted to go "check it out" in person. If a new rumor was circulating, I'd pounce on it like a dog on a bone to extract more juicy morsels of news. When my parents weren't looking, I'd dig holes in our backyard just to see what turned up.

When I was 13, I became so fascinated with how the workers were installing a new roof on our home that I waited until the roofers took a lunch break and then climbed their ladder to take a look. At the top, I suddenly felt the ladder collapsing around me. The next thing I knew, I was hospitalized with a broken arm and nose. Even that didn't stop my insatiable curiosity,

Today, some teachers and parents might label as *hyperactive* the kind of child I was. I still consider myself absolutely normal for my simple interest in just about anything and everything in my world.

Early on, my curiosity began to focus increasingly on all things religious. I would try to imagine what the world was like before God began to exist. That futile exercise inevitably led me back to the conviction that God must always have existed. *After all, how could God ever have been born? Did He have parents?* I wondered. *Preposterous,* I concluded.

I loved to read my Bible and then imagine what Jesus, Abraham, Peter, Paul, and all the other leading biblical characters must really have been like. One of my favorite activities was challenging my Sunday-school teachers on whatever point they seemed to be trying to make in the lesson that day. If they said *black*, I said *white* just for the fun of it—and also to watch them squirm.

When I was 9, I decided to "walk the aisle" at our church and make my public profession that Jesus was going to be my Savior and Lord for the rest of my life. I knew this was something I had to do because I had listened so intently to all the arguments my teachers and our pastor had given me about Christ as the only savior of the world. I truly wanted to be a follower of Jesus.

A few weeks later I was baptized in what had to have been the coldest water available in Oklahoma City in early March. When I slipped into my white baptismal gown, I was so excited and curious about the other baptismal candidates and what the congregation would look like from the baptistery vantage point that I forgot what my daddy had told me about removing my underwear before I put on my swimsuit to go under my robe. Since we had forgotten to bring an extra pair, he said I needed to conserve the dry ones I had on for when I would re-dress a few minutes later. Sitting in the pew afterward, the hour-long worship service seemed like an all-day event to my freezing, wet backside. To this day, I can still hear my mother's reaction when we got home and she spotted the telltale signs of my wet undergarments. The commotion almost over-shadowed the real significance of why I was in the water in the first place.

Reared in Southern Baptist churches, I thoroughly soaked up every activity (Sunday school, Training Union, Royal Ambassadors, church camp, and so forth) available to a young boy springing up in the 1950s. These forums offered me won-derful opportunities to ask questions, debate issues, and gener-ally investigate everything I wanted to know about the Christian faith. As soon as I was old enough, I signed up for a week at the Falls Creek Baptist Assembly, truly a rite of pas-sage for most Oklahoma Baptist teens of my era. This again presented more wonderful opportunities to ask questions and explore possibilities. I especially enjoyed trekking out into nature with my Bible in hand to pray and read the Scriptures and then to think about all the ramifications of what I had read.

Singing in the choir in one of the evening worship services at Falls Creek, I became convinced that God was calling me into some kind of special ministry. Since I couldn't imagine myself as a pastor and since I eagerly listened whenever I heard a "foreign" missionary give a testimony, I presumed God was saying that overseas missions was the calling for me. Having just read Tom Dooley's *The Night They Burned the*

Mountain about his missionary work in faraway Laos, I just knew that my life's work had to be that of a medical missionary, too. *I wanna be just like Dr. Tom Dooley*, I told myself. Years later I realized that Tom Dooley was a Roman Catholic—and good Southern Baptist boys weren't supposed to have Roman Catholic missionaries as their heroes. Nevertheless, to this day I still see Dr. Dooley as one of my spiritual mentors. Had he not died while I was in high school, I know beyond a shadow of a doubt that I would have tried to locate him and talk with him personally after I became religion editor of the *Houston Chronicle*. Such was and is my nature.

Somehow I failed to get the message that being a good Southern Baptist boy meant I was supposed to stay with like kind. During my teen-age years, I thoroughly enjoyed slipping out of my Southern Baptist church and driving over to visit the nearby Roman Catholic church for Christmas Eve Mass, the neighborhood Pentecostal church for an excitement-filled Wednesday-evening healing service, and the fascinating circular auditorium of the biggest Methodist church in Oklahoma City for a "cultural experience." In doing so, I wasn't aligning with the theology of any of these churches; I just found seeing what they did and what they believed fascinating. I found the burning incense at the Catholic church rather quaint and the unusual vocalization at the Pentecostal church rather humorous. I was not repulsed by them; they just made me all the more curious about why religious people did things so differently from each other!

* * * * * * *

About this time, two back-to-back events occurred that changed my life unalterably.

25

From as early as I can remember, my parents talked about my daddy's "heart condition." From time to time when Daddy was in the hospital, Mother would intimate that Daddy probably wouldn't be around when I was grown. That seemed almost as far-fetched as the story my parents told about how my daddy managed to contract this "heart condition." Daddy was 34 when the Japanese bombed Pearl Harbor and plunged the U.S. into World War II. Like his father and brothers, Daddy often had tried his hand at carpentry and was really good at it. As the U.S. geared up for war, the U.S. Navy pressed forward with forming and staffing the Seabees, otherwise known as the Naval Construction Battalion. Daddy was a natural fit for the Seabees, so he joined them and went off to war. He served in several battles in the South Pacific. His final battle occurred when General Douglas MacArthur made good on his promise to return to the Philippines. Daddy was there on the beach on the Island of Leyte, where today stands a huge statute in tribute to the great general's return. Daddy, however, suffered a massive heart attack on the beach during the early days of the battle and spent the next 11 months in naval hospitals, first in the South Pacific, then back home in America in the San Diego Naval Hospital.

Until later in life, I was somewhat embarrassed by this story. Other fathers got shot or gave their lives on the battlefield. My daddy had a heart attack in the midst of the war and had to be carried off the battlefield on a stretcher! Good grief! That wasn't exactly something I thought I should brag about.

Then about five years ago a friend loaned me a copy of a book about the history of the Seabees. The day I got it, I stayed up all night to read it. Much to my surprise, the book described the horrible stress under which the poor Seabees worked as they relentlessly followed the advancing soldiers onto the battlefields to build bunkers, airfields, roads, and all the necessary support facilities for our military. Though unarmed, the Seabees were targets for the Japanese as much as the regular soldiers were.

Then my eyes suddenly fixated on a statistic that instantly changed my thinking. The stress had been so horrible on these men that 10 percent of all Seabees participating in any given battle either suffered heart attacks or suffered mental break-downs from the stress they were under. The book said these wounded Seabees were considered as heroic as the men who had actually been shot on the battlefield.

Unfortunately, I never was able to tell Daddy what I had learned—that he really was a war hero after all. When I was 16, Daddy suffered a final massive heart attack and died quickly. That left my widowed mother with me and my two younger siblings to support.

On the heels of Daddy's death, Mother asked me to accompany her to the local Veterans Administration office to find out how she could collect on Daddy's $10,000 life-insurance policy. The nice gentleman at the VA who helped us stepped out of his office to go get Daddy's file. When he returned, his words continued to reverberate in my ears for many years later.

Daddy's heart attack was considered a battle injury—a "service-connected disability," the insurance man said. Since his death occurred because of this disability, the VA would pay for the college education of any of Daddy's minor children. The VA also would give my mother a certain amount of money each month to help her rear my brother, sister, and me until we reached college age.

All the way home, my mother and I kept comparing notes just to be sure we had heard the same words.

Because of Daddy's illness, Mother had to work as a government secretary to support our family. Money was in short supply. Living in Oklahoma City's southwest quadrant—not the more affluent north side that was situated across the Canadian River—we lacked material things that others seemed to have. People on our side of town didn't, as a rule, back then aspire to higher educations. I had presumed that I would have to work full time and go to the local state-supported college part time, if I was to attend college at all. When the VA paperwork was completed, I realized that the range of universities I could now afford to consider was far greater than I could ever have imagined. It had the feel of a major miracle!

Suddenly my world changed forever. I really could get the education to be the missionary I wanted to be! My first choice was the largest Baptist university in the world—Baylor University in Waco, TX—but it was out of reach financially. So I spent a year at Oklahoma Baptist University in Shawnee, OK, during which time something else amazing happened. As a part of President Lyndon B. Johnson's "Great Society" program, the Social Security program was extended so that a child of a deceased parent could continue to receive Social Security payments through his or her college years; previously the payments stopped when a child reached age 18. I was in the first group to qualify under the new law. The $40.40 I received each month from Social Security provided the exact amount of money I needed to be able to transfer from OBU to Baylor.

I have always been grateful to the Social Security program for this benefit. Subsequently, over the years I have never once complained about having to pay my FICA taxes. I thank God for Franklin Delano Roosevelt's wisdom in creating the program before I was even a gleam in my parents' eyes. Thus two different governmental actions had the role of helping fulfill God's purpose in my life in totally surprising ways. The Scripture promises that *the Lord will fulfill his purpose for me* (Ps. 138:8). In my case He used these governmental entities to do just that.

Many times the church sees itself as the exclusive be-all and end-all for God's work to be done in the world. Some church people think that the body of believers represents the sole major enabler to see God's will accomplished in human lives.

But in my career as a Christian journalist, I saw countless times in which God was at work using secular, or non-church, circumstances or events for His purposes, just as this happened with me.

After all, Jimmy Carter's 1976 campaign for the presidency was the event that for all times made the term *born again* a household phrase and gave Evangelicals an unprecedented public forum to explain the tenets of their faith. (I first met Carter, by the way, when he was a lone, unnoticed governor attempting to attract attention for his presidential aspirations.) Only heaven will reveal the countless numbers of people who turned to Christ simply because a candidate in a highly secular election made this concept a matter of public discussion.

Perhaps the clearest example in modern times of God using totally secular forces to accomplish His purposes is the incident I mentioned in the Prologue that occurred in the grand finale of the former Soviet Union, when Mikail Gorbachev, a non-believer, dismantled the Evil Empire in 1991. This paved the way for Christianity's rebirth in Russia and the former Soviet satellite countries.

* * * * * * * *

Although my dream of attending the brightest gem in Baptist education's crown was realized, my euphoria about pursuing a career as a foreign missionary was short-lived. It ended my first semester at Baylor when I took—and nearly failed—my first course in French. The final nail went in that dream's coffin when the next semester I took—and also did poorly in—my first course in Spanish. I by then was face-to-face with the reality that learning a foreign language was not something I could ever do. *What about that vocational call to the ministry I experienced that evening at Falls Creek?* I asked myself. *Did I only dream that God was speaking to me in this direction?*

My despair over this reality lingered until my junior year at Baylor, when on a lark I decided to take a course in religious journalism. By the middle of that semester I suddenly realized that I hadn't misunderstood my call to the ministry; I had simply jumped to conclusions too quickly about its taking the form of foreign missions. Everything I read and learned about religious journalism seemed to fit my personality, interests, and talents as though this form of Christian service was tailor-made just for me. The awareness flowed over me almost like another conversion experience.

Throughout the next three years God showed me repeatedly that a career in religious journalism was where I belonged.

Oh, yes, and about that original, long-ago calling that I thought was to missions. Years later, when I was named to direct the media operations of the largest missions-sending agency in the world—helping young, curious, missions-oriented journalists as I had once been—I realized, to my amazement, that God definitely hadn't once made a mistake. That missions yen that once motivated a fervent, 15-year-old boy at Falls Creek wasn't wasted after all.

In God's economy, nothing ever is.

Chapter 2

Union Card

Truth No. 2: Who you know, not what you know, is what makes the difference in religious organizations. Keeping one's union card highly visible while navigating the church in America is important.

Suddenly I was asking questions, checking things out first-hand, looking under every rock, and satisfying my curiosity about all things religious and secular more than I ever had before—and getting academic credit for doing it! All the behaviors that were by now second-nature to me were shaping up to be my life's work—and I loved it.

Just after I decided to enter religious journalism, I received a call from Dave Cheavens, chair of the Baylor journalism department, who earlier had guided me when I had been in the throes of my career angst. Cheavens had been the ideal person to understand my dilemma since he was the son-in-law of J.M. Dawson, the venerated former editor of the *Baptist Standard*, Texas' Baptist state paper, which combined the blend of religion and journalism that intrigued me. Cheavens wanted me to meet David McHam, Baylor journalism professor and adviser to *The Baylor Lariat*, the Baylor student newspaper. Shortly thereafter, *Lariat* Editor Tommy Miller invited me to join the newspaper's staff as religion writer.

Within weeks I experienced my first sense of *"for this I have been born,"* as I've already mentioned about my life verse found in John 18:37. I felt as though all the disparate parts of my personality and life meshed together positively in this new role.

Before many days, however, I began seeing that being a curious journalist did have some singular drawbacks.

Not long after I joined the *Lariat* staff, Roy Harrell, director of the Baylor Baptist Student Union, inexplicably resigned his job. Since this clearly was big news on the campus religion beat, I and another *Lariat* staffer, Kay Wheeler, were assigned to "dig out" the real story behind Roy's exit. All the beleaguered Harrell would meekly tell us about the development was, "It's sort of a separation." On further digging, however, we found Roy hadn't done anything bad except to get philosophically crossways with the powerhouse state administrator of the BSU in Texas, W.F. Howard.

What to do next? Cheerfully call Dr. Howard, of course, to get his side of the story, which we expected him to openly spill. That's when I shockingly learned that "top-dog" religious leaders don't cotton to being asked questions, especially about why they did something they thought was going to be kept quiet and behind the scenes. I was shocked by Dr. Howard's gruff and evasive response. He clearly wasn't prepared for some assertive journalism students at Baylor to pummel him with questions he didn't want to answer.

Rather than discourage me, the confrontation whetted my curiosity for finding out why this leader acted so furtively. It also educated me about future head-knockers with other religious leaders who disdain reporters shining a light on their inconsistencies and on their questionable actions. Some top-dog religious leaders have self-images that lead them to believe that somehow they are above accountability for their behaviors. I was glad that I learned this fact while I was still a young person because later on it helped me understand so many higher-ups that I would encounter in religious hierarchy.

A bit later I covered a BSU gathering that I thought would be just another boring club meeting. While I pondered what story I could possibly glean from this snooze of an event, one female student suddenly burst forth rather angrily that she wasn't about to say anything in the meeting "with *The Lariat* here." Since I quickly assessed that I was the only representative of *The Lariat* in the room, that really caught my attention. Eventually I was asked to leave the meeting so the young woman could say whatever she had in mind.

The next day *The Lariat* published my first-ever newspaper column, which questioned what gave with the BSU that was so sensitive that it couldn't be discussed "with *The Lariat* here." If the BSU had secrets, these needed to be shared with the wider Baylor student body, I reasoned. *Did it have anything to do with the director's having just left?* I wondered out loud for the campus to read.

The morning after the newspaper with my column in it hit the streets, David McHam stopped me on the sidewalk outside the journalism building and told me how much he appreciated what I wrote. He also told me he thought the experience would really help me understand what religion reporting was all about if I wanted to enter that profession.

It did. I was learning that behind the smiles and glad-handing of religious folks, all is not always as sunshine-sweet as it might seem. Religious leaders like to perpetuate a "positive" image by controlling what is known and what is said about their actions. This lesson has served me well for more than 40 years. Indeed, years later I am truly grateful to the hostile BSU students, though their remarks might have smarted at the time, for helping initiate me into this reality.

The school year ended shortly thereafter; when it did, I knew I was hooked on this new profession.

* * * * * * * *

The next semester began in a catastrophic way no one could have predicted. The presses that published the student paper had barely fired up for the fall when one of the biggest tragedies ever to occur on the Baylor campus hit. Baylor Chamber of Commerce pledge John Clifton died during a late-night, off-campus hazing incident.

The Lariat newsroom was electrified with the news. Even the *Lariat* religion writer was called on to join the team covering this story of behemoth proportions. The Baylor Chamber of Commerce men's service fraternity was and still is one powerful group on the Baylor campus. In my student days, its members were generally known for their antiseptic-clean images; many were preachers-in-training. Even today, some "Chamber pots" (a frequent campus nickname) who were there when John Clifton died are prominent in some churches and in Southern Baptist circles. Chambermen were *the* people to know on campus. John Clifton's death exposed the dark side of that organization.

My assignment was to visit the Baylor Student Union and conduct a series of "person-on-the-street" interviews to get campus reaction about what happened to Clifton. That's when I met Marie Mathis, the legendary leader of the Southern Baptist Convention's Woman's Missionary Union. Years earlier Baylor had hired Mrs. Mathis to run its student union, but everyone knew how much the school relished having someone of her denominational stature on the payroll and available to advise the administration on Southern Baptist life.

I commented to Mrs. Mathis that the normally abuzz student union building was eerily quiet that day after John Clifton died. In hushed tones she responded reverentially, "Oh, it's out of respect for Chamber."

"*Respect!?*" stormed *Lariat* Editor Tommy Kennedy when I returned to the newspaper office and reported my bizarre conversation with Mrs. Mathis. "Respect! John Clifton died because of what those 'pots' did to him. And she calls the somber mood on campus *respect* for Chamber?"

Indeed, the coroner's report later showed that Clifton had been required to drink a concoction of stuff too disgusting to describe. After drinking it, Clifton had to run alongside the other Chamber pledges, who had also drunk the brew. He started to vomit, and, as the coroner determined, drowned in his own juices.

I'm thankful that Mrs. Mathis taught me that even in the worst and most degrading of circumstances (that were, by that point, attracting national headlines that pounced on physical hazing at a Christian university), some religious leaders will try to advance an unrealistic, hyped-up spin for others to see and hear. To this day, I disdain such attitudes but appreciate Mrs. Mathis' personal and powerful indoctrination while I was still a young pup of a journalist.

With omnipotent Chamber furious at *The Baylor Lariat*'s persistent and dogged coverage of the organization's worst nightmare, *Lariat* staff members had to hang together like an army under siege. We learned about the *esprit de corps* that was necessary on a professional newspaper staff to produce a quality product day in and day out in the midst of public antagonism. Even though that year I bagged the best overall scholastic grades I'd ever brought home, I mostly remember spending what seemed like every waking hour either in the *Lariat* office or out rounding up stories to cover.

* * * * * * * *

Since I was in my senior year, my secondary focus was on getting ready for seminary, which I now planned to attend the next fall. Even though I had decided being a foreign missionary wasn't my true calling, I still believed I needed theological training to be the best religious journalist I could be. After toying with the idea of enrolling in a seminary in Wales on the British Isles, I determined to attend Southern Baptist Theological Seminary in Louisville, KY. All my Baylor religion professors vowed that Southern was where the "real action" was in Baptist seminary education in those days—that its professors were the most erudite and respected anywhere. I certainly didn't want to miss out on that kind of quality! Besides, I had an image of Louisville being "in the East" (anything above Arkansas was East to someone from the southwest side of Oklahoma City), which sounded exotic and alluring and somehow vastly different from where I had grown up. Because of my internal programming to check out, investigate, and explore the unknown, living in far-off Louisville sounded right up my alley.

This decision gave me my first experience with genuine, *prima facia* Baptist controversy—and was an early hint of the entangled years ahead for the denomination. To complete my seminary enrollment, I had to obtain a statement from my home church that it supported my sense of call to the ministry. I presumed that meant I needed a letter from Capitol Hill Baptist Church in Oklahoma City, where I had spent my growing-up years and which had ordained me into the ministry as part of my seminary prep. I wrote the pastor, Dr. Hugh R. Bumpas, and gave him a copy of the seminary's endorsement papers.

A few weeks later, Dr. Bumpas called me with some very disturbing news. The church had voted down my request. He quickly assured me that it had nothing to do with me personally—that the church supported and loved me very much. He said some in the congregation were greatly troubled by the "liberal" direction that they perceived Southern had taken in recent years. He said the opinion had been voiced that the church loved me too much to see me "thrown into the lion's den" with "a bunch of liberal seminary professors."

Dr. Bumpas said the church would approve my endorsement if I would switch and attend Southwestern Baptist Theological Seminary in Fort Worth because it was perceived as conservative. I told him I was truly convinced Southern was where God was pointing me. I told him I couldn't explain it, but this was something I felt deep in my heart. Dr. Bumpas lovingly agreed to support my decision and do what he could to help me.

Later I learned that Dr. Bumpas forthwith phoned Dr. Duke K. McCall, president of Southern Seminary in Louisville, and interrogated him directly about whether the rumors about liberalism at the seminary were correct. Dr. Bumpas reported to Capitol Hill Baptist Church that Dr. McCall assured him that Southern was not liberal but instead was bedrock conservative.

For years I wondered how a pastor of a relatively unknown church on Oklahoma City's southside would have the audacity to call the president of the oldest and most prestigious Southern Baptist seminary and inquire about liberalism on campus. Later I learned that Dr. Bumpas had served on the blue-ribbon SBC committee that wrote the 1963 *Baptist Faith and Message*, the denomination's doctrinal statement, which some today erroneously try to call a creed. I imagine Duke McCall didn't want to get on the bad side of this ostensibly backward yet influential Baptist from Oklahoma, so he must have told Bumpas the words he wanted to hear. Just after their conversation, my acceptance papers to seminary arrived in the mail.

* * * * * * *

Within weeks of that, however, another truly astonishing
event that shaped my destiny lunged down the pipe.

I knew the journalism faculty was worried that no clear-cut
candidate had emerged as a frontrunner for editor of *The
Baylor Lariat* for the next year. Given the upheaval on campus
in the aftermath of the painful John Clifton/Chamber episode
and the small but growing anti-Vietnam War sentiment among
students, the paper desperately needed a strong helmsman who
could fend off "liberal" accusations being flung at the *Lariat*
from many sides, including Chamber's well-connected friends
and alums who occupied some of the key Baptist pulpits in
Texas.

On a lark, I said one day to David McHam, "For two cents
I would stay here next year, go to graduate school in the religion department, and throw my hat in the ring to be editor of
The Lariat." Instead of brushing off my words, McHam
instantly whisked me to Dave Cheavens' office for me to
repeat what I had just said. Mr. Cheavens leaped from his seat,
pumped my hand enthusiastically (*practically hugged me* is
more accurate), and immediately pronounced his blessings on
the idea. He then pointed me toward the religion department's
office to visit with Dr. Ray Summers, the department chair, to
discuss graduate school. My head spun as I left Dr. Summers'
office as the reality of his concurrence soaked in.

A few days later, Dr. Abner V. McCall, Baylor president
(and no relation to the Southern's Duke McCall), strode
toward me on campus. He purposefully approached me, shook
my hand as though I were a long-lost friend, and said, "You
are a ministerial student, right? And a journalism major?" I
said *yes* to both questions. He patted me on the back and
walked off smiling. Stunned, I figured that either Mr.

Cheavens or Dr. Summers had paid a surprise visit to the president's office with the assuaging news of the new, palatable, dark-horse candidate for *Lariat* editor. Having a graduate-level ministerial student occupying the editor's office seemed to some to be the perfect antidote to the paper's recent fall from grace.

A few weeks later, Baylor students voted for my slate of electors for the Board of Publications, who then along with the journalism faculty and other faculty appointed by Dr. McCall named me editor of *The Baylor Lariat* for the 1968-1969 school year.

* * * * * * * *

Before I could write Dr. Bumpas and disclose to him that I was delaying seminary temporarily, a second major event occurred that illuminated another important quirk in religious life.

It arrived with a phone call from a denominational employee named Lynn Davis of the Baptist Sunday School Board in Nashville, TN. Lynn said he was looking for a college journalism student to spend the summer of 1968 working at Ridgecrest Baptist Assembly near Asheville, NC, as public-relations director for the conference center. He said Mr. Cheavens had recommended me. After I replied that I was interested, Lynn invited me to fly at BSSB expense to Nashville for testing and a formal interview.

The most important aspect of that trip, however, wasn't snagging the job but was a lecture Lynn gave me on denominational politics. Few people have ever talked to me so forthrightly and honestly.

I confessed to Lynn that despite my acceptance at

Southern, I still, deep down, harbored notions of attending seminary somewhere in Europe. He interrupted me rather brusquely yet almost paternally. "Louis, you need to understand some very important lessons about Southern Baptist life," he said.

"This denomination operates on the basis of union cards and networks. Your union card is your degree from one of the six Southern Baptist seminaries. Your network is your group of friends in the denomination who help out each other."

He didn't say *your conversion experience*. He didn't say *your testimony*. He didn't say *your prayer life*. He also didn't say *what you learn in seminary*.

He said, in effect, the *institution from which you receive your degree* and your *circle of friends within the denomination*. That was all.

It was enough.

What Lynn mentioned was not exclusive to my situation at that particular moment about a seminary choice.

A certain set of words or terms here or there, sprinkled among a person's credentials, can either signal a marvelous open door or can represent the kiss of death, depending on whom you know or where (and when) you went to school. Presumptions instantly will be made, labels unalterably applied, and stigmas put on.

Even today in Baptist circles, if an individual drops, for example, that he graduated from Southwestern Baptist Theological Seminary under the presidency of Dr. Russell Dilday, that simple statement, of itself, would communicate that he had received a vastly different type of theological education and would have a distinctly different set of denominational contacts than would a Southwestern graduate under the more recent presidency of Dr. Paige Patterson.

That very detail on a person's résumé could determine

whether the individual might or might not be chosen to write material for use in Baptist Sunday schools, named or overlooked for an SBC committee appointment, or considered or passed over for a church staff position.

Nor would this be something unique to Southern Baptist life. For example, among members of the Lutheran Church-Missouri Synod, mentioning that one attended Concordia Seminary in St. Louis while the cosmopolitan and urbane Dr. Robert Tietjen was president signals something vastly different about the person than would indicating that one studied there under Dr. Robert Preus, brother of the controversial firebrand conservative Synod president Dr. Jacob A.O. Preus.

* * * * * * *

At the time, when I first heard Lynn's comments, I thought they were mildly naive and humorous—that he didn't know squat about which he spoke. *Wouldn't Cambridge or Yale Divinity School appearing beside my name conjure up a higher level of respect?* I reckoned.

Before too long, though, I realized fourfold that Lynn was dead on. How blessed I was to be so "carefully taught" so early in my career! Years later, in a bizarre turn of events, when my blue-chip Baylor/Southern pedigree would be the one that netted me a peculiar form of reverse discrimination, I was thankful that Lynn's insights had, in their own way, prepared me for what lay ahead.

Chapter 3

Ecclesiastical Dog-Eat-Dog

Truth No. 3: Competition is alive and well inside the church as well as outside of it. Competition's ability to shape the church's past, present, and future can never be underestimated.

James L. Sullivan. Baker James Cauthen. Miss Alma Hunt. I met all these Southern Baptist luminaries and more during my summer job at Ridgecrest Baptist Assembly. Despite my expanding acquaintance with Southern Baptist bigwigs, my thoughts and focus were increasingly preoccupied with returning to Baylor in the fall.

Naturally I was eager to begin my much-anticipated stint as a graduate student in religion and editor of *The Baylor Lariat.*

But this longing for Waco was also piqued by a set of correspondence I received from overseas throughout the summer.

A group of Baylor students, led by one of my mentors, Dr. Glenn Hilburn of the Baylor religion faculty, was traveling through Europe and the Middle East during July and August. I was sick with envy that I couldn't accompany the group, but I lacked funds to pay for the trip, plus I needed my summer income to help cover my college bills.

However, my *Lariat* pal, Kay Wheeler, was one of the students on the whirlwind tour. A gifted writer and ever the resourceful one, Kay had managed to be named an intern for the *Baptist Standard* that summer. Her sole responsibility was to cover the Baptist Youth World Congress in Berne, Switzerland—one of the stops on the Baylor group's itinerary. Her coverage also included an interview with Billy Graham. I was devastated because I wasn't the one doing these jobs.

I soon realized that I could experience some of this trip-of-a-lifetime vicariously through Kay. I scraped up $5 to give her and included the admonition, "This is to pay for postcards and stamps for you to send me detailed reports along the way."

Just to be sure she remembered my request (and what the money was for!), I obtained the group's itinerary, including hotel addresses, so I could write her at each stop. Thus our letters crisscrossed over the ocean that summer.

After receiving several postcards from Kay, I began to realize that I was becoming overly eager to check my mailbox for her next correspondence and to write to her in return. I later learned that at that same time across the Atlantic, Kay became excited as well when she found my letters awaiting her at her hotel stops.

As she spins the story today, Kay's interest was fueled by Dr. Hilburn, who had taught us both in a religion course the previous semester and already deduced that Kay and I were ideal marriage partners for each other. "Well, look at this!" exulted the matchmaker dramatically as he delivered the mail to the tour group each evening. "Here's another letter for Kay Wheeler from Louis Moore. My. My. My!"

Actually, Kay says she had already fallen in love with me and decided I was the man of her dreams when I made my presentation to the Baylor Board of Publications the previous spring on why I should be the editor of *The Lariat*. A member of the board at the time, Kay said she admired my self-confidence under pressure as I fielded the board's questions. Dr. Hilburn's theatrics and my letters apparently played on that initial spark of interest.

In retrospect, the fact that the two of us ultimately would be drawn together was a true no-brainer. Kay, along with me, was one of the few practicing believers on the staff of *The Baylor Lariat*. Journalism isn't a profession that is particularly noted for attracting the pious. Being a bit cynical (about life in general and about religion in particular) is often part of the hard-nosed newshound stereotype. Especially during our college era, when nonconformity was the norm, *The Lariat* newsroom was a bit short on regular church attenders.

Kay was different in that respect; in many ways we were an obvious journalistic couple because of our similar backgrounds of growing up in Southern Baptist churches. Yet no one, including me, was any more driven than she was in her pursuit of a journalism career. Also like me, she considered Christian journalism to be her religious calling.

Just after I arrived back on campus that September, I (accidentally-on-purpose) encountered Kay. After she described a few adventures from her trip, I invited her to dine at my apartment to hear her entire European travelogue and her impressions of meeting Billy Graham.

Somewhere between the dinner, her voluminous number of photographs, and her descriptions of Graham, I lost track of the content of her speeches and concentrated totally on the person who was relating them.

Ah, young love! What euphoria! What bliss!

From that evening on, we were sure we wanted to share a future together.

Only one problem arose with that. We couldn't tell an absolute soul.

Lariat staffers were forbidden from dating each other. One or both of us—including me, the editor!—stood to lose our jobs if either of us breathed a word.

* * * * * * * *

To explain this seemingly bonkers mandate, I must eluci-
date the Green Beret-like training that student journalists
received at Baylor University during our era of the late 1960s.
Without question, it was unsurpassed by that on any U.S. campus.

Baylor's was a rigorous, brilliant, arduous, singular program that left its graduates unflinchingly prepared for any
work experience that might be thrown at them.

Considering the fact that late '60s grads like us were being
hurled out alongside such catastrophic news developments as
anti-war protests, racial unrest, and Watergate either under way
or on the near horizon, that's saying a lot.

All this stemmed from the fact that David McHam insisted
on running *The Baylor Lariat* as more than a campus newsrag.
He made it an utterly practical laboratory in life that taught far,
far beyond what anyone learned from our (almost irrelevant) J-
school textbooks. He desired that everything that happened in
the *Lariat's* third-floor news operation atop Harrington Hall
would simulate the constraints of a real-life newsroom on any
major daily.

Staff meetings (known as *blue alerts*) could be called on
an impromptu basis at the scandalous hours of 2 and 3 a.m. "to
get you ready for covering breaking news, which doesn't happen on banker's time," he would argue as he rousted us from
slumber with a wee-hours phone call. (When, years later, my
city desk plucked me from sleep to report in at 3 a.m. to cover
the shocking death of Pope John Paul I, I silently thanked
McHam for his cold-blooded preparation.)

Reporters' stories in the previous day's *Lariat* would be
unapologetically ripped to shreds in front of peers on a regular
basis. "The public won't spare your feelings when you mess

up; why should I?" McHam retorted if someone's lower lip quivered during a critique.

Rushing a sorority, singing in a campus chorale, running for student office while writing for *The Lariat*—McHam discouraged outside involvements. They limited a reporter's objectivity. Besides, he expected nothing less than total devotion to the newspaper business. Professional journalists, which we aspired to be in a few years, must be monofocused, he adjured. He didn't have much use for any of the other classes in our degree plans, either. Excusing ourselves from covering a story because we had a chemistry or a trig test the next day never really washed with McHam. He expected us to find time to attend class, study, and meet all other scholastic obligations somewhere between the minutes when we filed our late-breaking *Lariat* stories at midnight and the time we dragged ourselves back to work at noon the next day.

He taught us to pursue the truth at all costs and to report it with speed, creativity, integrity, but above all, accuracy. In *The Lariat* newsroom hung the motto, "Get it first, but first, get it right." The social conscience of the Baylor community—the students, the professors, the administrators, the alums—everybody—absolutely depended on what was read in the daily *Lariat*, McHam exhorted. To those initiated in Scripture, his manifesto sounded a bit like Proverbs 29:18, *Where there is no revelation, the people perish.*

Although no one could rejoice over a campus heartbreak such as the Clifton hazing death, McHam could hardly have invented more fertile soil for putting his student journalists to the ultimate test. Probably no other U.S. campus news event in modern history, except for something of the magnitude of the Kent State killings, the Virginia Tech massacre, or the Duke lacrosse team rape scandal, would give occasion to harden student reporters in such an unplanned refiner's fire. This subsumed gathering news under unthinkable deadline pressure, fielding bitter administrative backlash, crafting incisive, editorial calls-to-arms, snaring sensitive family interviews, cutting through public-relations platitudes, and thousands of other real-life complexities that *Lariat* reporters navigated during the hours and days that followed this monumental happening.

The proof was in the stellar Baylor J-school alums of our era, who ultimately assumed management roles at The Associated Press, United Press International, *Washington Post, Philadelphia Inquirer, Houston Chronicle, Cincinnati Inquirer, Fort Worth Star-Telegram,* and other major news outlets throughout the country, as well as on top J-school faculty. When he produced winners year after year after year, few could question some of his unorthodox manifestos.

And the little matter of McHam's intra-staff dating ban that was complicating love life for me and Kay in the fall of 1968?

Nothing personal, McHam might argue. Daily newspapers of that day and age simply didn't employ staffers who were married to each other. No point in going soft on student reporters and setting up scenarios that wouldn't be tolerated in a professional newsroom.

After all, the whole goal of training college journalists was the winnowing-out process—somewhat like Marine Corps basic training. McHam (who in private life had a heart of gold but was tough as nails in his drill instructor role) made sure only the strong survived. Those who didn't would wither quickly in the unrelenting heat of cutthroat professional journalism.

Thus, if Kay and I wanted to date, we knew we'd have to visit her parents 100 miles away in Garland for the weekend and pray we'd encounter no other Baylor students at the movie theater at NorthPark Mall. Everyone on the Baylor campus seemed to know about the oddball but unbending *Lariat* rule.

* * * * * * * *

The year I was *Lariat* editor plunged me deeply into the plight of African-Americans and the ugly racial prejudice they faced.

I entered Baylor the same semester and lived in the same dorm as John Westbrook, the first African-American to play on the Baylor football team. My editor year was when Baylor finally hired its first African-American faculty member, Dr. Vivienne Mayes. I gleefully wrote a *Lariat* editorial welcoming Dr. Mayes to the campus. I made certain the campus remembered that when the brilliant Dr. Mayes first wanted to attend Baylor as a student, she was rejected because of her color.

I also hired Willie White, the first African-American to work on the *Lariat* editorial staff. I diligently groomed Willie, who was also a ministerial student, as my successor—a mantle he assumed a year after I left Baylor. My personal friendship with Willie gave me the opportunity to see the civil rights movement through his saddened eyes. He candidly described what life had been like growing up on the other side (from me) of segregation. His story and that of his family was enough to make even the most calloused weep.

One day I was alongside Willie when the ugly truth about race relations in that era hit home. Willie rode to Houston with Kay and me for the annual Southwestern Student Journalism Conference. Kay's roommate, also a journalism major, accompanied us on the trip. Returning to Waco from Houston in my 1968 beige Volkswagen, the four of us stopped in at a small Central Texas cafe for lunch. Seated at our table, we realized all eyes in the restaurant were on us—and it wasn't just because of the attractive coeds in our company. Soon I realized the townspeople had drawn the erroneous conclusion that Willie was dating Kay's roommate, who was white.

Realizing we were "on stage" made the food the server brought us turn bitter in my mouth. I kept harboring the not-unrealistic fear that some rough, tough cowboy was about to arrive at our table and start punching at Willie and me. When we finished our meal and headed to the door, several redneck-looking patrons seemed to deliberately follow us into the parking lot. I breathed a "thank-You, God" when all four of us were safely back in my Volkswagen with the doors locked, the engine running, and the vehicle headed out of town. As I watched the restaurant disappear in my rearview mirror, I vowed to continue to fight the good fight for racial equality.

I often have wondered what the reaction on campus would have been if Willie and I had been beaten by one or several of those menacing cowboys. Would the cowboys have been the ones wearing the white hats, in the campus estimation? My strong beliefs about civil rights put me at odds with many people on the Baylor campus in 1968-69. (Much of this sentiment, unfortunately, sprang to light after the campus' less-than-mournful reaction to the assassination of civil-rights leader Dr. Martin Luther King.)

Sadly, Southern Baptists as a whole were not in the forefront of the civil rights movement, either. The SBC, in fact, embarrassed itself royally by opposing the 1964 Civil Rights Act. Despite a resolution in 1968 that reflected a 180-degree turnaround, the 1964 fiasco was such a blight that it marked Southern Baptists for more than three decades afterward. I left campus rueing the fact that I had not been even more aggressive in my *Lariat* support for equality among the races.

Some 25 years later, God honored my regret, as I found myself in a key position to influence the entire Southern Baptist Convention on this crucial issue. But in 1969 all I could do was feel remorse that I couldn't be a more efficacious, powerful voice.

* * * * * * * *

Being a graduate student in religion and editor of *The Lariat* afforded me the opportunity to explore other religious beliefs all around me. I enrolled in a graduate class on the history of the Roman Catholic Church. Students in the class were required to physically attend the celebration of a Catholic mass at a church somewhere in Waco. Again, this seemingly innocuous experience, undertaken to fulfill a class assignment, would not return to me void in later life.

That year I also took a course on Hinduism and Buddhism taught by Dr. James E. Wood Jr., the celebrated Baylor scholar on the separation of church and state. I remember the almost impossible time I had finding magazines and newspaper articles on both religions for my research papers. Americans apparently saw these groups as foreign and "over there," not as forces that would eventually become as prevalent as the Presbyterian and Episcopal churches just down the street.

* * * * * * * *

My year as editor accomplished the goals that I set for myself and the journalism faculty set for me. Although I managed to ruffle more than my fair share of administrative feathers, my term at the helm, overall, was considered a stabilizing force for *The Lariat*'s campus image.

A compassionate, in-depth article Kay wrote entitled "Baylor Chamber of Commerce: One Year Later," examining the new sobered, introspective mood of the service organization after its year from hell, went a long way to gain rapprochement between this powerful body and the campus media.

On my last day in office, I encountered Virginia Crump, Baylor assistant dean of students. She issued what I took to be a compliment: "I would not call you a popular editor, but I would say you have been respected." Given the inevitable tension that will always exist between the two entities on any campus—student reporters and school rule—*respected* was a term of pure gold. I had borne "witness to the truth" with my conscience clear, my calling intact.

* * * * * * * *

At year's end, the time arrived to pick up my much-delayed Southern Seminary plan, which had only one small, new wrinkle in place from the previous arrangement. I now would head off to Louisville as a married student, with my wedding to Kay set for Aug. 30, 1969, 10 days before the fall seminary semester began.

A few days into our January 1969 engagement, Kay and I ultimately had marched off to grovel before McHam, meekly confess to him our subterfuge, and let the chips fall. Over the noise of our knocking knees, he magnanimously pronounced that we could both keep our *Lariat* jobs after all, as he joked that he "obviously wasn't a very good reporter" if such a liaison could go on under his nose and he hadn't been able to sniff it out.

He didn't back down from his tough-love words of caution, however: newspapers wouldn't look kindly on our union when hiring time arrived.

Oblivious, we thanked him for his beneficence and invited this valued coach to be a groomsman at our wedding.

* * * * * * * *

Before either my marriage or seminary matriculation
occurred, I got my first taste of the shocking, dog-eat-dog
competition that I later would find is endemic in religious
institutions of all stripes. Interestingly enough, the campus job
that I was about to hold during my seminary days turned out to
be the subject of this up-close ecclesiastical wrangling.

In the spring of 1969, I had interviewed with Wesley M.
"Pat" Pattillo, Southern Seminary's public-relations man, who
was seeking a news director for the Louisville seminary and
also a managing editor of *The Tie*, the school's alumni magazine. Pat offered me the fabulous sum of $190 per month. With
our apartment rent set at $80 a month and my semester tuition
$80, this meant that Kay would still need to supplement our
income with a job of her own, but we were both OK with this
arrangement. Before my final spring semester at Baylor ended,
I had already said *yes* to Pat.

Just two weeks before our wedding, John Earl Seelig, public-relations director for Southwestern Baptist Theological
Seminary in Fort Worth, called with a mind-blowing counter-
proposal. He offered me the same position at his seminary that
Pat had extended at Southern if I would switch my seminary
locus and enroll at nearby Southwestern instead. Beyond
Southern's $190 a month, John Earl boldly offered me a start-
ing salary of $300 per month and also the opportunity to
remain near our family and friends. Kay's extra income would
not be necessary; she could continue on with finishing her
degree, which our marriage was disrupting.

For the second time (after Capitol Hill's initial balking at
my endorsement) a major pull was under way to keep me in
Texas and away from Southern Seminary. I certainly wasn't
winning any points with my future in-laws by planning to

whisk their daughter, a beloved only child, to another state more than 800 miles away. Southwestern's offer, even as our wedding gifts were being packed to ship to Kentucky, was a most perplexing, alluring 11th-hour struggle.

The matter wasn't helped by the fierce jockeying I suddenly saw ensue between the two seminaries and these two public-relations officials in particular.

Learning of the counteroffer, Pat rushed in to point out that Southern was Southern Baptists' oldest theological seminary; John Earl was equally speedy to remind me that Southwestern in Fort Worth was the largest seminary in the world.

John Earl immediately noted that Bill Moyers had held the PR job for which Southwestern was recruiting me just before Moyers was named press secretary to President Lyndon B. Johnson.

Pat promptly spouted off names of distinguished alums in his own news operation.

The two men stepped up the sparring and moved close to discrediting the other's offices. Courtly, courteous, but with a knife edge underpinning their tone, each tried to imply that I'd be happier with his own work and management style.

Surprisingly Pat never budged on his salary offer but instead relied on his and the seminary's credentials to woo me.

Years later I would experience this same kind of undercutting in almost every religious community I encountered. For example, as I made friends with youthful Rabbi Michael Leburkein and reported many times in my Saturday *Houston Chronicle* religion section on activities at his fledgling synagogue, esteemed fellow rabbi Hyman Judah Schachtel unfailingly would phone me on Monday mornings afterward. He would rail at me for not covering his larger, more prestigious congregation.

In the United Methodist world, I saw Charles L. Allen, megaprolific author and pastor of Houston's First United Methodist—the world's largest church in its denomination—wage a lifelong, futile struggle to become a bishop. The more diligently he tried to snare this coveted spot, the more hateful, venomous attacks poured out against him—claiming his church was too large, his ego too prominent, and anything else his competitors could manufacture. Despite his stature world-wide as a preacher and an author, Allen died without achieving his fondest desire. I find interesting and revealing the fact that the 2008 *Historical Atlas of Texas Methodism* scarcely men-tions Allen, despite the fact that this cleric saw himself the major force in United Methodism in the state if not the U.S.

* * * * * * * *

In the end, the certain, undefinable pull toward Southern Seminary that I'd found difficult to explain to my pastor, Hugh Bumpas, when Capitol Hill Baptist said it'd prefer I'd choose the Fort Worth seminary won out.

Although they had shed an immense and strategic spotlight on cutthroat church life, the men's competitive and thinly veiled sales-pitches ultimately counted for nothing as we yielded to God's still, small voice in the matter and continued on toward the Kentucky campus. Kay's parents gulped down their disappointment and stoically wished us godspeed as we heard Isaiah 30:21, *This is the way, walk ye in it,* personalized for us.

Only years later would I learn the full reason why I believe God steered me, against all odds, to the Bluegrass State with an inexplicable, unrelenting push.

Chapter 4

Smoking Pistol

Truth No. 4: Words unfitly spoken are like feathers shaken from a pillow. Once they're out, despite all efforts at damage control, they can never be put back into the pillow again.

When Kay and I arrived in Louisville on the heels of our honeymoon, I felt as though we were on another planet from the Texas-Oklahoma moorings that we knew so well. For one thing, we now reveled in autumns so astounding they would take our breath away. For people from our part of the world, anytime a leaf does anything except just hang there is cause for a banner headline. No one from our relatively monoseasoned states would have ever grasped that fall colors could be found in such a profusion of different shades.

Winter's extremes were different for us, as well. The below-zero mornings and chains for the tires of my little Volkswagen to negotiate icy roads were entirely new experiences. And I had once thought Oklahoma Januaries were straight off the North Pole!

Then we had the matter of the bedroom furniture in our rented, one-bedroom seminary apartment. The apartment, in the heart of married-student housing, with many of those couples being newlyweds, was equipped with twin beds only! For the life of me I couldn't figure why this was so. *Didn't Baptist preachers sleep with their wives?* I pondered. Resourceful Kay quickly remedied the situation by pushing the two beds together, turning the mattresses crossways, and adding a king-sized mattress pad and king-sized linens and pillows. Unless one looked closely, our tiny bedroom appeared as though it contained a real king-sized bed. From the get-go of our marriage, we were determined to do things our way and not conform to some asinine idiosyncrasies set by a religious institution.

If some of these matters seemed unusual to us, that was nothing compared to the seminary itself. Inside the school's majestic red-brick and white-spired colonial structures, the word *academic* had been lifted to the *n*th degree. Baylor's graduate school in religion had been academically challenging, but also had been fun, *laissez faire,* and enjoyable. Except for the *academically challenging* part, I would never describe Southern in any of those ways. Everything seemed so serious and uptight.

I also didn't take very long to realize why Capitol Hill Baptist Church in Oklahoma City had fretted that I would find "liberalism" on the campus. The so-called historical-critical method unabashedly ruled the day at Southern. This method teaches that the Bible is to be understood against the background of world history, not the Bible as the sole authority. The *critical* part was perhaps the most confusing. Every passage in the Bible was scrutinized not for its spiritual value but instead for whether it was authentic and really belonged in the text. Clear answers to simple questions about the Bible were difficult to obtain. If any professor at Southern in this era truly believed that Adam and Eve were real people, I never heard him or her say so in plain English. Even some professorial references to the biblical character Abraham left me wondering whether some professors believed Abraham had really ever existed at all. Theological tap-dancing was certainly the order of the day in Louisville during that era.

During my Introduction to the Old Testament class,

Professor Harold Songer said the seminary's purpose was to take apart young seminarians' faith and then at the end of the three-year Master of Divinity degree program to put it all back together again in a more mature, studied manner. The professors wanted to show us that academically examining everything was all a part of a responsible, educated Christian's life. I was taken aback by what Dr. Songer said, but I did appreciate his candor about the approach. At least I wasn't left wondering about his strategies.

I'll always believe that my fellow student, Joe Hornaday, was a tragic victim of this questionable method. Besides being Baylor graduates of the same era, Joe and I had in common the fact that we both lost fathers when we were teen-agers. Joe's father had died in an automobile accident; in Chapter 1 I described my own father's death from a heart attack. Many Saturday mornings during our first year at Southern Joe and I met at the seminary's gym to play handball. Our skills in the game were about equally matched; this made competing against him challenging and fun.

When I first met Joe during our college days, he was one of the most fervent, evangelical students on the Baylor campus. The word *conservative* fit Joe's theology well.

During our first year at Southern, Joe changed dramatically. Once a devout believer, he suddenly questioned everything—almost just for questioning's sake. By the end of our freshman year in seminary, Joe pronounced Southern "too conservative" for him. At the beginning of our second year Joe transferred to Vanderbilt Divinity School in Nashville, TN. The next spring Kay and I visited Joe and his wife in their apartment near the Vanderbilt campus. His hair was unrecognizably long, his demeanor bordered on obnoxious, he bragged about his major consumption of alcoholic beverages, and he appeared to be in rebellion against all things evangelically

Christian. I was shocked and disappointed in the transformation that had occurred in my friend. I found relating to the "new" Joe to be very difficult.

After that disturbing visit, I never saw Joe again. Several years later I heard the unthinkable story of how he divorced his wife and then took his life in the Arkansas gas station in which he worked.The news made me physically ill.

Somehow, after Joe's faith was "taken apart" by academia, he never was able to restore it. I've always wondered what would have happened to Joe had he gone to a seminary that did not try to remodel his faith but instead nurtured and reinforced it.

As a committed student I tried very diligently to honor my professors and the administration at Southern Seminary. I determined to separate the grain from the chaff, to soak up as many biblical facts as I could, and to dismiss professorial opinions as just that—opinions. After all, I didn't intend ultimately to be a pastor or church staff member, so I wasn't concerned about absorbing and promulgating the views I heard advanced there. I felt no obligation to line up behind any of my professors and become a clone of them. I was simply at seminary to acquire background knowledge to become a religious journalist.

Nevertheless, on more than one occasion, I reached my limit. One of these occurred in an advanced archaeology class I took as my last course at the seminary. The class involved a tour of the Middle East, including participating in an archaeological dig at Ai, one of the cities of the conquest by Joshua and the Israelites. The city today lies not that far from Jerusalem. Everywhere we went, the professor, Dr. Joseph Callaway, launched into a lecture about why what we were seeing could not possibly have been the authentic mountaintop, site, location, burial place, etc., referenced in the Bible.

One day, as we departed the bus to see the Old Testament city of Jericho, I asked whether we would be able to view any of the remains of the walls that the Bible says fell down during Joshua's siege of that city. Dr. Callaway responded that archaeologists could find no evidence whatsoever of a wall existing during Joshua's time and certainly no indication of a wall that fell down instantaneously.

"So, were there walls that fell down or not?" I asked. I don't remember Dr. Callaway's exact words, but I do remember the look on his face. It spoke volumes about how misguided and sophomoric he regarded my query.

(Interestingly, solid research since Callaway's time has gone a long way to confirm the fallen Jericho wall's actual existence after all.)

Because of my experiences in that class, I was not surprised years later when I heard the story that as the Conservative Resurgence noose tightened on Southern, Dr. Roy Honeycutt, then Southern's president, burned the midnight oil to find a way to get Dr. Callaway out of the classroom and into retirement before seminary trustees could press the archaeologist about what he really was teaching at the school.

I was personally fond of Dr. Callaway, although I puzzled at some of the things he said and taught. Among Southern professors who scoffed at literal readings of the Bible, he had plenty of company.

One Sunday at Louisville's Crescent Hill Baptist Church, where Kay and I and many faculty and students were members, Dr. William E. Hull, dean of Southern's School of Theology, preached his by-now legendary *Shall We Call the Bible Infallible?* To make a long story short, this guest preacher's conclusion was that we can't. I was rather dumfounded by his blunt assertions. I shuddered when I thought what would happen if folks back home in Oklahoma City could listen in on Dr. Hull's comments and thought processes in the sermon.

Dr. Hull's sermon eventually was preached or published in numerous Southern Baptist settings. As one might expect, the sermon began to cause an uproar.

I've always considered the Hull message to be one of the great miscalculations by the SBC's so-called moderate wing. It was delivered nearly a decade before the Conservative Resurgence (also known as the Fundamentalist Takeover) of the SBC began in 1979. It was preached at the heady, triumphant moment when what later became known as the moderate wing of the SBC controlled all boards, agencies, and seminaries of the Convention.

Some years hence, this sermon resurrected was like waving a red flag in front of a mad bull. To many conservatives, Dr. Hull's message was the smoking pistol they needed. They believed it proved beyond a shadow of a doubt what conservatives had been claiming for years: that Southern had a "liberal" bent, and even worse, that the SBC itself was turning "liberal." Seminary critics and emerging conservative leaders had to look no further than the sermon's text. The discourse reminded me of Martin Luther's 95 theses, which he posted on the door of the seminary at Wittenburg. Like William Barrett Travis at the Alamo, Dr. Hull drew the proverbial line in the sand. The vast majority of the seminary community wanted to stand with him.

And I was there, sitting in the congregation and hearing every word.

Down the years I've seen plenty of other examples of unguarded feathers let out of the pillow that later caused unmitigated harm that no amount of damage control could undo. Baptist evangelist Bailey Smith's offensive 1980 statement, "God Almighty doesn't hear the prayer of a Jew," might have been well-understood by his immediate audience, but the retelling of it in newspaper banner headlines did Southern Baptists centuries of harm.

Cecil Williams, the United Methodist pastor in San Francisco, was another who, while well-intentioned, smeared Methodists with his 1970s famous "Hookers Conventions" and ministries to prostitutes, pimps, and other sinners, which sounded too much like affirmation of their lifestyles than clarion calls for repentance.

* * * * * * * *

Pat Pattillo in the seminary's Office of Public Relations was a master mentor to hold for me a microscope over how a religious denomination operated. Pat was knowledgeable about all things Southern Baptist, at least as far as how political and bureaucratic mechanisms within the Convention worked. Pat's boss, Dr. Duke K. McCall, the seminary's president, held tremendous sway in the SBC. As I later learned is the case in all Baptist seminaries and many Baptist colleges and universities, one of Dr. McCall's means of influence was whom he invited to speak in the seminary's weekly chapel service. One had to be a true-blue non-fundamentalist to acquire one of the coveted invitations to speak from the Southern Seminary chapel pulpit. I could tell by the invitees that Dr. McCall and Pat certainly were not friends with the Convention's emerging conservative wing.

During my last semester at the seminary, two events occurred that illustrated the school's disdain for Convention conservatives, who at that time were dismissed as a fringe group of little significance. Only in the rearview mirror did I recognize what was taking place in both of these happenings.

One was the retirement of Joe T. Odle as editor of Mississippi's Baptist newspaper. Joe was thought of as the "last" remaining conservative, a.k.a. fundamentalist, in an editor's office in the SBC. His retirement sparked large celebrations in some quarters at the seminary. I did not care for the journalistic layout and design of the Mississippi paper under Odle, but later I also thought it a pity that all the state newspaper editors ostensibly had to be cut out of the same cloth.

The second event was heralded when one of my favorite professors, Dr. Jerry Vardaman, appeared at my office door and announced that Dr. W.A. Criswell, pastor of First Baptist Church of Dallas, had just revealed plans to start his own college. Listening to faculty reaction in the hallways for the next few days convinced me that some members of the Southern faculty prophetically thought the start of a small undergraduate school in classrooms at First Baptist, Dallas somehow portended unspecified difficulties for the seminary in the future. Little did these prophets or I sense what a major development the beginning of this upstart school would become.

I was already aware of the contempt the Southern faculty—and to a lesser extent the student body—felt toward Criswell, perhaps Southern's most famous alumnus and pastor of the largest Baptist church in the world at that time. Dr. Wayne Oates, Southern's lauded professor of pastoral care, at least had the courage to verbalize in class what others merely whispered in the hallways. He told a story about Criswell as a seminary student who loudly orated his practice sermons on Saturday afternoons in one of the seminary's larger halls. When the prof finished telling the story with all of his nuances, you knew Dr. Oates had at least two opinions about Dr. Criswell: that the preacher was obsessed with his public performance and that he tended to have a messianic complex (meaning that he thought he had an extraordinarily special—

albeit abnormal—role in God's kingdom). Dr. Oates' book, *When Religion Gets Sick*, illustrated what he thought were prime examples of emotional excesses among the clergy and laity. I quoted it over and over in the years afterward as I encountered many, many examples of what he described.

* * * * * * * *

I completed my seminary coursework in January 1972, but the next graduation exercise was not scheduled until May 1972. By May I was living out-of-state, on to other things, and not the least bit inclined to return to my alma mater for commencement. The ceremony overlapped with the annual session of the Northern Presbyterian Church in Denver, which I much preferred to attend. By that point my attitude was "been-there-done-that-got-the-union-card." I asked the seminary's registrar merely to send me my diploma.

I had gained much head knowledge from my M.Div. studies at Southern—biblical facts that would serve me well. I now had graduate-school credentials. Kay and I had profited from starting our married life in this new and intriguing part of the country; negotiating outside the comfort zones of our upbringings had been broadening. But spiritually I had grown little during that crucial, formative time of my early 20s.

Almost a decade would pass before I realized that my take-away from my Southern years was, curiously, more vast than I possibly could imagine—and had included a contribution I could never have identified at the moment I gave my parting glance toward the tree-dappled campus with its white, colonial spires.

Chapter 5

A Good Assumption

Truth No. 5: Church people rarely let a few solid facts stand in the way of a good assumption.

As I had approached the end of my seminary education, I struggled with *what next?* I pondered whether a ministry in Christian journalism had to be carried out only within the confines of a church or denomination or whether I could fulfill my ministerial calling while I worked on a secular daily newspaper. Pat Pattillo and others in the SBC bureaucracy argued forcibly that only within the denomination could true ministry be performed.

At home I witnessed a different perspective. When we arrived in Louisville, Kay joined on as a reporter for United Press International—the first female reporter in the Louisville bureau. Because she was married to a seminary student, anytime a religion story popped up on the UPI news agenda in the Kentuckiana region, Kay was asked to be on the scene. Sometimes I would tag along as she did her interviews and reporting.

The story I remember most was the spontaneous revival that broke out on the campus of Asbury Seminary, the Free Methodist school near Lexington, KY. Kay's story was picked up by the national UPI wire in New York and carried in newspapers all across the country and even around the world. She wrote an excellent account that merely told the facts, but the facts spoke for themselves: during special campus revival services, students became so inspired and Spirit-led that classes were dismissed, revival services went on continuously, and eventually students started disseminating in small groups to other campuses to spread the Good News of Jesus.

I believed that story was more beneficial to the Kingdom of God than were all the banal news and feature stories I had written the whole time I had been in the seminary's news office. It reinforced my feeling that denominational life would be too confining and too restrictive for one trained as I was.

Freedom of speech, freedom of expression, and freedom of press were visceral issues for me. My Baylor journalism training under David McHam had underscored these concepts to the point that they were part of my journalistic DNA. More and more I saw evidence that I could not be totally free working in a denominational setting, which has a vested interest in putting its own spin on the news.

One pivotal moment in my decision-making occurred with a developing seminary news event that I believe was dealt with poorly not only by Southern but also by the Baptist media. The issue erupted when Dr. McCall dismissed two music-ministry students for what was thought to be homosexual activity. The dismissal was supposed to be classified information. Somehow word leaked out; the Louisville dailies carried the story.

Bob Terry, associate editor of the Kentucky Baptist newspaper and a protégé of Pat Pattillo, called Pat to do a story about the matter for his own newspaper. I could hear Pat in the next office arguing with Bob on the phone about why the *Western Recorder* and all other Baptist state newspapers should drop the matter. Afterward, Pat appeared at my door and seemed triumphant that he had persuaded Bob not to print the story.

For me, the issue was not the subject of homosexual activity; the issue was freedom of the press. I could envision all sorts of other scenarios involving other issues in which truth could not be told. The more I thought about it and the more I looked around in the denomination, the more I concluded that freedom of the press and speech were simply not possible inside the SBC. I could not be a "witness to the truth" under such circumstances.

From that time on I never considered any field but secular religion writing/editing as my calling. Kay and I began praying that God would show us specifically what we were to do.

* * * * * * *

The answer seemed to arrive early in the fall of 1971 during my last semester at Southern. The managing editor of the *Louisville Times* invited me to perform a two-week "trial run" at being the newspaper's religion writer. We agreed that if I did well, he would hire me full-time starting the next February when I completed my degree. Until then I would work for the paper on a part-time basis.

I was thrilled with this awesome development. The *Louisville Times,* the afternoon counterpart to its sister paper, *The Courier-Journal,* had an admirable reputation in the industry. *The Courier-Journal* was long recognized as one of the outstanding regional newspapers in the U.S. To land a job of this stature as my first full-time employment out of graduate school was an unthinkable opportunity.

It carried one major drawback: If I took the job, Kay could not realize her own dream of joining *The Courier-Journal* or *Times* staff. When we had first arrived in Louisville, Kay lacked her undergraduate degree, so she was not eligible to work at the newspaper then. Her splendid credentials garnered at United Press during those 2 1/2 years plus the recent attainment of her bachelor's (through a creative mélange of correspondence and transfer courses back to Baylor) put her in a good spot to now move on from UPI and re-approach these two papers. David McHam's admonition about married-duo staffers being verboten on major dailies definitely rang in our ears as I began my part-time *Louisville Times* job with an eye to the future.

Nevertheless, I mapped out four *Louisville Times* stories that I wanted to write during the two weeks; I believed these exemplified my versatility and talents. One of those four was a story about the demise of Sunday-evening worship in the Louisville area. Much to my surprise, the *Louisville Times* played the story on its front page. I got the same great play with the next week's story about two Roman Catholic nuns who were African-Americans (a trailblazing situation at that time).

I was thrilled with my work experience so far and could already sense that the *Louisville Times* staff wanted to make it permanent. Kay and I were already discussing what her other (somewhat limited) work options might be in the Louisville area if the marriage restriction caused her to have to settle short of her newspapering goal.

* * * * * * *

During the second week of my "trial run," Kay and I were eating lunch together at our apartment when the phone rang with a scenario that would preempt all these plans entirely. It was from Don Pickels, managing editor of the *Houston Chronicle*. He said on the next Saturday he would be flying to New York City for the regularly scheduled Associated Press managing editors meeting. He wanted to know if he could stop in Louisville to talk with me about an opening he had on his staff. I told him about the arrangement with the *Louisville Times* and that I expected to be offered the job the next week. Advised about my availability via David McHam, Don said he planned to offer me a better position, which we would talk more about on Saturday.

Don concluded the conversation by saying, "And be sure and bring Kay with you to the interview. I want to meet her and interview her, too."

I was almost too stunned for words. *What about the marriage ban that was part and parcel of all newspapering?* McHam clearly had briefed Don about Kay's talents as well.

"You don't think I'm going to pay to move you to Houston and have Kay go to work for the (competing) *Houston Post,* now do you?" he asked quite firmly.

Our minds reeled. *Texas! Home! Both of us with full-time newspapering jobs—under the same employer's roof!* The *Houston Chronicle* (as an afternoon daily to the morning *Post*) lacked the national stature of the *Courier-Journal* and *Times,* but Houston was a bigger city with a more diverse religion community and more story possibilities. Suddenly our thoughts took off down an entirely different road.

* * * * * * *

From the moment we shook hands with Don Pickels as he stepped off the plane in Louisville, Kay and I never doubted what our ultimate decision was. Four hours later when we returned him to the airport, Don had bedazzled us away from Kentucky to join the *Chronicle* staff. Now more than 35 years later Kay and I both still regard Don Pickels as a prince among bosses. *Professional. Moral. Principled. Trustworthy. Honorable. Genuine. Kind.* Those words only begin to describe him. After Don Pickels, every boss either one of us ever had—including some very big names in Southern Baptist circles—would forever be compared to this truly great man.

One of the first things Don told us about himself was that he was a believer—more precisely, an Episcopalian Christian. He was extremely knowledgeable about religious events and religious life. He personally knew Bishop John E. Hines, who had recently been elected presiding bishop of the Episcopal Church. Hines had previously been bishop of the Diocese of Texas based in Houston.

After I talked with Don, I knew I was about to embark on an adventure of a lifetime. Unlike the *Louisville Times,* where I would have to report on other subjects as well, Don promised I could concentrate 100 percent of my time on religion. Also unlike the *Times*, the *Chronicle* promised a rather extraordinary expense account for travel to cover religious events.

And, as he had hinted, he was willing to hire Kay on the spot. He had an opening on the paper's county beat; he asked her to fill it. The *Chronicle* indeed had the same ban McHam had warned us about, but Don was willing to take a gamble on the two of us to see how it would work.

The only problem with the new job had to do with my predecessor on the beat—the previous religion editor, Janice Law. A few weeks earlier, City Editor Zarko Franks had fired Janice in a dispute over coverage of the local Galveston-Houston Roman Catholic Diocese. The dispute involved a controversial story about priests who were leaving the diocese to get married. Janice had protested her firing and claimed some decisions about the story were influenced by Franks' Catholicism. Janice had cried *discrimination* and appealed to the Religion Newswriters Association for assistance in fighting the matter. As far as Don Pickels was concerned, the case was closed.

Don also shared with me the disturbing stories of other former *Chronicle* religion editors. One had committed suicide. Another had been arrested in a pornography sting. During the first year we were in Houston, another former *Chronicle* religion editor was shot and killed by her husband during a domestic dispute. The more Don talked (and the more I learned later), the more I realized why he had mapped out a strategy to find a new religion editor who was trained in both journalism and theology and who felt a calling to a ministry in Christian journalism—and why he would move heaven and earth to get us there.

Don agreed to hire both Kay and me, effective Feb. 7, 1972, a week after I was scheduled to complete my final class at the seminary—the aforementioned Joe Callaway trip to the Holy Land that involved an onsite archaeological dig. Waiting from Oct. 15 until Feb. 7 to begin work at the *Chronicle* was excruciating for both of us, since our hearts already had moved to Houston. Don weekly sent us letters or called with updates on *Chronicle* life. The *Chronicle* arrived faithfully each day in our apartment mailbox. We felt as though we were already on the team even though we were nearly a thousand miles away.

* * * * * * * *

Our euphoria dissolved harshly on the late January day we returned to Louisville from Israel to begin our move to Houston. Tacked to our apartment door was a note directing me to "call Jim Newton at the Baptist Press office in Nashville." The note was labeled *urgent*.

When I called, Jim told me that Lester Kinsolving, an

Episcopal-priest-turned-religion-columnist for hundreds of secular newspapers, had written a column decrying the firing of Janice Law. In it, he had branded me, her successor, a fundamentalist Baptist preacher who had the audacity to believe in—horror of horrors!—the virgin birth. For the life of me, I couldn't figure out what Jesus' being born of a virgin had to do with my being hired at the *Chronicle*. Kinsolving had also sloppily referred to me as "William Moore" instead of Louis Moore. Of course he also hadn't bothered to get my side or to check out the facts in the case.

Jim Newton warned me to be scrupulously leery of proceeding on to Houston—that the entire Religion Newswriters Association was up in arms over what appeared to be the *Chronicle's* heinous dismissal of Law and likely would censure me personally if I took the job. He said the column had appeared in newspapers coast to coast. He said the copy he was reading at that moment was from the Honolulu newspaper.

Stunned by the announcement, I phoned Don Pickels immediately. Don was aware of the column and quickly explained the strange virgin birth reference. He said Kinsolving, in a telephone interview, had badgered him what Don and the new religion editor had talked about in the job interview. Don said the exact quote was "Oh, we talked about theology and such things as the virgin birth and the Trinity." Kinsolving asked Don whether I believed in the virgin birth. Don said *yes*. Kinsolving quickly assumed from that comment that I must be a flaming fundamentalist and that Southern Seminary, which later I learned he knew nothing about at the time he wrote the column, must be a highly fundamentalist school for allowing a graduate to hold such a ludicrous belief. Kinsolving vilified the *Chronicle* for hiring someone who no doubt would be narrow-minded in the place of Law, whom he esteemed.

Don said he was embarrassed by the unfair and sensational reporting by Kinsolving—a former cleric who should be more principled. Don heard my alarm that I would be unable to gain access to Houston's Roman Catholic community because of its heebie-jeebies over Law's parting story. Don agreed that things might be rough at first but soothingly assured me that I should proceed on to Houston—that over time, feathers could become unruffled.

On first blush we began having a thousand regrets for my turning down the *Louisville Times*. We also could not imagine why believing in one of the basic tenets of the Christian faith could cause such a national uproar. We also were surprised that no one in the Southern Baptist Convention either publicly or privately jumped to our defense. As we prepared for this new ministry which we believed deeply in our hearts was of God, we felt abandoned by the very denomination that had nurtured us and whose doctrines had affirmed the virgin-birth precept in the first place.

Meanwhile, back in Louisville, Pat Pattillo reported to me that he had been "jumped" by one of the Baptist state newspaper editors, Al Shackleford of Indiana, for my decision to depart denominational journalism for a career as a religion editor on a secular, daily newspaper. The implication in Pat's voice was that the painful cloud under which I now was assuming the Houston job was what I deserved for "leaving the ministry."

* * * * * * *

In one of his infamous, wee-hour staff meetings, David McHam had taught us a cardinal rule of reporting: never to assume anything. He reminded us the very spelling of the word *assume* implies what assumptions will do to a journalist—make an "ass" out of "u" and "me." In this baffling turn of events, assumptions appeared to be making an "ass" of everyone. We were reeling over what blind suppositions, unbalanced, knee-jerk reporting, and failing to check the facts could do, in such a brief time, to one's reputation.

We were not the only people who have found themselves victims of hurtful assumptions and stereotyping at the hands of church people.

One of the most nationally prominent incidents in U.S. history was the paranoia that John F. Kennedy, a Roman Catholic, would become a vassal of the papacy if he were elected President in 1960. While on the campaign trail, Kennedy had to refute this stereotype head-on in order to avoid a burgeoning national hysteria over the matter.

When now-legendary Southern Baptist pastor John R. Bisagno took the pulpit at Houston's First Baptist Church in 1970, great backbiting occurred over the fact that he was trained only as a musician and lacked a seminary degree. Bisagno, who underwent private theological tutoring to help overcome the stereotype, became a sage of a preacher and went on to develop Houston's FBC into one of the country's first megachurches.

Although Churches of Christ as a rule are noted for their fierce, stand-alone independence and for eschewing cooperation of any kind, I saw Houston's Churches of Christ in the 1980s totally set aside that conjecture and work together beautifully in the aftermath of a fellow church's bankruptcy—the exact opposite of how most people would have branded them.

* * * * * * * *

Stunned and shattered by the mysterious, assumption-spawned event that was impacting our young lives (as kids in our mid-20s), Kay and I continued to thread our way down that long, and by this point, bewildering road to Houston, with our once-promising world seemingly crumbling around us. We proceeded only because I remained impressed that I was doing God's will in my effort to bear *witness to the truth.*

The silver lining was that this debacle indeed *was* happening to us when we were kids in our mid-20s, when we could integrate this type of development into our psyches and steel ourselves to it.

This would be far from the last time that assumptions and stereotyping at the hands of those in the church would try me in the *furnace of affliction* (Isa. 48:10) in my professional career.

Chapter 6

Household Word

Truth No. 6: The ministry rendered in times of physical need by a local body of believers represents the church's finest hour.

Although shaking the icicles off Houston's Roman Catholic community would take years to accomplish, many others among the Houston religious seemed to welcome my arrival with (sometimes even overly) open arms.

One night after we arrived in Houston, we answered our apartment doorbell to gaze on none other than a rain-soaked John Bisagno, the prominent Houston FBC pastor I mentioned in Chapter 5, standing without an umbrella in the middle of one of the Bayou City's infamous deluges and asking whether he could enter so he could invite us to his church.

The mailbox of our apartment suddenly was stuffed full of letters from other Southern Baptist pastors (and those of other denominations in town as well) inviting us to attend (and join) their churches, too. Something about it reminded me of college fraternity rush, as all put on their best public-relations pitches to advance their congregations before us as we looked for local membership.

Since I continued to feel the censure of my professional colleagues in the still-fresh Janice Law conundrum, all this sudden courting by local church representatives was a breath of fresh air. No question about it—being wanted was a pleasant change.

We soberly and soon realized, however, that these invitations were not issued to Louis and Kay Moore, Mr. and Mrs. Average, Ordinary Christians who happened to work in Houston's downtown district and who needed a place to worship God and a church to love them and minister to them just like other Christians need. The invitations were issued to the religion editor of the *Houston Chronicle* and his wife. Having one with my job among their membership could be seen as an automatic foot-in-the-door to publicity, some surmised. That new and curious premise took some getting used to. *Role* was suddenly more important than who I was as an individual. Countless months would be required for me to understand how to react to this evolving situation of public persona—ego-boosting, but with its drawbacks.

Eventually Kay and I made our church-membership decision: we joined Willow Meadows Baptist Church in Southwest Houston. The pastor, Dr. Ralph Langley, had spoken on campus at Baylor when we were students. We felt an instant rapport with this popular, personable minister and enjoyed his biblically sound messages. His wife, Grace, became our dear, first Sunday-school teacher as part of a couples' class. Almost immediately, however, we were recruited out of her class to teach the college Sunday school. Just a little farther down the road in life experience than these students were, we found that this was a good, initial responsibility for us as we acquainted ourselves with our new home and church.

One day, as I sat alone on a pew in the church's auditorium, I heard my name sputtered quite vociferously in conversation. I suddenly realized that two women seated in the previous row—women whom I wouldn't know from a bar of soap—were busy spitting nails about ME! I heard one of them say, "That Louis Moore! I'd like to give him a piece of my mind . . ." and then continued her harangue. They seemed to not care for something that had appeared in that Sunday's *Houston Chronicle*. Actually, another reporter had written the article that peeved them. They had already begun to recognize my byline; they didn't like something in the paper; they somehow also had gleaned that I was a member of their church; so in their minds, all these loose ends became tied together—and I was at fault! For a few minutes I eavesdropped on the conversation and then leaned over and interrupted. "Hello, I'm Louis Moore. Do we need to talk about something?" I asked, overly buoyantly (and, I'll admit, a bit impishly.)

As their eyes widened to the size of plates, they were speechless for a long, long time. "Well, small world, isn't it?" one shocked conversant finally retorted, coloring. The sudden frost in their voices told me they didn't want to pursue the matter. I had clearly caught them red-handed in the act of gossiping. The lesson I had just learned was important for the future—being in the public spotlight can cause some awkward moments . . . and make me fair game!

* * * * * * *

After a few years at Willow Meadows I suspected that I needed to be out and about in Houston's church community on Sunday mornings instead of limiting myself to one church all the time. We resigned our teaching posts and then every Sunday for almost a year attended a church of a different denomination. First Methodist. First Presbyterian. Episcopal Church of the Redeemer. Emerson Unitarian. Memorial Drive Lutheran. On and on the list went. I needed to expand beyond my Southern Baptist heritage. This delightful period of dabbling in church experiences certainly acquainted me firsthand with the sumptuous array of local worship houses and offered some of the most memorable worship experiences of my life. Going from an Episcopal church one Sunday to an Assembly of God the next, then to a Roman Catholic church followed by a Unitarian church brought an interesting lesson in contrasts and painted for me a graphic picture of the field I was covering.

And of course, because my presence as religion editor was almost certainly recognized (I soon would begin a column that carried my photo) and my name was fast becoming a household word, I became instant celebrity. Clergy members fell all over themselves to greet me, welcome me publicly, and usually pursue me for church membership. The days of my worshiping in anonymity regretfully had passed!

As helpful as this pilgrimage was professionally, it also made us deeply aware of our own needs to return to being an ongoing part of a faith community that we could call our own. I tend to be a rather cerebral person, so I love to study, learn, and analyze situations, people, and institutions. But deep in my heart I yearned to feel connected to like-kind and to be able to minister to others and have this reciprocated.

The Bible says we need to *stir up one another to love and good works, not neglecting to meet together, as is the habit of some, but encouraging one another* (Heb. 10:24-25). The "stirring up of" and "encouraging" part was something we personally had missed while we gained head-knowledge of Houston's religious vitality.

Our rootlessness at this particular moment in our histories would soon have unfortunate repercussions. After a few years of living in Houston, Kay and I lost our first child that she was carrying. In the seventh month of her pregnancy, after (ever-organized) Kay already had bureau drawers lined with baby clothes and juvenile prints hanging on cheerful yellow nursery walls, our much-wanted baby was stillborn with a true-knot in its umbilical cord. As I write these words 33 years later, I still swallow back tears as I recall this unimaginable development.

I also still recall the sound of the almost palpable silence that deafened us because we had deliberately separated ourselves from the weekly fellowship with our local body. Though not maliciously done, this act left us without a group to nurture us and pray us through this severe loss. We had no immediate cache of believers to uphold us as we grieved and to be the earthly manifestations of God's grace to us. Several years had passed since we had had regular contact with our couples' class at Willow Meadows. By that time we had moved from our apartment to a home in far West Houston— too distant to continue to drive to Willow Meadows on the opposite end of town. Because of circumstances we had created for ourselves, the church did not have the opportunity to prove itself in what is typically its finest hour—physical ministry in time of need.

Anyone who has ever been on the receiving end of this type of practical lifeline can confirm how beautiful is the body of Christ when people need it most. Two friends of ours whose stories follow fully attest to the benefits of this type of ministry.

Almost from the time she was diagnosed with colorectal cancer, Tamara Rowland's Anglican/Episcopal church in suburban Nashville (as well as friends from her hometown in Franklin, TN, and a host of other believers within the global community) sprang into action. These made mammoth, detailed lists assigning families to take food for Tamara and her husband, Bob, and divided up caregiving responsibilities for the Rowlands' daughter, then 2. They also sent encouraging gifts and cards on a daily basis and literally prayed for her hourly throughout her ordeal. This ministry to the Rowlands went on for an entire year as Tamara underwent several surgeries, two bouts of chemotherapy, and one bout of radiation. Tamara says the ministrations represented God's showing His love through friends and family and allowed her to concentrate on her physical healing while she learned some vital life lessons.

Janet Nall observed this same kind of sacrificial self-giving when her Roman Catholic community, Sisters of the Holy Spirit and Mary Immaculate in San Antonio, rallied around her to take care of her elderly mother, an Alzheimer's sufferer.

A sister who lives in the Dallas area, Janet brought her mother to the community's headquarters in San Antonio for two weeks so Janet could enjoy a time of rest and replenishment and attend an out-of-town educational conference.

Janet said the members of her community and the staff at the headquarters cheerfully saw to her mother's total physical and social needs to give Janet, who is on leave of absence from her assignment in Zambia, a caregiving break from the unrelenting demands of looking after one with dementia.

* * * * * * * *

As we underwent the desperate, dark night of our lives after childbearing loss, certainly our family members and our work colleagues shored us up. Some clergy who were part of my beat wrote kind notes of concern. One of the most astute acts of ministry was from David McHam, not always one to quote Scripture, but who in this case enjoined us with the passage reminding that *all things work together for good to those who love God* (Rom. 8:28).

But our experience taught us never again to let ourselves be long without a local ecclesiastical family, even if we had to leave one congregation and join another to uncover the right church fit (and later, that's exactly what we'd find ourselves doing—again and again and—Did I say *again*?—again).

80

Chapter 7

Wrong (or Right?)-Way Corrigans

Truth No. 7: Religious conversion sometimes can be a baffling, yet genuine, two-way street.

Within Houston's religious landscape, its Jewish community represented my biggest surprise and personal stretching point. Until I moved to Houston (remember my southside Oklahoma City upbringing!), I could count on one hand the number of Jewish individuals I had even met or knowingly had been in a room with.

The same day Kay and I joined the staff of the *Houston Chronicle*, another twentysomething reporter named Marty Cohen joined the team, too. The three of us quickly became close acquaintances. Marty truly was my first friend of Jewish ethnicity. Outside the office, Marty and I had lunch together, went to movies together, and played pool together. I was riveted to his descriptions of what growing up Jewish was like. I felt sad when Marty and Zarko Franks, the *Chronicle*'s city editor, ended up on a collision course. After six months, Marty left the paper. I never heard from him again, but I've always appreciated the wonderful backgrounding insights he gave me into the Jewish experience.

During that same time I met Betty Zollars, the most evangelical Jewish person I've ever known in my life. Booming, boisterous, and aflame with enthusiasm, Betty was like a walking, talking matzo ball. She worked for a local public-relations firm, but her avocation clearly was advancing her Jewish faith.

She talked about her "evangelism" with such intoxication that I couldn't help but listen with high curiosity.

I was flabbergasted when one day Betty owned up that she had been reared United Methodist and had, as a young adult, considered herself a devout Christian. *How can that be?* I ruminated over and over. My Baptist roots had taught me the doctrine of "once saved, always saved." This new reality presented a major hurdle for me to overcome in my talks with Betty. She eventually persuaded me to write a story on the topic of other Houston Jews who had started their early lives as Christians. Many were Christian women who married Jewish men, but some were like Betty—an exuberant, utterly "born-again" Jew. Growing up I had been taught that Jews were the ones who become converts to Christianity. I remembered the "suck-the-paint-off-the-wall" national stir when actress Elizabeth Taylor converted to Judaism as she married Eddie Fisher, but I had never heard of proletarian Christians relinquishing their faith to become Jews.

Betty and the others to whom she introduced me were not Messianic or "completed" Jews—Jews who believe in Jesus yet who try to retain as much of their Jewish heritage as they can. Betty was a former Christian whose conversion, oddly, worked in reverse. For the first time in my life, I realized this *can* and *does* happen. I thought reporting on this circumstance would be eye-opening to other Christian believers and would set their antennae twitching.

As Passover 1973 approached, Betty invited Kay and me to attend her synagogue's large Passover seder, a ritual feast held on the first night of the Jewish holiday of Passover. In Houston synagogues often are *megasynagogues*—just as churches there are often beyond enormous. (After all, this *was* Texas!) My first seder was intriguing but not nearly as memorable as the debate that Betty got into at our table with a woman whose Jewish roots went back generations. In her usual delicious rush of zealousness, Betty expostulated that all Christians ought to become Jews. The other woman argued that the only authentic Jews were true sons and daughters of Abraham—born into Jewish families. Neither Betty nor I missed the implication: Betty's "real" Jewishness was brought into question. Christians would certainly question it, too. Fascinating!

Over the years, celebrating Passover seders at a Houston synagogue became a tradition in the Moore family. I became intrigued with the size, scope, and history of Houston's Jewish community and endeavored to editorially capture the heart of this citizenry. Among other stories, I covered a bris and bar mitzvah and did a photo essay and feature on a day in the life of an Orthodox family readying for a Sabbath.

I eventually decided to write a news story detailing the history of Judaism in Houston. The article unfortunately carried the offensive (as I later learned) header "The Jews Here." I was besieged with virulent letters and phone calls from Jews who protested, "When I saw that headline, I felt as though I was living in Nazi Germany again. I felt like the *Chronicle* was singling us out for persecution." *Huh?* I was stunned. *What gives?* I wondered. I genuinely had tried to tell a well-meaning story of how the Jewish community always seemed to have a geographical center, which over the years as Houston grew and prospered transitioned to different locations and neighborhoods within the city. I had quoted statistics from the National Conference of Christians and Jews noting that the average Jewish family's income in Houston was five times that of the average Houston non-Jewish family and even dramatically larger than that of African-American and Hispanic families. That was not something confidential that I had to dig out; it was readily provided to me. But my detractors had a good point; I needed to figure out Jewish sensitivities and elevate my consciousness, if necessary.

Also, at first I couldn't figure out the Jewish obsession with the Holocaust and Israel. Both topics seemed to evoke almost irrational responses and tap into caverns of emotion. I even was chided one time about referring to someone as "my Jewish friend." (I was supposed to say, *my friend who is Jewish.*) So, I started engaging in ongoing dialogues with various rabbis and other Jewish leaders in Houston to find out more about this horrific aspect of their history.

Years later, after I traveled for 10 days to the Soviet Union as the only Christian in a group of Texas Jews, I received a prestigious award from the Anti-Defamation League of B'nai B'rith lauding my singular relationship with Houston's Jewry. My dear friend, Tom Neumann, who headed the local ADL and invited me to make the trip with him, made the presentation. Texas' governor at that time (Mark White) was at the head table when I got the coveted plaque. That award touched me because I had worked so diligently to convince Houston's Jewish community that I was a friend and not just a narrow-minded, anti-Semitic, Southern Baptist bigot.

Actually I approached every religious and denominational group in Houston with the same curiosity and fervor that I did the Jews. Though certainly still solid in my own personal, Evangelical religious persuasion, I set as my goal to write about every religion and every denomination represented there. I did not keep actual charts, but I mentally measured, *When was the last time I wrote about the Mormons? Or the Jehovah's Witnesses? Or the Churches of Christ? Or the Church of God in Christ? Or the Muslims? Or the Hare Krishnas?* I developed a host of contacts and sources in all of these communities. I found the plurality of Houston's religious life truly captivating.

As I mentioned earlier, I arrived in Houston just in time for the opening of the first mosque, which served as a catalyst for mosques not just in Houston but around the country. I stayed long enough there to see the proliferation of mosques in Houston as well as the emergence of Islam as a major factor in Houston's religious life. It all began in a small, brick, two-bedroom cottage in Houston's Montrose area. The small band of Muslims who arrived in Houston because of Houston's connection to Middle-Eastern oil dressed like Houston businessmen of that era. They bought the house and turned it into a mosque because they needed somewhere they could worship Allah and practice their faith. As I watched the Islamic faith burgeon there, I realized that someday Muslims would outnumber the Jews in Houston and elsewhere in the U.S. Then I began in columns to wonder out loud what implications this had not only for Houston but also for our nation as the axis of religious life in America shifted so dramatically.

Early on I observed an odd, emerging kinship between Houston's new Muslims and some members of Houston's African-American community. Though of Middle Eastern descent, Houston's Muslims warmly embraced these African-Americans who wanted to join their faith. The movement was particularly pronounced inside Texas prisons in which African-American inmates began adhering in significant numbers to Allah and Islam. This, too, was a national trend that most traditional church leaders chose to ignore rather than face directly.

I was struck with the serious realization that churches for the most part disregarded the young African-American males—who were then and still are disproportionately represented in our nation's prisons and jails—while the Muslims were busy winning converts and building bridges to black followers.

85

Why would someone such as Betty Zollars reject her strong roots in Christianity to become a Jewish, female Billy Graham wannabe? What was so alluring about Muslim beliefs and practice that black males (usually from homes with some Evangelical connection) would be so drawn to the worship of Allah?

Later, as a vice president of an SBC agency, I'd visit Mexico with missionaries to find a huge local core of former Southern Baptists who turned their back on these roots and now embraced the Mormon faith. *What's the deal?* I pondered. What were our churches doing, or not doing, that would pave the way for and enable these reverse conversions in droves? Why were people so disenfranchised with the faith that had been instilled in them since childhood?

For that matter, why eventually would churches dot the landscape with marquees calling themselves, among other titles, "Family of Faith," "Koinonia Fellowship," and "Household of Love"? Why, if one probed further, would these worship houses reveal they were former mainline congregations that wanted to dodge having *Southern Baptist, Presbyterian, United Methodist*, etc., humiliatingly linked to their monikers?

Years would pass before I could get my mind around, and would find myself personally smack-dab in the middle of, the *why*s of this turnoff.

Chapter 8

Go to Your Brother

Truth No. 8: If those who lead the church could pick one passage of Scripture to jettison from the entire Bible, Matthew 5:23-24 probably would be at the top of their list.

Although it was then known by the somnambulant title, the "Church *Chronicle*," the weekly religion section that I inherited actually was one of the oldest, largest, and best-developed of its kind in the country for that day. Major metropolitan dailies were just beginning to emphasize the religion beat and to devote set-apart pages in the paper for religion news. Even though the *Houston Chronicle* was far from the largest newspaper in the country, it already was on the map in this regard. My task was to kick it up several notches to even greater respectability.

Because I at first was a one-person operation, I had to write, edit, design, and oversee the entire production of the Church *Chronicle*, whose alliterative name I upgraded to simply "*Chronicle* Religion." My task, I discovered, was arduous. I realized that I had to rely heavily on news services and feature syndicates to help me fill all the space in my large number of pages, especially since I also was expected to write daily news stories for the front page and other sections of the *Chronicle*.

About six months into my job, the Greek Orthodox Archdiocese of North and South America held its annual convention in Houston's Rice Hotel, across the street from the *Chronicle* building. I wasn't quite sure what kind of feature story I would write about this still rather mysterious body, whose members wore formidable, flowing, black robes. Many had enormous, Eastern European-like beards and looked like something out of the opening scenes of *Dr. Zhivago*.

One benefit of covering the event was getting to dine at one of the toniest multi-course formal banquets I've ever attended in my life. As each person destined for the head table entered the room, a spotlight followed the person to his or her seat amidst high drama. The food was to die over—literally.

After we finished the main course, I spotted the wait staff hoisting trays of the dessert—gorgeous plates of 600 bosomy, icing-bedecked baked Alaska—into the huge dining hall. Just as the trays of the flaming delicacies were paraded though the doors, billowy robed Archbishop Iakovos jumped suddenly to the podium. He blurted that he'd just received word that the Patriarch of Constantinople (the pope of this body) had just died. Iakovos began weeping theatrically and then fled the dining hall in an emotional eruption of grief. The Greek Orthodox priests rose in unison from their tables and, in a fever of respect for the late leader, instructed the waiters to return the still-flaming baked Alaskas to the hotel's kitchen.

I, too, felt like weeping, but not so much for departed Patriarch Athenagoras. I had already been salivating for some of the amazing sweets that now were destined for the kitchen garbage disposals! I thought that surely this treat would be my well-deserved reward for sitting through a boring meeting so far. Seeing this dream go down the tube (or into the dumpster) might have been one of the saddest moments of my life.

Then it dawned on me: I had stumbled into a "local angle" on an international event—something reporters can only dream of happening. I may not have feasted on the anticipated baked Alaska, but at least I had a story. Before that point, the prospects had looked bleak.

For the next several days my articles about the death of the patriarch and the local reaction appeared on the *Chronicle*'s front page. Even the feature I planned for the religion section got swiped for the main paper. Before the week was over, I had written 10 separate stories as daily coverage.

When my religion section appeared at the end of the week, no *Louis Moore* byline appeared anywhere. I was just too tired and overwhelmed (maybe I was still grieving my lost baked Alaska) by everything else I had done in recent days, so I had used the religion wire service copy to fill up my space.

As I prepared to leave the office on Friday afternoon, Dan Cobb, the *Chronicle*'s crusty, pipe-smoking news editor, cornered me and lambasted me for not having a local bylined story in the religion section. Weary as I was, I thought he was rude, completely insensitive to my situation, and just downright mean.

Nevertheless I walked away from our conversation vowing to myself that as long as I was on the newspaper's payroll, *Chronicle* Religion would never appear again minus my byline. From my briarpatch of guilt, for the next 14 years I made good on my commitment. If I wanted to take a vacation, it could begin only after at least one bylined story was written and left behind for the section front page. Years later when I was burned in a freak propane accident while our family camped in Colorado, I wrote my weekly column from my hospital bed (dictating it to my wife because my hands were too badly burned to be used on a keyboard).

Dan Cobb's diatribe was just the right motivation I needed to propel me to write my own stories about national and international religious events. No longer would I be satisfied to print someone else's stories and bylines in my religion section. That meant I had to bone up fast on all the major religion stories occurring worldwide.

In this context I learned about the theological squabble under way in the Lutheran Church-Missouri Synod, a denomination about which I knew very little.

The *St. Louis Post-Dispatch* and several other newspapers in America's heartland were noted for specializing in this story. The *Post-Dispatch*'s much-ballyhooed coverage was led by Jim Adams, a former Roman Catholic priest who was by then married and a father of several young children. One of my goals was to become as adept at, if not better than, Jim was at covering the story.

The Missouri Synod was embroiled in a controversy over the infallibility of the Scriptures. The issue involved how literally Scripture was to be interpreted. Leading the charge against so-called moderates in the synod was the Dr. Jacob A.O. Preus, a feisty, fiery fellow with a demeanor more like that of a firebrand politician than a pastor.

The first time I met "Jack" Preus, we connected well. I found him conversant and quotable. He didn't equivocate on his stands or his words. He said what he meant and meant what he said.

The fight in the Missouri Synod pitted Dr. Preus against Dr. Robert Tietjen, president of Concordia Lutheran Seminary in St. Louis. Tietjen was considered the synod's leading moderate. I did not find Dr. Tietjen particularly friendly or easy to quote or understand.

Most religion editors, including Jim Adams, had the exact opposite reaction to the two men. In their estimation, Preus was the villain and Tietjen the saint.

At first the split in the synod between the moderates and conservatives seemed about 50-50 among both the laypeople and the clergy. Everything pointed toward a major schism in the 2.7 million-member denomination.

The battle divided the national church body but also the

state synods and even local churches.

At the heart of everything was the issue of how the Bible's authority was to be viewed. Conservatives took the position that the Bible was infallible in all matters. The moderates said some passages were allegory and begged not to be understood literally. Around and around they fought.

Since newspaper people often have liberal leanings, the conservative Preus was soon at odds with most of those on the U.S. religion beats. He believed he had been maligned and misrepresented by most reporters. Since I always had easy rapport with him, I soon found myself in a tiny league of writers to whom Dr. Preus would even speak.

One Sunday night in January 1976 Dr. Preus was in Houston to preach at a local Lutheran congregation. I took Kay, now pregnant again and in her ninth month with our expected son, with me to cover Preus' message. Preus, himself the father of 10, seemed impressed that I had brought my great-with-child wife out on a wintery night as I covered his message. This seemed to further my good relations with him.

The first time I attended the Texas Lutheran synod meeting, Dr. Preus was scheduled to be a keynote speaker. As usual he and I had a cordial interview; I got several "scoops" on what his plans were for removing moderates from the synod leadership.

My discussions with Dr. Preus, however, did not sit well with Dr. Carl Heckmann, president of the Texas Synod of the Lutheran Church-Missouri Synod. In the hallway afterward, Dr. Heckmann, a noted moderate, verbally bludgeoned me for trying to stir up trouble by interviewing Dr. Preus. In a nanosecond the conversation went south.

The next morning at breakfast in the hotel, Mrs. Heckmann approached my table and whispered, "My husband wants to visit with you today to apologize for his behavior last night.

He had no business speaking to you the way he did. I reminded him afterward that our son, Mark, is a journalism student at the University of Texas and wants to be a newspaper reporter like you. I asked my husband how he would feel if someone spoke to Mark that way."

She went on to confide that she understood what a terrible spot I was in trying to cover evenhandedly two warring denominational factions. Nothing I could do would please either side completely, she avowed.

I was shocked by her words. She was the only religious leader's spouse who, in my entire career, ever cast even the mildest aspersion on her husband in my presence and acknowledged that being in my role was difficult at times.

As his wife had assured me, Dr. Heckmann later that day pulled me aside in the hallway and apologized for his intemperate remarks. He said he would never want any church leader to speak to his journalist son, Mark, in such a thoughtless way.

I accepted his apology as graciously as I could.

Ironically and parenthetically, a year later Mark Heckmann applied to the *Chronicle*, among other newspapers, and was hired as a general-assignments reporter there. Shortly thereafter he, even more ironically, was assigned to be my assistant.

In a still stranger turn of events, Mark substituted for me in 1976 and 1977 at the annual meetings of the Baptist General Convention of Texas. In those years the BGCT was embroiled in a controversy over whether to allow churches that had become charismatic (neo-Pentecostal) to send messengers (thus official recognition) to the BGCT meetings. The BGCT emphatically and by a wide margin rejected the charismatics. Fortunately during this controversy I never knew of any BGCT leader who spoke rudely to Mark Heckmann as had happened to me in his father's denomination.

Because I now was Mark's supervisor, over time Carl Heckmann and I became good friends. I grew to truly love the Heckmann family. Years later after I had left the *Chronicle* and was living in Plano, TX, and shortly before his death, Dr. Heckmann deliberately sought me out to have lunch one last time. We recalled and laughed about our first encounter in that Austin hotel hallway so long ago. Aware he was nearing the end of his life, Dr. Heckmann wanted me to reassure him again that I had forgiven him for his remarks and held no lingering grudge.

In retrospect I believe Dr. Heckmann was one of the finest Christians I have ever known. Only a secure person of strong character can admit error forthrightly without qualifying, parsing words, or trying to wiggle out of clear wrongdoing. This minister truly followed Jesus' admonition in Matthew 5:23-24: *"Therefore, if you are offering your gift at the altar and there remember that your brother has something against you, leave your gift there in front of the altar. First go and be reconciled to your brother; then come and offer your gift."*

At the time this happened, I was 30 years old. As I experienced Dr. Heckmann's exemplary act of contrition, I might have expected that I would run into his brand of magnanimity among religious leaders again and again. I remember thinking that others out there, who immerse themselves in Scriptures daily and are so intimately aware of the teaching of Christ, would also model this type of biblical peacemaking.

I needn't have wasted my time waiting for this to happen. *Mea culpas* do not roll trippingly off the tongues of people of the cloth. Proper, sincere, clerical public apologies that I've witnessed or even remotely known about are few and far between. W.A. Criswell, a vocal supporter of segregation in the 1950s, apologized later for being on the wrong side of the race issue, although he did so long after many in the public eye were reversing themselves all over the place. His was considered less than a Damascus-road experience.

In Jim Bakker's book, *I Was Wrong,* the former televangelist apologizes for a wrong understanding of the prosperity gospel and for leading others astray by teaching them to "fall in love with money."

More than 30 years after it happened, Billy Graham apologized publicly for making what is considered now an anti-Semitic remark while he talked with President Nixon; their conversation was recorded on the infamous White House tapes.

In his popular discipleship series, *MasterLife,* author and Southern Baptist missions leader Avery Willis recalls a much-lauded time in Indonesia in which, during a worship service, a great movement of reconciliation broke out among missionaries and others. Missionaries and their leaders stepped to the mike and confessed publicly, while others tearfully approached friends in the audience privately and sought forgiveness for hurts and wrongdoing in the missions community.

The *Chronicle,* like other newspapers, regularly printed retractions when it found it had misrepresented facts. Certainly, from time to time in my 14 years there, I had to swallow my pride and publicly apologize in print for something that wrongfully made its way into my coverage.

But in my own, individual experience, in my more than four decades of observing the church at work, Lutheran official Carl Heckmann stands alone as the *only* leader of any religious denomination to ever extend to me any type of personal "I was wrong"—an utterly horrendous but regretfully not surprising commentary on the followers of Christ.

* * * * * * * *

The battle in the Missouri Synod raged throughout most of the 1970s. I saw Dr. Preus often and stayed on the cutting edge of developments in that denomination. In fact, I wrote about the controversy so often, some *Chronicle* readers were convinced I must be Lutheran.

One headline I wrote—"Those fighting Lutherans"—seemed to personify the situation. My friend and colleague, Gary Haaland, associate pastor of Memorial Drive Lutheran Church in Houston—the largest Lutheran church in America at that time—advised me that the headline offended many Lutherans not affiliated with the Missouri Synod. He said the strife within the Missouri Synod was embarrassing other Lutherans who wanted to live together peaceably.

The Missouri Synod eventually did split. The rupture was nowhere near the size of what many had expected. The moderate wing managed to pull away only a small number of churches and followers when it eventually fled the denomination to form its own enfeebled synod, which never amounted to much.

In so many ways the Lutheran Church-Missouri Synod catfight was my "learner" schism preceding the war that soon would splinter my own denomination, the Southern Baptist Convention. What eventually occurred in the SBC had an eerie parallel to the previous Missouri Synod scuffle. I was glad this chapter in Lutheran history at least had happened on my watch so it could prepare the way.

I remember that when the acrimonious Missouri Synod fight was at its peak, I remarked almost prophetically to my fellow reporter, George Rosenblatt, that if the SBC ever became embroiled in such a heinous war, I would rather quit my job than be forced to cover it. I confessed that I couldn't imagine how I would respond if I had to watch my own people at each other's throats as viciously as the Missouri Synod members were knifing each other.

Regrettably, years later, I was an eyewitness to SBC behavior that made the Lutherans' battle look like a Sunday-school picnic.

Instead of getting to bolt, I had to brace myself and be there—covering every mumblin' word.

Chapter 9

Nowhere to Go but Up

Truth No. 9: When God promises He'll take care of your enemies, He's talking about church people, too.

To other reporters on a newspaper, someone who might actually *want* to cover religion had to be some kind of serious weirdo. Among news staff members, who were sometimes cynical and—putting it mildly—heathen, the beat itself was usually the brunt of major, deriding humor.

Thus I was eager to meet other people who shared my true passion for reporting on the subject. I wanted to know how religion editors on other secular daily newspapers conducted their jobs. The society for such professionals was the Religion Newswriters Association, composed of journalists from United States and Canada.

Naively, I decided to attend the annual RNA meeting in Atlanta when it met in May just after I was hired in February 1972. I knew that the Lester Kinsolving column decrying the Janice Law firing and hinting that I was untrustworthy because I dared to believe Jesus was born of a virgin was still on the front burner with RNA members. I knew that some people still thought I was wrong to take the *Chronicle* job after what they believed was the questionable ousting of one of their closest confreres.

But I had to be in Atlanta anyway on assignment to attend the annual convention of the Quadrennial General Conference of the United Methodist Church. *What harm could be done for me to just drop in to the RNA meeting that convenes while the Methodists are in session?* I reasoned. *After all, to know me is to love me.* I was gutsy enough to think that I could, in one-on-one relationships, make inroads into this group.

In the Methodist-meeting press room beforehand, however, some colleagues cautioned me that I wouldn't dare attend the RNA meeting if I valued my life. They said anger against the *Chronicle* still ran extremely high. One colleague bluntly adjured me to "stay out of the way for a little while so you won't become the scapegoat and victim of this situation." When Lester Kinsolving would enter the press room, he would shoot me a glacial glare and refuse to speak. Several other religion reporters seemed to view me with alien eyes. I yielded to the words of warning and decided not to risk my luck with what appeared to be a cold-blooded group. Discouragement suffused me. While others attended the RNA meeting, I stayed in my hotel room alone in my pity party. I watched television and called Kay every few hours to tell her how lonely and disappointed I felt.

The morning after the RNA meeting concluded and with the United Methodist meeting continuing, a few of my peers, having realized I indeed had not joined them at a single RNA event, must have sensed how inhospitable this looked. A few suddenly went out of their way to encourage me to stay the course. "Just do your work and do it well, and you will earn the respect of your colleagues," I heard Associated Press Religion Writer George Cornell saying to me.

I was stunned that someone with the stature of Cornell, considered the dean of religion writers, would give a nod in my direction at all.

At the moment I heard these words, something clicked within me. I vowed to myself that with God's help I would someday lead this organization that right now was wiping its feet on me. With my nose to the grindstone and determined to succeed, I worked early morning to late at night in the denominational press rooms. I began trying to scoop all my colleagues so that others would take notice. I vowed to write stories that would convince them all.

Whenever a colleague stepped over the Maginot Line and deigned to chat or, on rare occasions, invited me to share a meal, I hoped that meant I was getting somewhere with my peer relationships. That posed a new set of problems. I quickly discovered that most of my colleagues were regular drinkers of alcoholic beverages. Since I did not imbibe, I tried diplomatically to steer around the issue. I did not want that fact to become another red herring as the theological issue of the virgin birth had been.

On one occasion when I was with a group of about 12 fellow religion editors at a bar in Dallas, I quietly ordered a soda; then when the server demanded that our party be issued only one check, I covered my tracks by volunteering to be the banker for the group and collect the money for the bill and tip. My action was a ruse to divert attention away from my non-alcoholic drink. Eventually my peers seemed to accept the fact that I would not be their drinking buddy but could still have convivial fellowship with them when I was invited.

Among my new friends was Bill Reed, religion editor of the Nashville *Tennessean*. Bill was one of only a few African-Americans on the religion beat of a secular newspaper anywhere. Since Nashville is the epicenter of Southern Baptist life, Bill wanted to look sharp when he covered that denomination but also felt handicapped with his lack of knowledge because he was not one. He quickly observed that, given my background and experience, I might be valuable help to him. Until he retired years later, Bill deliberately inserted himself next to me in the press room at all SBC and other denominational meetings. I would coach him on Southern Baptist intricacies.

To my surprise, Bill was a bigwig in RNA. In 1976 he was elected president of the organization. Out of his gratitude for my helping tutor him in Baptist life, Bill got me involved in one special committee assignment as a way I could begin establishing my worth to the group. I participated in this "toe-in-the-door" maneuver but still kept a low profile.

* * * * * * * *

During 1975, I produced some especially outstanding religion sections that I believed demonstrated excellence in news coverage. I submitted them to the prestigious contest for RNA's Harold Schachern Memorial Award for the best religion sections during the previous year. I knew that the deck was still likely stacked against me and figured I didn't have much of a chance to win, but I couldn't imagine that anyone had sections any more scintillating than those I submitted.

My stories included such resourceful work as an interview about the religious life inside a Texas prison, local clergy responding to the revelation of Nixon's profanity, evangelical revival services held by a Catholic church, a federal crackdown on church-bond funding, the opening of the first Hindu temple in Houston, financial retirement woes for some pastors, the cancer battle of a top Presbyterian executive, and others.

For almost three days I almost literally held my breath while I knew the contest committee was screening everything.

Then I got the announcement—the *Chronicle* indeed had WON THE SCHACHERN! Only three years earlier, for fear of reprisal, I had boycotted the RNA meeting. Now, I was one of the organization's top award winners!

This event seemed to turn the tide for me and the *Chronicle* in busting down the door to RNA acceptance. Even Lester Kinsolving offered his terse but significant congratulations. In a short but momentous first conversation, we agreed to bury the hatchet and let the Janice Law incident take its rightful place in RNA history.

The year 1975, the same year the *Chronicle* won the Schachern, turned out to be a watershed period in my career. In April, I received the National Religious Public Relations Council's annual media award for outstanding religion coverage on a secular daily newspaper. That award made me a "fellow" of RPRC, which meant I had a lifetime honorary membership in the organization. I was the youngest reporter to win that award, which was presented at the Washington, D.C. Press Club.

Those two remarkable accolades in 1975 were bright spots in the dark year that had begun with the personal loss of our first baby, mentioned in Chapter 6. They ushered in the sunshine of early 1976, which kicked off with the February birth of our son, Matthew—healthy and at term!

* * * * * * *

Winning the Schachern award broke the ice and cleared the way for me to become more active in the organization. Then in 1978, Bill Reed called and said he wanted to nominate me to be RNA treasurer. I was flabbergasted. The protocol was that every two years RNA officers seemed to move up a step in the leadership—secretary, then treasurer, then second vice president, then first vice president, then president. I was shocked that Bill wanted me to skip a level and start with holding the treasurer's post first. I told him I hesitated to go around the organization's previous lock-step patterns. I feared I'd make myself vulnerable again if proper channels weren't followed. With Bill's calm assurance that he would smooth any difficulties for me, I agreed to the nomination.

After being elected unanimously, I assumed the role as if it were my part-time job. Whereas previous treasurers operated in a rather hang-loose manner, I set about to organize, upgrade, and professionalize the office. Today, RNA is extremely corporate, with a staff of its own—far beyond what I ever dreamed. Back in 1978 RNA was a very loose-knit organization; the treasurer's records reflected this. Numerous members were behind in paying their annual dues because no one had systemized the process. Financial reports were embarrassingly skimpy to non-existent. Unlike today, where many of RNA's awards are endowed, back then the organization's endowment of $5,000 was insufficient to fund from interest the three RNA annual award contests, which paid a mere $100 each.

Two years later when I moved up to be RNA's second vice president, I felt pleased with the status of the treasurer's records and funds that I turned over to my successor. Perhaps my greatest accomplishment was getting the ball rolling for what today is RNA's premier annual award, the John M. Templeton Award for Progress in Religion Reporting. Mr. Templeton, who at that time was one of the world's richest men, visited my office at the *Houston Chronicle* to propose funding such an award. Establishing this award took more than five years because a few key members fought against the idea and said that naming an award for someone outside the organization was compromising and a potential conflict of interest. Most RNA'ers today would probably have trouble believing that the much-touted award was voted down twice before finally being approved on a trial basis.

As RNA's first vice president I also was chair for the organization's annual contests. Other RNA officers were on the contest committee, so I became a committee member immediately after I was elected treasurer. This meant that for eight years I was involved with overseeing the organization's contest for the best religion section, the best religion reporter, and the best religion reporter on a small newspaper.

The more than 200 religion reporters I knew were uniquely gifted individuals whose work reflected their widely divergent personalities. Although at least one, Virginia Culver of the *Denver Post*, was outspoken about her atheist beliefs, most were practicing members of their religious denominations. Marge Hyer of *The Washington Post* and Ed Briggs of the *Richmond Times-Dispatch* were Episcopalians. Helen Parmley of *The Dallas Morning News* and Russ Chandler of the *Los Angeles Times* were Presbyterians. Roy Larsen of the *Chicago Sun-Times* and Ken Briggs of *The New York Times* were United Methodists. *The New York Times* seemed always to have a Jewish person in one of its religion-reporting slots. Only a handful of religion reporters were Evangelicals. Most of my time in RNA, I knew of no other religion editors or writers who were affiliated with the Southern Baptist Convention. This worked to my advantage, since I became useful for others to pick my brain.

* * * * * * *

In 1984, at the age of 38, I became the youngest person in the organization's history to be elected president of RNA. I accomplished the goal that 12 years earlier I had made with clench-jawed determination. At that year's end, the *Los Angeles Times* media critic wrote a front-page series on religion editors on U.S. secular newspapers. David Shaw's article contained the quote, "Moore is eminently fair, many in the field say." He noted that among my peers I was the most outspoken about my Christian faith and active in the practice of my personal religious beliefs. He then made the broad statement that despite my personal expression of faith, my colleagues scored me high for professionalism and abilities.

Newspaper executives throughout the country who were looking for new religion writers began calling to seek my opinions about potential hires who I thought were the best in the business. Newspapers called me for quotes about the state of the religion-writing profession.

From the bottom of the heap, when I felt too beaten down to attend a single RNA session, I had risen to "Mr. RNA," as my colleague Helen Parmley, religion editor of *The Dallas Morning News,* called me. Without my having to engage in flagrant confrontation, God had taken care of my enemies, as He promises in 2 Chronicles 20:15-17: *"Do not be afraid or discouraged because of this vast army. For the battle is not yours, but God's . . .. You will not have to fight this battle. Take up your positions; stand firm and see the deliverance the Lord will give you."* In this case those *enemies,* as I earlier pointed out, were among the practicing faithful. (Remember, religious people were the ones who nailed Jesus to the cross.) I didn't have to rise to their bait or exchange verbal unpleasantries. Steadily, methodically, using my God-given talents to disprove their claims—that conservative Christianity would taint me from covering my beat with integrity—won the day.

Among people who have seen this promise from God's Word borne out in their lives, I have been in stellar company.

As Baylor president from 1995-2005, Dr. Robert Sloan was shamelessly vilified for his efforts to turn the university toward a slightly more conservative bent. A Scripture, *By Him are all things made* (John 1:3), etched in stone over the new state-of-the-art science building, symbolized Sloan's efforts to make Baylor's Christian moorings more a part of day-to-day campus life. Forced to resign because of pressure from an unrelenting old guard, Sloan became a modern-day embodiment of Jesus' warning (John 15:20) that His followers would know persecution just as He did. Houston Baptist University snapped Sloan up in a heartbeat for its presidential vacancy; the final story has not been written about what the visionary Sloan will be able to accomplish at HBU under his leadership. In the face of extreme character assassination, Sloan remained a model of Christian deportment. God fought the battle for him; his enemies have been unable to derail Baylor's ambitious 2012 plan, of which Sloan was the architect. It remains the blueprint by which Baylor presses on toward the upper echelons of higher education.

When Cardinal Joseph Ratzinger arrived at the Vatican from Germany in the early 1980s, he was greeted ignominiously by the curia of that day (who even sarcastically emphasized the *Rat* syllable in his name). While I found his writings and statements fascinating, many in the U.S. press corps recoiled at many of his positions. One wondered how long this maligned cardinal would remain in Italy before he was sent back to his home.

Despite the negative press and negative attitudes in the Vatican bureaucracy, Pope John Paul II continued to rely on Cardinal Ratzinger's skills and rewarded him for his fidelity and for their mutual perspectives on the church. Though the men were somewhat similar in age, by the time John Paul died in 2005, Ratzinger had risen above the controversy and was poised to succeed the charismatic pope. God took care of his enemies, as the formerly defamed Ratzinger was elected Pope Benedict XVI.

* * * * * * * *

While I breathed a prayer of thanks for God's provision in helping me overcome these severe RNA roadblocks, I couldn't help pondering what lay beyond my 40th birthday, when I would be a "former" RNA president. Would I simply "drift" for the next 25 years into retirement? Would I quickly become a "has-been" in what is generally regarded as a young person's profession? Or would I find some new mountains to climb?

Personality tests show that I am not the kind of individual who sits quietly and easily on the sidelines. The two years as RNA president, which began in 1984, provided me with a rare opportunity to think about the future in a way not afforded me during the trauma that first greeted me and that I had to conquer. I began to envision what might be beyond the next hill.

But soon I would be snapped back to reality and away from indulging in these mind trips. I first had to continue navigating my way through one of the greatest professional challenges of my life—far more of a threat to me than the irritating Kinsolving/Law/RNA tangle.

Staying afloat would take every ounce of my energies and focus.

Chapter 10

An Episcopal Priest!

Truth No. 10: God has friends in all kinds of places.

In the same *Los Angeles Times* story that described me as "eminently fair," media writer David Shaw also described one of my happiest journalistic experiences: dining with a Catholic bishop who said he was certain, from my writing, that I was an Episcopal priest!

Shaw noted that in my time as *Chronicle* religion editor, I also had been mistaken for a Catholic, a Jew, a Methodist, an atheist, and a Hare Krishna—"all of which he takes as testimony to his professionalism," the *LA Times* reporter wrote.

Clearly someone who pegged me in any of these ways never read any of my impassioned columns during the height of the Southern Baptist fracas, in which I decried the fact that my own denomination was going berserk before my very eyes.

But I can't help myself—I did love to cover a good Episcopal story, especially since I had so much typecasting to overcome about this particular body. I had always thought of Episcopalians as a very narrow group representing the wealthy, well-heeled, and hoity-toity.

In September 1973 I attended my first Episcopal General Convention held in Louisville, my old stomping grounds. The pomp and ceremony, clergy vestments, and the prevailing attitude in the Episcopal House of Bishops (lay people get to participate in the House of Deputies) certainly reinforced my regard of this denomination as one of money, education, and political stature.

But the Episcopal convention's decision to rewrite its definition of *marriage* was anything but narrow! Previously *marriage* was defined as a set of vows taken before a clergyman followed by one act of sexual intercourse producing a lifelong marriage commitment. The new definition spoke of ongoing spiritual, psychological, and sexual recommitments by the married couple. Little did I realize then how revolutionary the convention's alteration of the *marriage* definition would be. By today's standards, that change seems rather miniscule and archaic. But it launched the basis on which mammoth changes impacting the Episcopal Church's approach to marriage, divorce, women's rights, homosexuality, and other issues emerged.

Back in Houston, I began to learn more and more about Episcopal churches and discovered how much individual congregations can vary from each other.

One Sunday I attended Houston's Episcopal Church of the Redeemer, which broke ground for the introduction of the Charismatic (neo-Pentecostal) Movement into the Episcopal Church at large. Across the front of the church's sanctuary was painted a huge mural of Jesus with outstretched arms. From the building appearance alone I could have been in an African-American congregation instead of a predominantly white, Episcopal church. The church's music was like the fare one hears today in "contemporary" services everywhere. Back then, of course, in the early 1970s the music was thought unusually evangelical and confessional and regarded as revolutionary.

People at Church of the Redeemer greeted each other with warm, expressive hugs and embraces—not the frozen, formal handshakes I had expected. Nothing in the church's demeanor was stuffy or snobbish.

Most interesting of all was when the congregation sang "in tongues" with almost wanton gaiety or when individuals spoke in unintelligible utterances during worship services. When that happened, I had to look again to be sure the bulletin said "Episcopal."

If what went on inside the church's walls was unusual and busted preconceived images, what transpired outside the church's walls was truly remarkable. Many of Redeemer's members lived in what the church called *households*—homes in the surrounding neighborhood that resembled religious communes. One church family provided the "core" for the home, but others, including married couples and singles, lived there, too. As the Book of Acts describes the early church, these households shared *all things in common* (Acts 2:42-47). Residents pooled their money and shared their cars. Some felt "called" to work in secular jobs to raise funds to allow others in the household to hold all sorts of ministry positions.

On several occasions I was invited to dine at household tables at Redeemer church. The people seemed to relish in being together for the innocent enjoyment of pure fellowship; an amazing spirit of intimacy prevailed.

The households sponsored a ministry in the Fourth Ward Clinic in Houston's Montrose area. Doctors, nurses, and other medical personnel who lived in the households and worked in the clinic provided free medical services for Houston's poor. Doctors at the clinic spoke of praying for patients and literally seeing broken arms mended and illness healed. I found their testimonies eye-popping.

As intriguing as everything was at Episcopal Church of the Redeemer, it also seemed surreal. Over the centuries Christians have been troubled by those Book of Acts descriptions of early Christians holding everything collectively and sharing all. In other places in other centuries when Christians have tried to duplicate the Acts setting, their idealism eventually collapsed.

At the time I couldn't pinpoint why I felt vaguely troubled and doubtful about this Houston movement's success. Years later I understood why. What began as a harmonious Christian community eventually turned into a squabbling, litigious environment where distrust replaced certitude and pragmatism replaced idealism.

Households became places in which people were expected to conform to the standards of the authority figure in the home—where addicts were reformed not by love but by stern discipline. (Sound like a Jonestown precursor? It's what happens in many churches when the excesses of good are overdone.)

My greatest disappointment with Episcopal Church of the Redeemer occurred when nearly three decades after I first visited there, the married pastor of the church in the 1970s confessed publicly to having had, during that time, an ongoing homosexual relationship with a young man in the church. I was shocked at the revelation, as I'm sure many others both at Redeemer and in Christian communities around the world were. Brotherly love became too brotherly; the forging of intimate relationships went askew. What looked so model on the outside was entirely different up close.

* * * * * * *

In another sector of town was John Bradshaw's innovative Sunday-morning class at Palmer Episcopal Church in the Rice University area. Bradshaw was in the vanguard of blending psychology with religion in the church setting. A recovering alcoholic, John brought the term *dysfunctional family* into the mainstream and laid the groundwork for what eventually became the self-help and recovery movement in churches across the country. Today, John is an international speaker/author on recovery ministries and personal growth. Looking back, I feel honored that I interviewed him when he was just beginning the long road to fame and fortune.

* * * * * * *

Unlike the two churches just mentioned, St. Martin's Episcopal Church in Houston's silk-stocking Memorial area bespoke wealth, education, and political clout—at least my image of America's Episcopalians had *some* grain of truth in it.

Like Palmer Memorial, which birthed Bradshaw, and Church of the Redeemer, which birthed the modern communal-living movement, St. Martin's Episcopal was known throughout the country as well, but for an entirely different reason. Its most celebrated members were George and Barbara Bush.

Each Easter, St. Martin's held a series of six Monday-evening Lenten worship services. I was amazed when one year I was invited to be one of the six speakers. I estimated that a Monday-night service at an Episcopal Church would be a snoozer and probably would draw a crowd of no more than 25 persons. Imagine my surprise when I showed up 30 minutes before the worship service and couldn't find a place to park because the church's lots were full! As I looked out over the congregation that night, I could not see a single empty seat in what was the largest Episcopal sanctuary in Houston.

The bigger surprise occurred several weeks later when the Rev. J. Thomas Bagby, longtime rector at St. Martin's, informed me that each year the congregation votes on which of the six Lenten speakers it wants to invite back to speak at services in the year to follow. I'm glad I didn't know I had been engaged in a popularity contest! I was humbled when Dr. Bagby told me I won the vote and would have a repeat performance. This established a warm relationship with St. Martin's, which ultimately provided one of the most unique experiences of my life.

One day a call from Dr. Bagby invited me to attend a private breakfast in his office before the worship service on the first Sunday in the new year, 1984. He said he wanted me to meet the guest speaker—the Vice President of the United States.

Kay and our by-then 7-year-old son, Matthew, accompanied me to St. Martin's. I intended simply to allow Matthew to peek into the pastor's office to glimpse at the Vice President before we directed our son to the church's program for children. Before I knew it, George Bush spotted Matthew and raced to the door to shake his hand. The Vice President leaned down, compared the pattern on his necktie with that of Matthew's, and schmoozed him thoroughly.

When George Bush finished preaching that morning, Kay, Matthew, and I accompanied George and Barbara to their limousine. George again treated Matthew as though the Vice President were a grandfather or a very special friend.

After that, I never doubted the political strategy of baby-kissing. After he met George H.W. Bush, Matthew couldn't have beamed more if Jesus Himself had been in the pulpit of the church. When the first George was elected President, Matthew, by then a teen-ager, celebrated as if his close buddy were living in the White House. He was certain Bush remembered him even yet. The night George the First lost his re-election bid, no one in the Bush family could have cried more bitter tears than did our own son. No wonder I had a reverential place in my heart for Episcopalians!

* * * * * * * *

Christ Church Episcopal Cathedral in downtown Houston provided some additional insights into the diversity of Episcopal life. Before I arrived in Houston in 1972, John E. Hines had been the church's rector. He ultimately became the local Episcopal bishop, with his headquarters at the cathedral. Hines next ascended to be Presiding Bishop of the Episcopal Church in the United States. In the early 1970s he set loose the revolution that propelled the Episcopal Church onto its current liberal path.

After Bishop Hines left Houston, the cathedral's attendance and influence waned significantly. The first time I attended services there, I was appalled to see so few people in the pews. I knew from the rumor mill that the church had a large endowment which accounted for its manicured lawn and impeccably maintained buildings. But without people it was a beautiful but empty shell, with a great stasis eating the very life out of it.

Several years later J. Pittman McGehee arrived to take the cathedral reins. Like me, Dean McGehee had grown up in Oklahoma City, only in a more prosperous section of town. We were about the same age. I immediately liked him but wondered what he possibly could do to restore life to a wealthy but clearly wilting inner-city congregation.

His first act was to open the church's dining hall as a noonday restaurant for downtown workers. Instead of serving church cooking, Pittman hired the best Cajun restaurant in Houston to operate the restaurant. Soon the place was abuzz with Houston's downtown crowd. I still go back there to eat lunch when I'm in Houston.

Noontime worship services and art shows were added. Sunday services there became packed with people who found the weekday events so enticing, they decided to learn more

113

about what the church offered. I personally know of some individuals who found Jesus after a lifetime of rejecting Him because of being drawn back to the church through Christ Church's and Redeemer's ministries.

* * * * * *

As I look back on this era, however, their intriguing diversity is not what most stands out about the city's Episcopalians.

While under the red-bricked spires of Christ Church Cathedral, the groundwork was being set for Bishop Hines to take the Episcopal Church in the U.S. to the far left, two blocks away, under the dome of another landmark, worked a man who headed an embryonic movement that ultimately would take another major U.S. denomination on a decided course to the right.

The two men who soon would lead these two movements would traverse the same downtown Houston sidewalks, eat in the same restaurants, and hobnob with many of the same influential people, but they eventually would cast markedly different, long shadows over two major American church bodies.

A stone's throw from Hines' Christ Church office on San Jacinto Street was the Harris County Civil Courthouse, which housed the courtroom of State District Court Judge Paul Pressler.

The hands on the clock were ticking while Pressler quietly gathered forces and prepared to emerge on the stage of history of Southern Baptist life. When he did, this denomination—the denomination of my upbringing, the *true* denomination of my heart—would be shaken to its very core.

Chapter 11

Of Plans and Popes

Truth No. 11: Even popes of all stripes, try as they might, are unable to micromanage all the life events that surround them.

While these two major movements were taking shape, I still was saddled with one of my original problems on the beat. I found that only one obvious solution existed to dealing with members of Houston's Roman Catholic community.

Ignore them.

Undeniably, this was excruciating for me, because my interest in Catholics extended, as I mentioned, back to my high-school visits to the local Catholic church on Christmas Eve and later to the Catholic-history class masterfully taught by Dr. Glenn Hilburn at Baylor.

As a Southern Seminary student, I enrolled in a Roman Catholic history class offered at St. Meinrad Catholic Seminary across the river in Indiana. St. Meinrad was one of six theology schools in Kentuckiana that banded together and let their students co-op elsewhere.

I longed to study alongside men preparing for the Catholic priesthood. Unfortunately I couldn't complete these plans at St. Meinrad's because Kay and I had only one car. We were unable to figure out the logistics for me to make the 150-mile roundtrip four days a week for a month.

When I worked that two-week trial stint at *Louisville Times*, the story about the two African-American nuns who wanted to break away from traditional racial and sexual stereotypes was one of my favorites.

With all these encounters (or near-encounters) fresh on my mind, I arrived in Houston eagerly looking forward to covering the Roman Catholic Diocese of Galveston-Houston.

Instead I found the local Catholic diocese almost paranoid about media coverage. As I mentioned, conflict still hung over the *Chronicle*'s firing of my predecessor when the diocese allegedly complained about Janice's stories on Catholic pastors leaving the priesthood. The *Chronicle* management was eager to prove that it had not succumbed to pressures to tone down its Roman Catholic coverage. The Catholic Diocese of Galveston-Houston saw the national controversy over the firing of Janice Law as added proof that reporters were dangerous hombres with which to deal. Diocesan leaders believed they had been unfairly dragged into the hubbub and were embarrassed. To my face they vowed they had nothing to do with the firing. That was the same position everyone in the *Chronicle* management took, as well.

After a few unfulfilling forays into Catholic coverage, I decided my best approach would be benign neglect—in other words, for my first year or two on the beat I focused on Protestants, Jews, Mormons, Jehovah's Witnesses, etc. I deliberately chose to write on Roman Catholics only when I couldn't avoid doing so.

Shortly the strategy worked as I had hoped. At my *Chronicle* desk one day, I picked up my phone and heard the voice of Bishop John Morkovsky, head of the local diocese. He told me about a Catholic-related story he someday hoped I would cover. He even invited me to visit him in his office. Fellow reporters were astounded to hear that the bishop had phoned. I knew that the *fullness of time* had arrived to turn the limelight on the Catholics again.

Patiently and quietly I developed some exceptionally good sources to help guide my Catholic coverage. One of these sources tipped me to a major national/international development occurring in Houston. A local convent had been caught in the grip between too many elderly sisters in its ranks and too few young women wanting to become nuns. With her bank account lean, the mother superior had gone to the local state welfare office and pled for financial aid for aging nuns who desperately needed medical care that the local convent could not afford.

My nuns' story appeared on the front page of the *Chronicle*. Several weeks later the *New York Times* carried a story very similar to mine about the Houston nuns' application for welfare. That story never mentioned that the news first appeared in the *Chronicle* under my byline. I was content to know that I had broken the story and that a paper as prestigious as the *Times* had followed behind me.

Houston Catholic priest John McCarthy, who later became bishop of the Austin, TX, diocese, was also an excellent contact. John returned my calls promptly and talked to me on the record or off the record—whatever I needed. (By the way, he was not the source for the nuns on welfare story.)

By 1978, I felt at ease covering local Roman Catholics in both positive and negative stories. The Vatican still seemed far away and beyond my reporting skills. That was soon to change.

The shift occurred with the death of Pope Paul VI in 1978. The *Chronicle* played the story on its front page. I wrote minimally about it. Then the cardinals meeting in Rome elected Pope John Paul I to head the church. His Italian background and track record seemed another *ho-hum, nothing-new-here* decision.

Four weeks later, Dick Friedman, the *Chronicle's* overnight news editor, awakened me sometime around 3 a.m. "The pope has just died," he informed me.

I responded, "Good grief, man, that happened about two months ago!" Thinking the conversation was someone's idea of a practical joke, I almost hung up the phone. But Dick pressed on: "Louis, the new pope was just found dead in his room at the Vatican. We don't know what happened exactly, but I think you need to return to work right now."

I quickly dressed, drove through the darkness to the *Chronicle* building, and started reviewing the news stories flowing out of Rome about the sudden death of Pope John Paul I and his 33-day papacy. I put together a brief story cataloging all that had happened in Rome during the past eight weeks. More importantly, I was snagged by the story.

"I want to go to Rome to cover the election of the new pope," I begged the *Chronicle* news editor.

"No way," he responded. "We don't have that much interest in it for us to spend the kind of money necessary for you to go to Rome right now."

I hung on the *right now* and became determined that I ultimately would achieve my goal. For the next few weeks I followed the papal election from afar. When I received word that the official white smoke had puffed forth from the Vatican chimney, I raced to my TV to watch Polish Cardinal Karol Wojtela appear on the balcony as Pope John Paul II. Goosebumps spiked on my arms and chest. I knew something incredibly significant had just happened.

A few weeks later I saw a brief announcement that Pope John Paul II would make his first trip outside the Vatican and would travel to Mexico. I determined I would not miss this event if I had to swim the Rio Grande to get there.

Don Pickels approved my request to go to Mexico City for the pope's visit. He even authorized photographer Carlos

Antonio Rios to travel with me. I felt fortunate to have Carlos, a Hispanic-American, along; at one point in his life Carlos had studied to be a Catholic priest.

Carlos and I arrived in Mexico City about 24 hours before John Paul's plane was scheduled to touch down on the Mexican tarmac. That gave us plenty of time to rent a car, check into our hotel, obtain our press credentials, and survey the city for the pope's arrival and stay.

That night as I slept in my sixth-floor hotel room, I jolted awake to a strange sensation which I presumed to be the onset of Montezuma's Revenge. I felt dizzy and somewhat disoriented. Reaching for my bedside lamp, I was startled to hear it crash to the floor even before I touched it. Then strange, female voices materialized in the hallway outside my door. I peeked out to find a half-dozen nightgown-clad women fleeing down the hallway and shouting in British accents, "It's an earthquake . . . it's an earthquake!"

I threw on my overcoat, jumped into my shoes without donning any socks, grabbed my briefcase, then headed back to the door to follow the scurrying women. I encountered Carlos screaming, "Help me with my cameras!" We raced into his room to rescue what we could.

With multiple cameras around our necks and other equipment in our hands, we bounded down the six flights of stairs in what felt like an old-fashioned cattle stampede. People in pajamas, nightgowns, robes, or merely their underwear pushed and shoved everywhere.

Moments later we stood in the cold February night air on *Avenida Juarez* in Mexico City. We watched police, firefighters, and other emergency officials racing to calm the crowds and checking for injuries and damage. After about 45 minutes the police gave the *all clear* to return to our rooms.

As Carlos and I climbed the six flights of stairs, we

encountered my colleague, Helen Parmley, religion editor of
The Dallas Morning News, who was calmly descending.
Whereas in my haste to depart the building I had not bothered
to comb my hair or even put on any trousers, Helen was her
usual picture of perfection—hair coiffed just right, clothes
neatly arranged, and makeup perfectly outlining her face. She
said that by the time she dressed and preened, all the excitement seemed to be over.

Helen asked if we wanted to join her over coffee. We told
her that after our disruption, we were in no frame of mind for
socializing. She proceeded on to the first-floor coffee shop
while Carlos and I marched up the remaining stairs to check
on our possessions left behind.

A few years later during another major earthquake in
Mexico City, this same hotel where we had stayed for the
papal visit crumbled to the ground. After hearing that, I've
always been grateful I raced out of the shaking building as fast
as I did—even sockless and unkempt.

The Mexican media didn't miss the irony of the earthquake
on the morning of the pope's arrival. "The ground shakes as
the pope arrives," heralded one newspaper headline in
Spanish.

Unable to resume sleep because of all the excitement,
Carlos and I decided to head out early to the Mexico City airport to try and get a front-row seat for the papal landing.

At the airport Carlos made a wrong turn; we somehow
ended up on what appeared to be a runway instead of a street.
A small Lear jet passed within 50 feet of us and jolted us into
reality that we were definitely in the wrong place. We attributed our mistake to our lack of sleep. We finally parked very
near where we were told the pope's plane would stop on the
runway for him to deplane. We walked over to and stayed at
the bottom of the portable stairway airport officials planned to

use for the pope's arrival. Keep in mind this was John Paul's first trip outside the Vatican to anywhere except Poland. Security was minimal or virtually nonexistent. Nobody checked our credentials. They looked at our official Vatican press badges and accepted that we were who our badges said we were.

When PJP2's plane finally arrived, Carlos and I were well-posited at the bottom of the stairs waiting for him—clearly, almost alone among the press! I started to ask the pontiff a question when suddenly John Paul slipped to the ground in the scene I described in the Prologue. When he rose, he began greeting the more than 50 Mexican Catholic dignitaries all dressed in red and black.

Up close I easily could see John Paul's famed, riveting blue eyes. They reminded me of Billy Graham's. His hair was prematurely snow white. His complexion was smoothly pallid but with a distinct ruddy undertone. In his billowy cassock the pope looked every bit the part of a holy man. I could tell immediately why he had been chosen for the job.

In what seemed like only a few seconds, John Paul completed his greetings, then donned his red cardinal's hat, mounted the back of an open-air platform truck, and prepared for his unprotected ride into downtown Mexico City. I was amazed at the lack of formal security.

As his motorcade proceeded through the streets of Mexico City, the crowds waiting to greet him seemed to grow larger with each passing intersection.

Carlos managed to secure a seat alongside other photographers in the back of another open-air truck that followed just behind the pope-toting truck. That gave him a fabulous location for his snapshots. That also meant I had to drive our rental car by myself through the streets of Mexico City. At first I was a little leery of driving in a foreign city, especially one as crowded as this one, but I quickly gained my "sea legs" and actually enjoyed the freedom of having my own set of wheels.

For the next five days Carlos and I followed the pope everywhere he went—in a well-orchestrated array of churches, public arenas, and meetings with political and religious dignitaries. Only 58 at the time, John Paul had ebullient energy and Superman stamina. His trim physique and athletic good looks labeled him the "keep fit" pope. How any human could go nonstop as he did in Mexico for so long without having to take a bathroom break puzzled us. We speculated that he must have a portable urinal strapped on under his street-length robes.

The pope's visit to Puebla, to the Catholic seminary about 100 miles from the capital, turned out to be my first real encounter with the wildly competing international press corps. At the seminary John Paul addressed the bishops of Latin America for the first time. Back then—in 1979—Liberation Theology was the rage among many priests and in the majority of Catholic seminaries in the Americas. Briefly, Liberation Theology refers to the church utilizing secular, political means to help the poor and downtrodden. Some called it *socialism*. Others called it *communism*.

John Paul was clear: "Jesus Christ was no revolutionary. And His priests are not to be revolutionaries either."

The international press was electrified with his words. Headlines flowered all over Latin America, on the East and West Coasts of the United States, and in Europe saying John Paul had denounced Liberation Theology and forbade priests to be involved in any way with social or political activities. Reporters immediately labeled the pope as a radical conservative who would make Pope Pius XII look liberal. Back in the States, many reporters wondered aloud if U.S. priests involved in politics, such as Father Robert Drinan of Massachusetts—the first Catholic priest in to serve as a representative in the U.S.

House of Representatives—were about to be defrocked or forbidden to enter the U.S. capital or even Washington, D.C. again.

A few of us reporters based in the U.S. Southwest didn't
see the pope's words as drastically conservative or backward
as did our contemporaries. Further into his speech, the pontiff
seemed to encourage radical political change in Latin America.
What I noticed immediately was that he seemed to embrace
the words *Liberation Theology* but with a sense of giving them
a new meaning as defined by himself. Over the next years as I
traveled and covered the pope, I began to see clearly that this
was his ploy—to write his own definition of politically controversial topics.

After his speech, the bishops of Latin America held a
reception for the new pontiff. The pope's security remained
extremely loose. I apparently was the only newspaper reporter
in Puebla that night who was dressed in a three-piece suit. I'm
still not sure why I chose that attire that day, but I was glad I
did. Other male reporters in jeans and rumpled shirts were
quickly singled out by the pope's staff and kept at least 50 feet
away from him. Nobody, however, tried to set any boundaries
on me. All day long I had been able to move freely from the
press quarters to the actual areas where the pope was greeting
people and making speeches. Despite the fact that I wore my
press badge in plain view, my corporate-looking suit appeared
"Vatican" enough that I could enter the reception hall unim-
peded and could stand in the papal receiving line.

When John Paul was only two people away from me in the
line, I reneged. Fearing I would be close enough for someone
official to read my press badge and to panic, I forfeited what
ultimately would be my first—and last—opportunity to ever
shake his hand. I feared that engaging PJP2 in conversation
would blow my cover and risk my being impolitely escorted
out of the hall. I quickly sidestepped the line and busied

myself with refreshments nearby. From there I was able to observe John Paul's interaction with his Latin American bishops and archbishops and to engage in small talk with Mexican church officials who seemed not the least bit bothered by my presence.

That night I learned an important lesson: If a reporter dresses and acts like the people he or she is covering, the reporter is more likely to see more, gain more information, and be treated better than other reporters who prefer the more casual look.

On our return trip to Mexico City that night we joined the pope's motorcade as it slowly wound through huge crowds of people who built warming fires on streetcorners while they waited patiently for this lifetime experience.

It was a lifetime experience for me as well—a Southern Baptist boy from southwest Oklahoma City riding in the pope's motorcade on his way back to Mexico City from a history-making Latin American meeting.

I couldn't imagine my career in religion journalism getting any better than this!

Not long afterward, in 1981, I, like everyone else, was stunned with the news that an assailant had shot Pope John Paul II in St. Peter's Square in Rome. I was sorry I had not been on the scene for that development but was not surprised because of his passion for pressing the flesh and the less-than-circumspect security. Even all the well-choreographed events surrounding someone of a pope's stature could not be totally predicted.

* * * * * * *

This same period of time also brought me up close to

Southern Baptist's pope, Wallie Amos Criswell, pastor of Dallas' First Baptist Church. He had a limitless vision for his church, which made many people liken First Dallas to the Vatican.

These same people saw Madalyn Murray O'Hair, the famed atheist from Austin (she could have been likened to the atheists' pontiff, too, I guess), as the devil's handmaiden. Though Evangelicals said they "loved" Madalyn and prayed for her soul, many hated her with a passion reserved for their special enemies. Inevitably the Baptist and atheist "popes" had to meet. When they did, sparks flew.

One weekend I traveled to Dallas to cover a WFAA-TV debate between Dr. Criswell and Mrs. O'Hair. Not particularly fond of either (from my Southern days I remembered Wayne Oates' Criswell stories), I suddenly found myself sympathizing with W.A. because I found Madalyn not to be a nice person in the least. Uninvited, she interrupted my interview with Criswell and spoke harshly to me. She critiqued my questions as well as his answers. During their televised debate Criswell became so indignant with her interruptions that he finally blurted out, "If you would just shut your mouth, woman!" Some thought that even in this, he was far too restrained.

About a year later, Madalyn's office called and asked whether I would do a story on her as she visited Houston. I agreed yet immediately doubted my wisdom in this. For several hours beforehand I prayed that God would give me grace to avoid becoming angry at her as I had earlier in Dallas. I concluded that she got some kind of jollies from razzing people, especially preachers and journalists.

As Madalyn arrived at the *Chronicle* with son Jon and granddaughter Robin and saw me poised to interview her, she immediately demanded that I find another reporter to do the story. She said that from our previous, mutual meeting with

Criswell, she was quite certain that I was a Christian and therefore wanted to avoid me. God indeed gave me the special peace I needed to remain calm in the midst of her furor. I told her that I had not made the appointment with her—that her office had arranged the meeting with me specifically. I told her she was free to leave. For about five minutes she continued ranting. Finally, after she saw I was nonplussed, she insisted that I take notes. She stormed against Christians, church people, preachers, and everything else that apparently crossed her mind.

As she ceased talking, I expressed sympathy for the recent loss of Madalyn's husband, Richard O'Hair. I asked her where she thought Richard had gone after death and whether she believed she would see him again.

"He's dead. That's it. Death is the end," she hissed at me.

Years later I remembered her haunting, pathetic comments after I read that she, Jon, and Robin had been murdered and their bodies chopped up and buried by some con artists who tried to steal the O'Hairs' money.

I wondered how W.A. Criswell had avoided choking her much earlier.

* * * * * * *

Throughout the years many have asked me whether, indeed, Wallie Amos Criswell had masterminded the Southern Baptist Conservative Resurgence. They presumed that the Baptist pope was behind the scenes pulling the strings of every move that occurred. They imagined that his lackeys were merely enacting Criswell's edicts and that all conservative strategy certainly emanated from a command-center office at First Baptist, Dallas.

126

One certainly would be correct in saying that Criswell was the grandfather of the movement, because his conservative, literal-interpretation ideology had spawned huge followings and girded his adherents for action as they marched off to war.

But almost from its very inception the movement already was taking on a life of its own—even well beyond Criswell's micromanagement ability.

The tide of turning that was about to roll over the world's largest Protestant denomination was, almost from the get-go, careening out of the control of even its powerful pontiff's hands.

Chapter 12

The President Next Door

Truth No. 12: You can never judge a future church (or any other kind of) leader by his or her cover.

Back in Houston after my Mexico adventures with John Paul, I had hopelessly contracted the "pope" bug. I was pleased when Bishop Morkovsky of the Roman Catholic Diocese of Galveston-Houston lauded my "pope-in-Mexico" coverage. He seemed amazed that a Southern Baptist (by now he had figured out my background) would express such delight at covering his church's peripatetic leader. I vowed to keep in touch with the Vatican and lobby the *Chronicle* management for the funds to travel on any more of the pontiff's overseas trips.

Lest anyone fear I was becoming a wild-eyed papist, however, let me clarify that I never agreed with everything I saw and heard out of Pope John Paul II. On occasions when he preached on the end times and on the love and sacrifice of Christ, I would remark to myself, *He could have delivered that sermon in most Protestant, including most Southern Baptist, churches and fit right in.* Then, when he began expostulating on Mary, the mother of Christ; the saints; and other such topics, I would shake my head in disbelief. Once I heard him rattle off so much Mariolatry in one setting that I had to excuse myself and go outside for some fresh air. While Mary certainly was a key player in the life of Jesus and in the early church, she was not—and never claimed to be—equal with her Son.

She knew the Holy Spirit had given her the special gift of Jesus to rear.

I liked what John Paul said about communism. I thought his view of free-market economics—a great appreciation for entrepreneurial small business and a fear of large corporations—rather novel. I liked what he said about capital punishment and abortion. I admired what he said about loving the poor and treating all people fairly and justly regardless of race, creed, or nationality. I liked much of what he said about families, except for his pronouncements on birth control. I thought his stands on war were courageous though sometimes a bit naive. I was concerned about his comments on the role of women in the church. And his view of church structure certainly differed from the Baptist concept with which I grew up.

Over the years many have asked me whether I thought the pope was saved. My answer: "Absolutely!"

At the time John Paul lay dying in his apartments off St. Peter's Square in April 2005, we were in a deathwatch for Kay's mother, who outlasted PJP2 on Earth by only five days.

We drew comfort from realizing that Mable Wheeler and Karol Wojtela—both blood-bought children of God and equals before Him—would be members of the same heavenly freshman pledge class!

Despite any misgivings I might have had about parts of John Paul's theology, I found him to be a truly extraordinary church leader who was destined to cast a lengthy shadow over our era of human history. I looked forward to my next opportunity to observe him more closely.

* * * * * * * *

I didn't have long to wait. The Vatican soon scheduled a

papal trip to the United States for the next fall. I was one of the first to apply for press credentials to accompany John Paul on his visit to six American cities—Boston, New York, Philadelphia, Washington, D.C., Chicago, and Des Moines.

As things turned out, more than 10,000 reporters from newspapers, TV and radio stations, and other U.S. and world-wide media outlets applied for credentials to cover this American tour. Obviously I was not the only newsperson with a growing fascination with PJP2.

I was fortunate to receive one of about 100 special Vatican press passes and to be invited to travel in the press corps accompanying the pope. When I arrived in Boston to begin the tour, I was excited to learn that we would travel in a caravan of three 727 jets nicknamed Shepherd 1, Shepherd 2, and Shepherd 3. We were told each would have Secret Service agents on board. The pope and his staff were on Shepherd 1. I was on Shepherd 2.

The lax security we had encountered in Mexico was now replaced by top-notch U.S. surveillance. Not only were the Secret Service protecting the pope, local police were every-where. Today I still marvel that I—as well as others including ordinary people on the street—once had wanton free access to PJP2. After that brief period, he was shielded as though he were the Hope Diamond.

As things were slowly revealed, the press corps was a part of the Secret Service's complex security plan for the pontiff. Each time John Paul moved from one city to the next, Shepherds 1 through 3 were loaded and moved simultaneously onto the runway for departure. Once away from the terminal the Secret Service would order the planes scrambled on the runway until we got into takeoff position. Each time we departed in a different order. After observing this phenomenon and querying Secret Service, I deduced that they were trying to confuse anyone who might be planning to shoot down the pope's plane. The three planes looked exactly alike, except for the names painted in small letters on the sides. Somebody wanting to harm the pope would have had to have known precisely which of the three planes the pope was on. I admit I was a bit apprehensive when I realized my plane—Shepherd 2— was one of the two decoys.

The flotilla of planes had its special moments as well. At one point when airborne, Shepherd 2 was ordered to get in front of Shepherd 1 so we could land first. As we edged by Shepherd 1 in mid-air, I could spot John Paul peering out of his own plane window and absorbing a breathtaking view of America's heartland. That truly was a Kodak moment!

John Paul seemed to thrive on the arduous schedule which supercharged him from early morning until bedtime late at night. I was 25 years younger than John Paul and merely a reporter tagging along—not the central player—but I was wiped out by the pope's killer travel schedule. When we finally arrived in Chicago after stopping in Des Moines for a full day of activities, I was so tired, I decided to repair to bed early (about 11 p.m.). The next morning I learned that about the time I was turning off the lights in my hotel room, John Paul had stood on the balcony of his host home leading gathered admirers in several hymns and sacred songs. Reporters who saw him said he looked refreshed and ready to celebrate for the entire night.

* * * * * * * *

When John Paul went calling on the nation's First Couple—Jimmy and Rosalynn Carter—we in the traveling press corps had ringside seats on the White House lawn.

Five years beforehand—the last time I had seen Jimmy Carter in person—circumstances had been highly different. I happened to be assigned the hotel room next to his in Dallas for the 1974 Southern Baptist Convention annual meeting. Carter, then the Georgia governor and his local church's messenger to the 1974 SBC, had hung around the SBC press room that year and seemed almost overly eager to engage reporters, but no one was paying him much mind.

On the Friday morning after the meeting ended, Carter and I happened to emerge from our hotel rooms simultaneously. I ended up walking side by side with the governor (and a lone Georgia state-trooper bodyguard) as we traversed the length of our hotel hallway. The two of us and the trooper were the only three people riding the elevator together to the ground floor. All the while the affable Carter, with my press credentials in plain view, smiled and chatted with me. He was in no rush and even seemed to want to linger in the lobby to continue our conversation.

Throughout this, however, I kept thinking, *What's with this guy? I've gotta excuse myself. He's the governor of Georgia. I'm a newspaper reporter in Texas. None of my readers are gonna give a flip about him. I've got to get on to something significant that I can use to file my story.*

I shook off Carter and scrambled off to a breakfast meeting where Vice President Gerald Ford was to speak. I figured my readers surely would hang on every word of what the Vice President of our nation had to say.

Imagine my thoughts five years later as I stood on the White House lawn and watched the fellow I thought such a lackluster player as he now welcomed Pope John Paul II for his first visit to the White House! (That was, of course, after Carter defeated incumbent Ford to win the presidency.)

Just about that same time, a personable but ordinary seminarian who also liked to attach himself to newspeople showed up at my *Chronicle* office bearing press releases for evangelist James Robison. In looking back, I probably gave this 21-year-old visitor the same sort of obligatory attention that I had given Carter in 1974. The lad visited several times and always seemed loath to leave, but I couldn't size up this "flak" (as we called PR people) as amounting to much more than being a lifetime hanger-on to the high-profile religious.

Oops, guessed wrong again! That former effusive "flak" is now former Arkansas Gov. Mike Huckabee—who became a hard-charging contender for the GOP U.S. presidential nomination in 2008.

I occasionally would visit in the Lakewood Church of pastors John and Dodie Osteen, who were at the helm of a minor, fledgling, suburban Pentecostal congregation in North Houston. They may or may not have mentioned that they had a teen-aged son as they tried to convince me, usually unsuccessfully, that their church was worth a *Chronicle* story. However, the son that this obsequious couple may or may not have mentioned turned out to be Joel Osteen, who ultimately bought the Houston Summit (Compaq Center) professional basketball arena as the headquarters for his by-then world-famous Lakewood Church. Now an internationally known televangelist, Osteen commands $13 million book advances. *Who knew?*

One of the most unlikely-to-succeed fellow ministry students in my Baylor classes was an unimpressive swain named Joel Gregory. His demeanor, voice, and grasp of his subject would typecast him as the probable pastor of—at the most—a lifelong stream of county-seat First Baptist churches. Gregory worked to polish his diction, his preaching mannerisms, and his intellect, as his "can-do" mettle achieved for him his religion Ph.D. Imagine my surprise when ultimately I looked up and saw him as the succeeding pastor to W.A. Criswell!

For decades I would remember these lessons. Never under-estimate a soul! 1 Samuel 16:7 reminds us of this when it says, *"The Lord does not look at the things man looks at. Man looks at the outward appearance, but the Lord looks at the heart."* That random-looking guy you brush off might morph into someone special—such as your future boss, a future televange-list, or even the future President of the United States.

* * * * * * *

By the time John Paul returned from the U.S. to Italy and I to Houston, I was completely captivated by this dynamo pope, the Vatican, and Rome. I now was on high alert for any other papal trips that I might join.

I soon spotted a news release saying Roman Catholic Church leaders in Canada were preparing to welcome the pon-tiff to their country. I immediately called Canada and obtained information on how to get a seat on the press plane accompa-nying John Paul's coast-to-coast pilgrimage. Much to my delight I was again invited to join the pope's traveling press corps, so off I flew to the great frozen North.

A few weeks after the Canadian adventure, John Paul returned to this hemisphere to the Dominican Republic for a specially called conference of Latin America bishops. I was there again dutifully trying to ferret out what little news leaked from the closed-door meeting.

I next began, in earnest, to explore ways to at last get to the pope's home base. In November 1985 the coveted opportu-nity occurred. The *Chronicle* dispatched me to the Vatican to cover the 25th anniversary celebration of the start of Vatican Council II, which John Paul commemorated with a special Synod of Roman Catholic bishops from throughout the world.

For nearly a month I trudged the labyrinthine Vatican halls and personally interviewed many top Vatican officials. John Paul, however, remained elusive. From his lofty balcony perch, he kept his distance from the media. He let reporters cover only orchestrated events and never intermingled with us. I thus was left to always wonder what John Paul was really like as a person. His reputation and image were enormous. He was truly larger than life. I finally concluded that he must be satisfied with his depiction as more of an institution and public persona than as a real human being.

While in Rome and exposed to the Vatican's way of doing business, I realized how deeply political so much of what happens there really is. Although I—five Papal trips later—had been exposed to megadoses of the Vatican and Catholics, I realized that I would still need decades to master Vatican protocol and politics in order to understand the true innerworkings of the Roman Catholic Church. I was sure it had the side the public saw and then the veiled, ugly underbelly. I concluded that understanding this denomination from the inside out might have to be a lifetime pursuit.

* * * * * * *

I soon would be seeing a religious denomination from the inside out, all right—but not the Roman Catholics. As my own—the Southern Baptist Convention—began positioning itself at the epicenter of what would be the major religion news story of the 20th century, uncovering its ugly underbelly didn't take much pursuing. It would hardly be veiled at all.

Chapter 13

Never a Straight Line

Truth No. 13: The shortest distance between two points is never a straight line.

After her first day on the job in February 1972 as the *Chronicle*'s courthouse reporter, Kay arrived home recounting, "I believe the judge in the case I covered today must be a believer."

I asked her why she was so sure.

She replied that no one, apart from the Christian experience, could have kept his or her cool in dealing with the likes of the infamous Candace Mossler Garrison, whose civil hearing had been on the docket that day.

Garrison was the widow of wealthy Houstonian and banking magnate Jacques Mossler. In 1964 she and her lover, Melvin Lane Powers, had been acquitted in Mossler's murder, thanks to the illustrious defense of top criminal attorney Percy Foreman.

Although many still believed Garrison conspired to murder Jacques in this high-profile, sensational case, Candace went free—and now was wrangling over an estate matter with Mossler's children in a state-court battle. Kay described Garrison as having been highly theatrical in her courtroom performance that day.

Time after time, Kay recalled, the presiding judge addressed this aging drama queen firmly yet calmly despite her tirades, some directed at him.

Thus the name of *State District Court Judge Paul Pressler* was first introduced into casual conversation in our home. In the weeks and months ahead, Kay would return with other such stories of Pressler's magnanimity under duress during courtroom theatrics.

Even more impressive was the fact that Pressler invited reporters to his chambers for rare but helpful backgrounding sessions, either before or after one of his hearings. He believed that their coverage of cases in his court would be more factual (and his rulings more accurately relayed to the public) if he helped interpret legal phrases or maneuvers for them. While never delving into the facts of the case or tipping his hand as to his ultimate verdict, Pressler's patient, off-the-record briefings did walk the courthouse press corps through easily misunderstood aspects of the law. This sort of heads-up made Pressler well respected among print and electronic journalists alike. Many judges looked on the presence of reporters as but a niggling annoyance and a cross to bear. While Pressler at all times remained judicial and wasn't one to chew the fat over a cup of coffee in the courthouse lunchroom, he didn't run from the press. That distinguished him from many others Kay covered.

This type of casual, news source-to-reporter dialogue about civil cases was the milieu in which Kay and her colleagues on the county beat forged relationships with Pressler in the early part of the 1970s. Actually, before I ever even made his acquaintance or had any idea that this person whose name Kay occasionally dropped was a growing factor in Houston's Southern Baptist life, Kay would end up having known this jurist for more than three years.

In the scheme of things, however masterfully Pressler guided reporters to "get it right" in their respective media outlets would end up mattering little. Comparatively speaking, he would be minimally remembered for the judicial decisions he rendered in his fifth-floor courtroom just down from the elevator.

His virtuoso performance in another drama is what would forever inscribe the *Paul Pressler* name in the annals of history. That drama was rapidly moving ahead just on the horizon.

* * * * * * * *

As much as I enjoyed traveling with Pope John Paul II, attending Episcopal conventions, and heading overseas with friends who were Jewish, nothing quite compared to attending the annual Southern Baptist Convention. Because I was a graduate of Southern Baptist institutions and because I personally knew so many of the key players in the denomination, I had the proverbial "leg up" where covering the SBC was concerned.

I attended my first Southern Baptist Convention annual meeting in 1972 in Philadelphia. I was awed by the size of the press room set up to accommodate the secular and other outside press. I appreciated the professional way it was administered by Jim Newton and W.C. Fields, the then-leaders of Baptist Press. Those running the press room were helpful and speedily provided information that reporters needed. I could tell immediately I was going to enjoy covering this meeting every year.

My first awareness that everything was not as it seemed occurred that first meeting when I received a copy of the SBC president's address, to be delivered by Dr. Carl Bates, pastor of First Baptist Church of Charlotte, NC, and then-president of the SBC. The written speech was embargoed until after the address. *Embargoed* meant reporters could use it to follow along as Dr. Bates delivered his message without having to actually take notes, but no one was supposed to write about the sermon until it had occurred.

I was stunned to read where Dr. Bates, in essence, was planning to tell fundamentalists in the Convention to either shut up or get out. His message was directed at a group of pastors and laypersons known as the Baptist Faith and Message Fellowship. Basically this group was beginning to point out instances of liberalism in Southern Baptist life and was urging a return to what they saw as fundamental Baptist beliefs. Instantly I knew that his battle cry would be the newspeg for the speech.

But as I listened to Dr. Bates speak, I was even more shocked to see his "shut-up-or-get-out" section was nowhere in his actual message as he spoke.

I quickly queried W.C. Fields, who coyly noted that perhaps someone had suggested that Dr. Bates eliminate those inflammatory words.

Why would Bates write the sermon and Baptist Press publish it for the media with what was clearly Bates' strongest punch line, yet Bates deliver it without uttering the key words? I wanted to know. That seemed to me like a very strange way to do business.

More than 35 years later, I still consider providential the fact that Dr. Bates' sermon was my introduction to how Southern Baptist Convention politics operated—sometimes through instances of passive-aggressive behavior. Passive-aggression is not just a human trait but also characterizes some church bureaucracies. A full decade before the Convention exploded in a major fight between conservatives (fundamentalists) and moderates (liberals), a pitched battle was brewing between the Convention's moderate leadership and a conservative faction. Out in public the message was subtly delivered to the media but never actually stated for messengers to the meeting to hear with their own ears. Bates' embargoed speech signaled to the news media that the Convention leadership wanted to be rid of those pesky, irritating theological conservatives. But to be able to point the finger and say it in clear English would have been too confrontive and would have stripped the veneer of majestic sweetness that sat enthroned in the SBC. Thus the aggressive high point was delivered in a passive fashion.

Ver-r-r-r-ry interesting, I mused.

Nevertheless, each year after 1972, I looked forward to the SBC as it moved from city to city, coast to coast. I enjoyed seeing old friends and making new acquaintances. During the 1970s, only newspaper reporters from the South and Southwest bothered to attend the annual SBC meeting. I could count on always seeing my counterpart (who changed about every two to three years) at the *Houston Post* and reporters from *The Dallas Morning News, Dallas Times Herald, The Atlanta Journal-Constitution, Memphis Commercial Appeal,* and the Associated Press. Reporters from *Time, Newsweek, The Washington Post, The New York Times,* and *Los Angeles Times* seldom put in an appearance. At that time the SBC was considered a regional denomination with little happening that would appeal to the wider secular and religious American audience.

The SBC's image problem was illustrated beautifully in a headline that ran in the *Chicago Tribune* in 1976 when Jimmy Carter was running for U.S. President. "Who are the Southern Baptists?" it read. One can't imagine a headline that said, "Who are the Roman Catholics?" or "Who are the Episcopalians?" But in the Northeast and Western U.S. in that era , the question "Who are the Southern Baptists?" was most appropriate. Rank-and-file Americans simply had little exposure to this denomination.

Besides thoroughly enjoying fellowship with my colleagues from other newspapers in the so-called Bible Belt, each year I expanded my network of contacts in the SBC and knowledge of how the Convention worked. I was careful to include corporate insiders as well as sidelined and minimalized dissidents. I also deliberately sought out sources and contacts reflecting the wide array of theological perspectives active in the Convention in that era.

Before 1979, the SBC was a superbly operating, well-oiled bureaucracy—a wonder to behold. The people who later became known as *moderates,* or the entrenched establishment, were in their heyday. They held all the key positions in the Convention. Agency trustees were chosen because they were reliable corporate players who weren't interested in rocking the boat and in causing denominational agency heads insomnia or nightmares. Agency heads were groomed and moved up the career ladder in predictable, corporate fashion. Many in the SBC leadership could trace their professional roots to the Baptist General Convention of Texas, a marvelous training ground for future national denominational executives. With more than 2-million members at that time, the Texas Convention was the size of many national denominations and wealthy enough to support a good-sized bureaucracy of its own.

On the one hand I admired the corporate style of SBC leaders then. They were all intelligent and capable graduates of Baptist colleges and universities as well as Southern Baptist seminaries. My friend and mentor Lynn Davis was exactly right when he had advised, "The SBC operates on the basis of two things—union cards and networks." As I mentioned earlier, Lynn described the *union card* as a degree from one of the six Southern Baptist seminaries. Because of their size, Southern and Southwestern seminaries seemed to be the dominant schools. At the peak of their prominence and power, Convention moderates truly reflected a well-educated and literate clergy.

On the other hand, the growing undercover dissident movement within the SBC was not difficult to miss, though with an unpracticed eye many media and Southern Baptists were still oblivious to it. For all the smiles and glowing reports on the surface during the 1970s, the dark clouds of a developing thunderstorm were roiling and boiling just below the surface.

I took special note of a situation that occurred in 1976 when the Convention bureaucracy and leadership seemed to gang up on a renegade Memphis, TN, pastor named Adrian Rogers. That year, six of the largest and most influential Southern Baptist state newspapers editorialized against Adrian ever holding a leadership position in the Convention. They said his views were too reactionary and out of step with mainstream Southern Baptists.

Although their particular beef with Adrian, pastor of Bellevue Baptist Church in Cordova, TN, was amorphous and difficult to pinpoint, basically they disliked the fact that he questioned the way SBC business was done in the "good-ole-boy system" without room for outsiders.

Also, Adrian and some others were beginning to finger some specific slippages—decrying what they believed was creeping liberalism at certain seminaries. Although some dismissed these charges as a witch hunt, I hadn't forgotten my experiences in the early 1970s at Southern, with professors who took a less-than-literal view about certain Old Testament people and happenings that I described earlier.

If I had attended another seminary, such as Southwestern, where lines were less succinctly drawn, I might have dismissed the conservatives' growing concerns. I was beginning to see that if in 1969 I had taken that attractive, proffered job in the Southwestern news office and never headed East, I might be hooting at Adrian and others, too. But the troubling parts of my Southern education were causing outcries such as Adrian's to hit a resonant chord. I had been there on the occasion when a Southern dean delivered his "smoking-pistol" message in Louisville. Deep in my heart, I knew these complaints were valid.

I found curious the fact that these antagonistic state newspapers "unendorsed" Adrian, since for decades they had refused to openly endorse candidates for national leadership positions, except in some deftly subtle ways such as well-placed, carefully constructed, passive-aggressive comments. Now they were out in full force lobbying *against* a possible candidate. *Why?* I wondered. I also knew that kicking Adrian was favorite sport among some Convention bureaucrats and leaders. I felt very sorry for him.

To understand this more clearly, one must know the formal protocol in the SBC in the 1970s. A person seeking an SBC leadership did not announce his candidacy straight out—and especially did not say publicly that he was seeking a Convention position. Such direct communication would have been the "kiss of death." Instead, the politically correct language was to murmur humbly with bowed head, "Brother So-and-So" or "Some friends of mine have asked me to allow them to place my name in nomination for Convention president (or vice president, or whatever). After prayerful consideration, I have agreed to let him/them do so." It was all spoken in dulcet tones surrounded by excruciatingly courteous Southern gentility and self-deprecation, but anyone listening carefully knew exactly what strategy was being communicated.

Even when candidates were, behind the scenes, twisting arms like crazy to get elected, they still publicly followed this prescribed, lock-step subterfuge. I saw the whole system as corrupt and sickening. *Why can't people just say what they mean and mean what they say?* I often wondered both privately and in print. I remembered that Jesus in Matthew 5:37 said, *"Simply let your 'Yes' be 'Yes,' and your 'No,' 'No'; anything beyond this comes from the evil one."* For them, the shortest distance between two points was never a straight line.

I personally shook my head every time I watched the charade being played out. I really wondered whether pastors who played that game really thought I or other reporters—or even other Southern Baptists—were too dumb to see through their back-slapping deceptions.

Baptists did not have the corner on the market in passive aggression. Other denominations had this strategy down to a slick science, as well. One of my favorite United Methodist news sources was Woodrow Seals, a prominent federal judge in Houston as well as a leading lay member of the United Methodist Church. In the late 1970s Seals tipped me to a controversy he knew was about to spout at the annual upcoming Methodist annual conference. After I wrote the story and arrived at the meeting, I realized that Bishop Paul Galloway of the Houston-based Texas Methodist Conference and Seals were, in fact, the ones at odds over the issue and personified the flap that was brewing. The bishop issued a blistering salvo at me for writing the story and for airing this dirty laundry. Seals had several opportunities to clear the air and advise the bishop that it was actually he who had instigated the story, but instead Seals publicly denounced me and the article and left me in an embarrassing spot. Too late I realized I had been the victim of a passive-aggressive political *tour de force* in the world of Methodism.

My best friend in the ministry in Houston was a Lutheran pastor whose career later was sunk by a flagrant passive-aggressive machination when he transferred pulpits. In respect for his family, I'll not use his name but tell the story here in the same way I did in my *Chronicle* memorial column about him in 1983. This pastor, called away to West Texas to a new post, was unable to shake the influence of the immediate former pastor of his new church. Though outwardly welcoming and cherubic, the Lutheran predecessor refused to emotionally step aside from his old congregation and caused unmitigated behind-the-scenes ills for my friend. Unable to get his sea legs in the community after relocating his family and pulling up roots from a stable church situation, my pastor friend became depressed, which led him to suicide. This appalling and unnecessary waste of a precious life haunts me and others still.

Joel Gregory met the same type of passive aggression when he attempted to succeed W.A. Criswell at First Baptist, Dallas. Joel's personal website, *www.gregoryministries.org*, outlines a candid assessment of what transpired when Criswell would not actively distance himself from the post he'd held so many years. Gregory ultimately resigned and refused to recant, even when his deacon body voted not to accept his resignation. Although Joel today is a popular professor at Truett Seminary in Waco and still is regarded as a master preacher, his career and personal life went through some wilderness years in the interim.

* * * * * * * *

The passive-aggressive history of the SBC establishment—attack to the back and not to the face—is what caused the unprecedented, direct bombardment on Adrian Rogers in 1976 to rivet my attention. I had never before seen anything quite like it. Most newspaper reporters ignored the story, but I called

Adrian at his office in Memphis to interview him about the Baptist newspaper editorials. I can still remember the hurt, sadness, and pathos in his voice as he tried to explain his reaction to being jumped on and beaten up publicly and so severely by denominational journalists. I never doubted for one minute that these state editors acted in concert with Convention leaders, who saw the "rising star out of Memphis" as a serious problem and/or threat.

I also took special note of a situation involving Bob Holbrooke, a small-town, South Central Texas pastor. Holbrooke was the first Southern Baptist I ever knew who adamantly opposed abortion. He did so out of a genuine concern for the unborn. Later some Baptist leaders erroneously labeled Larry Lewis, Richard Land, and a few others involved in the Conservative Resurgence as the *original pro-life Southern Baptists*. These men certainly did their part in steering the SBC onto a pro-life stance, but they were antediluvian compared to Holbrooke. Bob founded Baptists for Life. I once said in a newspaper column that Bob's group could hold its annual meeting "in a phone booth." He did not take offense because he knew he had scant following and was fighting a David-and-Goliath battle.

At the Southern Baptist Conventions in the mid-1970s, Holbrooke haplessly presented resolutions opposing abortion. At that point in history the SBC was tilted more toward a pro-abortion stance. I found listening to some Convention leaders tap-dance around the issue to be amusing. They would proclaim the Convention was *pro-life* and then proceed to support every exception possible including the "mental health of the mother" (a catch phrase for pro-abortionists at the time).

The SBC leadership recoiled at Holbrooke. The SBC media either ignored him or mocked him. I liked Bob and thought he deserved at least a fair hearing. He and I both knew he was by far "a voice crying in the wilderness." But even a lone, dissenting voice deserves to be treated decently.

Once after I wrote about Bob, I received a phone call from Robert O'Brien at Baptist Press asking whether I realized that Bob Holbrooke was a one-man organization and a voice with little support in the SBC. The implication was that I was violating some unwritten rule by even mentioning in the *Chronicle*'s news columns Bob's name and his cause. I was greatly offended by this apparent effort to silence Holbrooke by trying to browbeat me into not writing about him. It did not succeed.

Perhaps because of my stories about Adrian Rogers and Bob Holbrooke, Bill Powell, founder of the Baptist Faith and Message Fellowship, obtained my home phone number and started calling and leaving messages (some might call them "news tips") for me about what he perceived as problems in the SBC. I never was quite sure why I gave him a hearing. When I asked around in the SBC about Bill, I was told he was a man with a cause because the Home Mission Board had fired him. I learned he was on a personal crusade and vendetta against his former bosses. I may have given him an ear because I really didn't believe everything in the SBC was as rosy and peaceful as the denominational leaders and Baptist media types tried to portray it as being. Or perhaps I just felt sorry for him. I could see in him the same attributes that Woodward and Bernstein probably saw in Deep Throat, their Watergate source. Bill may have been angry, but he could also cut to the chase on SBC issues. He knew "where the bodies were buried," as the cliché goes. He had an excellent grasp of SBC people and issues. He was always transparent, so I recognized his agenda even as I listened to his tales and insights about the SBC leadership. I could sense he had more to his stories than simply being a deeply wounded Southern Baptist with an axe to grind.

By that time—the mid-1970s—the two major players in the Conservative Resurgence—Judge Pressler and Dallas theologian Paige Patterson—were definitely among my circle of acquaintances, but I never discussed the SBC with either one of them until their movement was well under way in 1979. Before May 1979, if someone had queried me about either of Dr. Patterson's or Judge Pressler's opinions about life in the SBC, I would have pled ignorance. I simply had no idea they felt so strongly.

* * * * * * * *

I ultimately met Judge Pressler in 1975 because, quite honestly, I was needing a feature-story idea for an upcoming religion section. Kay heard me puzzling aloud over my search and suggested I visit the courthouse to see what I could learn about the judge of whom she spoke.

Kay still had engaged in no conversations of a personal nature with the judge, since journalists are taught that to enforce objectivity, they are to keep personal references away from conversations with news sources if such matters are not germane to the story. But at home she continued to share impressions about how she believed this jurist modeled Christian deportment.

She described how Pressler, during a recent trial, had suddenly rushed from the courtroom because of a family emergency. Afterward the judge's bailiff told Kay this urgent departure was because one of his daughters had just broken her leg in a Colorado ski accident. Kay thought that displayed the reactions of a dedicated Christian father—that he would postpone a trial to help his injured teen-ager get home.

"I've heard that he is a member of a Baptist church and is a Sunday-school teacher there," she reported some time later.

So, having learned early in our marriage to listen to my intuitive wife, I called the judge's office and made an appointment to see him.

As he entered his chambers for our chat, Judge Pressler quickly removed his long, black legal robe revealing a business suit and eased into his recliner for a lengthy conversation affirming his Christian faith and discussing whether it impacted his judicial decisions. But in our more-than-an-hour conversation, he said nary a word about the SBC.

* * * * * * * *

Until May 1979 I also knew zilch about Judge Pressler's relationship with Criswell College President Paige Patterson, ultimately his compadre in the takeover coalition. I had, however, met Dr. Patterson a few years after I first interviewed Judge Pressler. This occurred when I decided to write a feature story about W. A. Criswell and First Baptist Church of Dallas. That story was to be headlined "The Baptist Vatican." While I made arrangements to be at First Dallas for several days, Dr. Criswell's office informed me that Dr. Patterson would be my host. I had the distinct impression that Dr. Criswell's secretary was trying to steer me toward writing about Criswell College instead of Dr. Criswell himself. I saw the college as tertiary in importance—third behind The Man himself (Criswell) and the church. I had yet to buy into the Southern Seminary paranoia about this small, private, Christian school.

Arriving at First Baptist, Dallas, I was directed immediately to Dr. Patterson's office. I was surprised at his youth, his Western boots, and his bush of red hair. I found him to be friendly and bright as a button and not much like the corporate climbers and shakers in the moderate-dominated SBC, even though he was the son of retired Baptist General Convention of Texas exec Dr. T.A. Patterson. As with Pressler, Patterson cheerfully stuck with my agenda and made no mention of his concerns within the denomination.

* * * * * * * *

I had little contact with either man again until four years later, when Pressler and Patterson suddenly cannonaded forth on the playing field as the two kingpins in the effort to shift the Southern Baptist Convention into a more conservative direction. I was shocked. When I mentioned Pressler's role to Kay, she asked me if perhaps I might have him confused with someone else. We never saw it coming.

What I did know, however, is that they were, by that point, in good company—with numbers of aficionados growing by the day. I also knew, sadly for the denomination, that in many cases, they were dead right.

Chapter 14

Helping the Cause

Truth No. 14: You can't always judge a denominational faction by its label.

Although the growing storm would separate the sheep from the goats and would force most every Baptist church in Houston to align itself, one way or the other, choosing the politically correct "side" in the SBC split was never the Moore family's top priority in trying to find a local church to call our own.

Identifying a body of believers that would accept our unorthodox lifestyle was. How things ultimately shook out defied all liberal-conservative stereotypes.

I've already discussed how our first church, Willow Meadows Baptist in southwest Houston, eventually was unworkable for us because we moved far away. Our new home, plus the arrival of a baby boy who didn't tolerate long car rides, caused us to pull up roots there, though we admired Ralph Langley's spirited preaching and enjoyed the fellowship. One Sunday morning, a speeding ticket I got while I raced the clock to arrive at church on time clenched our decision. We knew we must change to a closeby congregation in our far-west side of town.

We settled on Tallowood Baptist in Houston's prosperous Memorial area. We thought attending church alongside people in our neighborhood, with whom we might rub shoulders at the grocery store and at other events nearby, was a good idea.

It had numerous families with young children. The five-minute commute was tolerable to a hungry, indignant toddler who was eager to dine as soon as church was over.

A few months later Kay went back to work, as planned, at the *Chronicle* after her one-year maternity leave. In Kay's presence, friends in our Tallowood Sunday school class made negative comments that were both insulting and insensitive to employed mothers. Most other young mothers in the church did not work outside the home. Her Sunday-school class prayed that another employed mom wouldn't make the same "mistake" Kay did and "abandon" her baby to a daycare center. When Kay tried to explain that her work as a journalist was a calling and that our decision to be a two-paycheck family was made after much prayer and seeking God's will, it went right over other couples' heads. We knew then that this church selection had been a major blooper on our part. The monoculture church reflected its very corporate neighborhood, where higher income levels found most wives comfortable as stay-at-home moms. Kay's situation as a committed professional was very foreign.

(Ironically both Willow Meadows and Tallowood ultimately became identified as "moderate" Southern Baptist churches. This type of label was on one hand puzzling, since we found few, if any, really progressive attitudes there.)

Fortunately Tallowood was at that moment establishing a new mission church in the suburbs near Katy, about 12 miles west of our house. We liked the idea of being a part of a church start and saw a graceful exit out of a dead-end situation, so we joined the formation of the Kingsland Baptist mission. With everything so new, we thought we could help shape attitudes and guide people to a more enlightened approach. After all, the two-paycheck lifestyle such as ours was fast becoming the wave of the future, as women began to return to the workforce in droves. It was not a lifestyle that was about to go away. This new body could be on the cutting edge of the way people were now living.

Starting a new congregation from scratch was thrilling. We initially met in a day-care center housed in a manufactured building sitting in the middle of a dirt parking lot. The first Sunday Kingsland (which ultimately also wore a "moderate" brand) held worship services, Houston experienced one of its memorable floods. The dirt parking lot turned into a sea of mud. When our first worship concluded, other men and I took off our coats, ties, shoes and socks, then rolled up our trouser legs and waded through the water and mud to, one-by-one, bring our cars to the church's front door to pick up our wives and children. You might call that a true "bonding" experience.

Setting up folding chairs and arranging a makeshift platform for the preacher and song leader was fun. At first we met only on Sunday mornings, which gave me flexible time to attend other churches as part of my responsibilities at the *Houston Chronicle.*

Soon the new mission church grew so large we discussed adding Sunday-evening and Wednesday-evening services, hiring additional staff, and constructing a new building. We had hoped Kingsland would become a creative alternative to traditional Baptist churches in the Houston area, but weekly the church was becoming more and more like its mother church and other by-the-book, cookie-cutter Southern Baptist congregations.

Because we were employed parents with limited time, we wanted to spend every spare minute with our son, Matthew. We were unable to make major time commitments to teach Sunday school, sponsor fellowships, or serve on committees. This didn't sit well with the ambitious pastor, who told us rather pointedly: "*Love* is spelled T-I-M-E." We got the message that he thought we ought to be at church endlessly (in all fairness, an attitude probably required of church-start pastors to get a congregation growing).

He also seemed to little understand my professional circumstances as I disappeared to go on papal trips and non-Baptist denominational conventions. Instead of seeing me as a valuable resource with a vast knowledge of Christendom, he wanted members to fit into tidy little boxes that met church expectations.

After conferring with Kay, we decided the time had arrived to look yet for *another* new church home. *But where? And what kind?* Since we had contacts in Lutheran, Episcopal, Methodist, Churches of Christ, and denominations throughout the city, we even questioned whether we ought to remain Southern Baptists.

As Kay and I began looking around Houston at other couples who were in our same situation, we realized we were not alone. We began to query dual-income couples at other churches about how they dealt with these acceptance issues and how they ultimately found the right congregations that worked for them.

Again, the label issue arose. I would call pastors I thought to be the most open-minded and innovative and be told no dual-income couples attended those churches. I would call the most narrow-minded theolog in town and be given numerous names.

The result was our book, *When You Both Go to Work,* which shared not only our story and struggles but the stories of various other two-paycheck couples from all denominations who managed to stay active in their churches. Because we were on the cutting edge of what ultimately would become a majority lifestyle, we wanted to write a how-to book that would answer questions such as, "What does the Bible really say about women working?" and "How do I balance all my time commitments to keep church in my schedule?" The book got huge media exposure throughout the country. As I said earlier, even television's *PTL* with Jim and Tammy Bakker aired us live—just before the Bakkers' empire crumbled.

* * * * * * * *

As we had begun conducting interviews for our book to ferret out answers for ourselves, Ken Chafin, pastor of South Main Baptist Church near downtown Houston, called to tell me about a new worship service his church was starting on Friday nights. It was designed to take the place of Sunday-morning worship for families who felt a time crunch on weekends. South Main had numerous young, employed couples who, like us, sought ways to spend more time with their children. Having church commitments met by the Friday-night worship service gave them the entire day of Sunday to spend with their families.

I went to South Main to hold interviews with staff in charge of starting the new services, which included dinner, worship, and special classes to replicate Sunday school, only on Friday. I left the church not only with a story for my religion section but also with a probable solution for the Moores.

Soon Kay and I visited the new Friday-Night Live program to investigate for ourselves. We not only enjoyed and found our niche in Friday-Night Live, but we were able to attend Wednesday-night supper and prayer meeting at the church because the church was situated near downtown Houston and close to the *Chronicle* offices.

Ken, the church staff, and other church members seemed to resonate fully with my wider role in Houston's religious community. When I was off attending a Methodist General Conference or traveling with Pope John Paul II, these Southern Baptists were enthusiastic affirmers. They prayed for my travels and asked for a full report on all I had experienced. Instead of demanding that I earn my stripes on church committees, they appreciated the unique role I contributed as one whose life experiences were richly different from that of the average member. They asked me to sponsor enrichment trips to Buddhist temples, Hindu pagodas, and Jewish synagogues in a comparative-religions class for South Main members.

South Main, in an odd sort of way, fit the "conservative" mode perfectly because of its huge emphasis on soul winning and evangelism. Even before the term was coined, Friday-Night Live worship services were *seeker sensitive* to draw in potential converts. Services at this hour attracted unchurched downtown office workers and people who responded well to this needs-based worship time. Though later SBC's "Mr. Moderate," Ken Chafin was a passionate soul winner who at one time held the Billy Graham endowed chair as a seminary evangelism professor. His sermons were peppered with stories about people he'd introduced to Christ that week. Yet this church with priorities that would, in many ways, line up with those of the conservative movement was the one, above all others, that greeted our cutting-edge "liberal" two-paycheck lifestyle with comforting, affirming acceptance.

Just another case in which labels didn't mean diddly.

In other denominations, we also saw examples of this.

Years later, when Kay and I were in Birmingham, AL, on business, we worshiped in St. Luke's Episcopal Church in which our former Baptist pastor, John R. Claypool, was now rector. Claypool had been senior minister at Crescent Hill Baptist Church in Louisville when we were seminary students. Disenchantment with Baptists plus a failed marriage had sent him transitioning to train for the Episcopal clergy. Once one of Southern Baptists' brightest risers and known broadly for his brilliant preaching and writing, he quickly got on the fast track in this new denomination. Many expected that this stellar cleric would even, in his lifetime, be elevated to bishop. We wondered how the priesthood had changed Claypool and how his learned yet impassioned preaching style had evolved under this new stamp.

Despite the high-church liturgy, the vestments, the genuflecting, and the other trappings of this "liberal" body, Claypool's compelling message that day could have preached in just about any Southern Baptist church. It was laced with "conservative" themes—salvation in Jesus Christ, His love and redemption, and the need for people to have life change through Him. These Episcopalians little realized that their prized, sought-after catch would always be just a basic ol' Baptist preacher at heart.

Father Ralph A. DiOrio of Massachusetts is a faith-healing Catholic priest—a cleric whose ministry is but a Catholic warm-over of the late ultraconservative Kathryn Kuhlman's "miracle services." Though from the "liberal" tradition, DiOrio's evangelistic itinerant ministry urges people to "make the issue of God and your soul the most important priority of your life." *Very un-Catholic,* many might say.

The Bible reminds us of a labeling instance even in the life of Jesus: *"Isn't this the carpenter? Isn't this Mary's son and the brother of James, Joseph, Judas and Simon? Aren't his sisters here with us?" And they took offense at him* (Mark 6:3).

I don't want to minimize the fact that some serious theological differences ultimately were at stake in the Conservative Resurgence movement. My Southern Seminary experience and later awareness convicted me that a new wind clearly needed to blow through Baptist life. Some major drifting had occurred from bedrock Baptist fundamentals—drifting that needed to be made right.

But I also know that labels often reveal little about a person or a particular church body. Paul Pressler and Ken Chafin later would become mortal enemies in the battle for the denomination. These two Houstonians ultimately would personify the two most polarized sides—the yin vs. yang, the Bush vs. Clinton, the warp vs. woof—of the conflict.

But if you had sat the two of them down in the same room and—side by side, point by point—painstakingly grilled them on each issue in their individual theologies, you would have been hard-pressed to find a dime's worth of difference between the so-called ultimate conservative and liberal.

And that's the way it was again and again, person after person, in my experience. In their hearts, they were far more alike than different.

* * * * * * * *

Although he was adept at keeping separate my roles as parishioner and religion editor, Ken got no greater rush than when he could serve as valuable news source. One of his tips, unfortunately, led me into the absolute teeth of sick, sordid denominational life. It happened because of a new wrinkle in the news-release "embargo" issue I mentioned earlier.

In 1982, when conservative Bailey Smith was running for re-election as SBC president, he routinely gave a copy of his planned presidential address to W.C. Fields of Baptist Press. As usual, a copy of those remarks went to religion reporters with the typical "embargo" stamp mandating that the speech could not be used until after it was delivered. On first glance, I could see Bailey's message contained a predictable scathing attack on the "liberals," but, knowing weeks would pass before I could release it, I filed it away for future use.

Then Ken Chafin called and insisted that he talk with me in person. Ken was one of the earliest alarm-sounders about what was abrew in the Convention and was up to his armpits in the fray long before the average Baptist was. When I arrived at his office, he had a copy of Bailey's "embargoed" speech lying on his desk. He said W.C. Fields—who was supposed to hand off the speech only to reporters—had deliberately also circulated it to "concerned" Convention leaders, including Ken, who were gravely bothered about the ongoing potential divisiveness. He said Convention leaders wanted the speech leaked to the public before the annual meeting began; this would rouse opposition. He asked me to write a news story immediately. My news peg would be that a copy of the hair-raising speech was circulating throughout the Convention's agencies, institutions, and leadership and that plans were under way to derail it.

I was dubious about writing the story, since I had never violated an embargo. For several days I left untouched the copy of the speech Ken slipped me.

Shortly afterward Ken called again and pled his case—that the story urgently needed to appear. Polite but resolute, Ken said if I wouldn't write it, he and others planned to approach Helen Parmley at *The Dallas Morning News*. Since the previous year Helen had broken the headline-grabber on Bailey's "God Almighty does not hear the prayer of a Jew" statement, Ken felt certain Helen also would report this denominational news if I wouldn't. Knowing the competitive penchant among journalists, I was sure she would, too.

Still unsure what to do, I took both copies of Bailey's prepared remarks to Dan Cobb, the *Chronicle*'s news editor, and asked for an opinion. Dan reasoned that Baptist Press's Fields had already broken the embargo by circulating the message widely within the Convention. He rationalized that if the President of the United States had prepared a speech and then his press secretary had circulated it far and wide within the government and within one political party before delivery, Dan and other news editors would rule that the press secretary had invalidated his own embargo. Dan urged me to write the story and write it quickly. I did.

Bailey and the leaders of the Conservative Resurgence were furious. I had let the cat out of their bag, so to speak.

When I arrived at the SBC meeting, Bailey confronted me hotly. Beet-faced and shaken, he fumed and harangued for all to hear. Publicly W.C. Fields chided me in front of the entire press room for releasing the story. I was dumfounded by his remarks. Ken had identified W.C. as the source of the leak; now W.C., admitting nothing, was publicly berating *me* for the reportage. I knew Ken to be a political operative with his own agenda, but I had never known him to be untruthful. In fact, I thought of him as brutally honest. *Why then would he lie to me now?* I wondered. *Or had he?*

Almost from the opening gavel in New Orleans, at the podium Bailey unfurled a copy of the *Houston Chronicle* and before thousands pummeled me and the *Chronicle* for publishing the speech story. (*Were those shouts of "Crucify him!" I heard in the distance?*) He never mentioned Fields' role in circulating it to opposition leaders long before the story hit the streets.

Loyal Ken, appalled at the "shoot-the-messenger" sentiment that prevailed at the meeting, suddenly became pastoral. Tracking me down in the SBC press room, he vowed that he would take the microphone on the convention floor, defend me, and admit his complicity. He said he would clarify that he was the one who had slipped me the copy of the speech that

W.C. Fields had slipped him to pass to those who were against Bailey.

Amazingly, I appealed to him to hold back. Journalists have primal convictions about their confidential sources; when this relationship is endangered, we go into auto pilot. Painful as this was for me, a principle was involved here: a news source should never be identified, despite the hysteria and personal attacks. If Ken unveiled his role, all future contacts between the two of us would be suspect.

Kay, busy strolling our new daughter, 8-month-old Katie, was with me in the SBC meeting hallway the next day when W.C. and his wife appeared in our line of vision. Fields stopped, sidled up to me, and interjected, "If you ever report what I'm about to say to you, I will deny it, but what you did helped our cause. I appreciate it very much."

Helped our cause! His words, which he may have thought would be marginally comforting, felt like a meat cleaver hatcheting through me. *Our cause*—as though his and his cohorts' interests were mine, as well! Journalists have no *cause* except the cause of truth. The very idea that I would want to advance a certain side in this issue was ludicrous. I had no side except that of fair reporting. I felt horribly set up and exploited. I couldn't believe the duplicity of his words and the depravity of the entire situation!

I also couldn't fathom that the president of the Southern Baptist Convention, who could have used his bully convention-floor pulpit to advance any God-anointed spiritual plea on his heart (how about, *Go out and win souls to Jesus*?), had given even one second's worth of his prime time to take a cheap shot at the news media!

In this situation, everybody wore black hats.

Everyone that is, except the *Chronicle* management, which steadfastly supported me and never batted an eye that we were right in publishing the story. Ever the white knight, Don Pickels assured me that this smear tactic that had discredited me would eventually fade from everyone's radar screen. Lesser editors would have cut and run and left the reporter hanging when controversy hit. I'll never forget the *Chronicle*'s undergirding me in this tenuous time. My superiors affirmed that I indeed had borne witness to the truth in difficult circumstances.

But, again, once the feathers are out of the bag, they can never all be re-collected and stuffed back in. On the Bailey Smith incident, many in the denomination would have very, very long memories.

Chapter 15

Woo, Pig! Sooie!

Truth No. 15: Animal Farm is more than just an accommodation for livestock.

With my early 1979 papal travels to Mexico City and Puebla now history, my calendar reminded me to start preparing for the Southern Baptist Convention to be held in my own backyard—Houston's Summit—that June. I admit that I was still starry-eyed over having been on the circuit with Pope John Paul II; by comparison, settling back in for the forthcoming Baptist meeting seemed quite lackluster.

I presumed the Convention would feature its predictable fare: the election of one of the "good ole boys" as president and a feisty debate over dreary resolutions such as selecting the meeting city for 1988. After covering the SBC for the *Chronicle* for seven years, the denomination seemed lockstep. Those in charge appeared still to have a firm grip on things.

Though I had seen the first foregleam of discontent, signaling that the denomination was not quite as unified as the Convention's leaders tried to portray, I couldn't see how, short of a full-scale civil war, things were going to change.

The real rumblings began in late April before the June meeting. The Deep Throat murmurings on my answering machine said the natives were restless. *So what does that mean?* The information indicated discussions were being held that could unleash a mighty earthquake in the denomination. *Right*, I thought skeptically.

I started listening more closely to the distant drumbeat but still was wary. *Wouldn't want to go jumping at shadows and mistake Bill Powell and Bob Holbrooke for a revolutionary army. After all, these are the guys who hold their meetings in cubicles,* I told myself.

The first real confirmation arrived when the *Baptist Standard* reported and Baptist Press followed that Paul Pressler and Paige Patterson were out speaking in churches and trying to rouse the mighty sleeping conservative giant within the Convention.

Baptist Press called them *ultraconservatives* and minimized the possibilities.

I started making phone calls and soon discovered that the drumbeat was louder and stronger than I had suspected. *But what's Judge Paul Pressler, the fellow I interviewed about being a Christian jurist, got to do with this? And how is he tangled up with that carrot-topped cowboy I met in the president's office at the fledgling Criswell College in Dallas?*

In response to my phone call, Pressler invited me to his home in the affluent Memorial area villages of West Houston. Calmly and matter-of-factly he explained his concern that the Convention had drifted too far to the left. He enlightened me about the partnership he had forged with Paige Patterson since 1977, after he visited key pastors who were concerned about the denomination; his support for Adrian Rogers after Adrian's castigation by the ruling denominational leaders; and how he indeed had trudged throughout the South for the past several months and held meetings anywhere he could gain a hearing to convince people to travel to Houston and rise up against the establishment.

After the 1979 SBC meeting, when swarming converts from the Pressler whistlestop tour literally took the meeting by storm, Pressler personally apologized that he might have minimized to me beforehand the size and extent of the movement. Indeed, he had downplayed the possibility of success, which I later learned was vintage Pressler political style.

The ruling party, whose members later were tagged the *moderates*, responded with its own form of calm assurance that only a handful of natives were truly restless and this, too, would pass without much impact. As far as they were concerned, this little "tempest in a teapot" would amount to nothing; they would sally forth with the reins of the denomination squarely in their hands.

Thus, I began to see the faint outline of the differences that would ultimately decide the fate of the nation's largest non-Catholic denomination—Pressler demurring and devaluing the size and extent of the upheaval; the moderate leaders misreading the tea leaves and underestimating the strength of their enemy.

I also quickly sized up that Patterson, formerly pastor of First Baptist Church in Fayetteville, AR, was the minister/academician who would major on the theological issues in the conflict while Pressler was the strategist who would steer and guide as though he were staging an election campaign.

Months after the SBC rebellion erupted, the *Chronicle*'s executive editor, Everett Collier, summoned me to his office to disclose, "I've been reading your stories about Paul Pressler and the Southern Baptists. There's something I want to tell you. You may not know that Paul Pressler is the grandson of the late, great Judge E.E. Townes, who ran the Texas Democratic Party out of his hip pocket. I remember when Paul was a young lad and would ride around with his grandfather as Judge Townes ran his political machine all over the state. As I've read your stories, I clearly can see that young Paul learned what the grandfather was teaching. When I look at your stories today about the grandson, I see the grandfather."

The second week of June 1979, Southern Baptist denominational leaders and their well-educated, affluent followers headed to Houston for what many believed might be a "little unpleasantness" that could be stopped quickly. Few had any inkling of what lay ahead for them.

At the same time pastors and laypeople from small, often rural churches who had felt disenfranchised by what they felt was the exclusion of the ruling party made their way to the Bayou City, too. They arrived believing the time was at hand to "take back" the denomination, which many believed had been stolen from them.

Later, Baptist state editors would complain that these "new" messengers were "bused" to the SBC meeting by the Pressler-Patterson coalition, a fact that Pressler always steadfastly denied. Critics completely ignored the fact that huge numbers of Convention employees and their spouses, representing the party in charge, had arrived in Houston by commercial aircraft using tickets purchased with Cooperative Program money—often given by the same churches whose pastors and laypeople had to ride the aforementioned mythical buses.

I would eventually liken the rebellion to what happened in George Orwell's famous novella *Animal Farm*, the satirical allegory in which the farm animals rise up and overthrow the human owners of the farm because they have had enough of the owners' corruption and power abuses. I'm certainly not likening the small-church pastors to farm animals, even though people of the new group were definitely of a different ilk than were members of the ruling Baptist aristocracy at the time. But their gripe was simple: they could cite specific times in which students in certain Southern Baptist schools were being taught things different than what the Bible says. They could identify occasions in which professors mocked students who held to inerrancy of Scriptures and believed that conservative traditional Baptist beliefs were not being adequately presented as students were taught. They believed that those in charge had not been willing to listen to these concerns; therefore the rebel forces had no other choice except to try to effect change through SBC processes.

* * * * * * * *

By tradition, Southern Baptist Conventions are preceded by the SBC Pastors' Conference. The conference starts on Sunday night and concludes on Monday evening for the convention to begin on Tuesday morning. It consists of sermons from a slate of pastors carefully (and politically) selected beforehand so that messengers can hear the "best" of Baptist preaching. Before the 1979 SBC meeting, the emerging conservatives had cleverly and quietly moved into certain leadership positions of the Pastors' Conference. Unbeknownst to the denomination's ruling party, the cannons were already loaded and ready with ammunition on opening night.

Evangelist James Robison fired the first volley. It included one diatribe after another against the Convention's "liberals." In a column I once had called Robison "God's Angry Man," a phrase he embraced, picked up, and used in his publicity. That night he clearly was the budding conservatives' "Angry Man." The crowd leapt to its feet with cheers and war whoops. Near where I was seated, some pastors literally stood in their seats in passionate support as Robison spoke. They jumped up and down with vociferous "amens" and affirmations such as, "You tell 'em, James!" and "Preach on, brother!" Kay vowed that from where she sat, she distinctly heard yells of, "Woo, pig! Sooie!", the famous spirit cry of the University of Arkansas

Razorbacks. Kay felt that this type of unorthodox exclamation symbolized the tone of what at some points became a near melee. At strategic moments in the sermons, people spontaneously broke into hollers of whatever pet exclamations they knew. I had never seen a staid, Southern Baptist crowd so animated or carry on like this.

Then W.A. Criswell took to the pulpit. He first attacked Convention "liberals" and then proclaimed, "This is going to be a great convention if for no other reason than to elect Adrian Rogers as our president." With his usual moonlight-and-magnolias, silken Southern coyness, Criswell later denied that he had "endorsed" Rogers ("Wah, ah nevah endahssed the lad."), though everyone in the large assembly hall knew exactly what the SBC pontiff had meant by his remarks.

Convention bureaucrats in the meeting hall looked wan and startled. I felt electrified as I did when John Paul II was elected. I could feel the goosebumps dot my chest and arms. I knew this SBC wasn't going to be your grandfather's Oldsmobile. This 1979 SBC could be on the par with the earth-shaking election eight months earlier of the world's first Polish pope!

I assessed quickly that because of the direction this SBC meeting was turning, I needed to stay as close to Pressler as I could, so I did. The news that likely would emerge from the meeting suddenly seemed to be tied to this one man's coattails. In fact, after the next night's Pastors' Conference concluded, the judge invited me to accompany him to a "special little get-together of friends" at a cafeteria in Houston's emerging underground tunnel system. When we arrived at the "little get-together," I saw that the place was packed to the rafters with "new" messengers to the meeting. I realized that we were there after the restaurant's closing hours. That would be one of many times I would marvel at how effective Pressler was at always having the right resources available at the right moment.

What I remember most about that late-night meeting was the prayer time: Everyone dropped to his knees and prayed. The person who voiced the prayer specifically asked God for victory the next morning at the SBC meeting. The prayer contained no platitudes asking for peace, prosperity, and harmony. The petition minced no words. These people were there to win.

Off I went to the *Chronicle* building to file my story for the next day's paper. Returning home well after midnight, Kay's report told me volumes that I might not have learned trudging up and down the convention's hallways for days. After she left the Pastors' Conference with our houseguests, a pastor friend and his wife from a smaller church in the South, these friends disclosed that they, too, had actually been lured to this year's SBC by the same forces that Robison described. They were there to see that "liberalism" be routed from the Convention's seminaries, particularly Southern. *So now even my own home has been infiltrated by the rebellion that is under way,* I thought. Kay and I, looking at each other, asked ourselves, *Just how big and widespread is this thing, anyway?*

I remembered a quote I had read from a book about the restoration of the British monarchy after the days of Oliver Cromwell in the 17th century. A description stuck in my mind. It read, "The desire of the people had begun to push up like green shoots through the earth. Across the water the exiles had waited, shivering and hungry through the coldest and most poverty stricken winter of all. Then the miracle happened and spring burst forth."[1]

Did some exultation akin to *Woo, Pig! Sooie!* emerge from these exiles' lips? Is this what was happening at the 1979 SBC before my very eyes, as those who felt exiled marched on

Houston to take back what they thought was theirs?

Finally, attempting to snare a few hours' sleep before I had to be back at the early morning meeting, I startled awake at 6 to my bedroom phone ringing. My sister, Mary, relayed to me that my mother's only surviving brother had been murdered at his Oklahoma City home during a break-in! Because of my mother's fragile health, I needed to leave at once to drive to her townhome about five minutes away so I could tell her in person about this tragedy.

Before I hung up from talking with my sister, however, I advised her that I wasn't at all sure that I'd be able to travel to Oklahoma for Uncle George's services. Based on what had happened the previous night at the Pastor's Conference, I shared that I likely could be ensconced in one of the biggest religion news stories of the century and could hardly step aside from it at this very moment.

I couldn't believe I was hampered from being with my family in the sad crisis of my uncle's slaying because my own denomination was getting ready to explode all over itself!

* * * * * * * *

The next morning, back at the SBC, the looks on the faces of the unsuspecting ruling-party members spoke volumes. Dressed in their finest, they arrived in Houston for the 1979 Southern Baptist Convention expecting to have a wonderful time dining in the city's finest restaurants, seeing old friends, and doing what they were accustomed to doing at an annual meeting. This included back-slapping in the hallways, catching up on the latest gossip of who was being considered for what pulpit or denominational post, and culminating the visit with a special service led by Evangelist Billy Graham in Houston's shiny Astrodome.

Paul Pressler, Paige Patterson, Adrian Rogers, and their friends were set to spoil their party.

When I arrived at The Summit and encountered Pressler, he invited me to his skybox at the very top of the building overlooking the convention floor. It wasn't his personal skybox; he had just "borrowed" it from friends who loaned him the key and gave him *carte blanche* permission to use it as he wished. Once again I definitely was seeing the connection between the SBC meeting being in Houston and Pressler's incredible knowledge of and resources in the city!

The skybox became command central for the Conservative Resurgence. Because of Kay's and my history with Pressler, I would be the only secular or denominational newspaper reporter granted complete and unfettered access throughout the meeting to the skybox, thus becoming truly an eyewitness to religious history in the making. On Tuesday of the SBC meeting, after I convinced *Chronicle* management that I sensed I was up to my armpits in one of the biggest religion stories of contemporary times, other *Chronicle* reporters were sent in to undergird me. Assistant City Editor Tommy Miller, who once hired me as a cub reporter for *The Baylor Lariat*, was recruited to be my main helper. Miller actually had grown up in the same church and high school in Beaumont, TX, with both Paige and Dorothy Patterson. In adulthood he was no longer a practicing Southern Baptist but because of his roots continued to hold a deep curiosity about the SBC. The Pattersons seemed pleased but surprised to see their old friend with a reporter's notebook in hand covering them. At various times he was with me in the skybox that would forever remain an icon in Baptist history.

Kay, whenever she had time and could be at the meeting, was granted admission to the skybox, also. But of necessity she had to divide her time between her regular reporting job at the *Chronicle;* caring for our son, Matthew, 3; and ferrying my mother (who under normal conditions cared for Matthew when we were in a bind) to the airport for the family drama that was under way 500 miles north in Oklahoma City. Of course Kay was still also hostess to our houseguests, who by now were wide-eyed at the events unfolding at the SBC meeting.

* * * * * * *

I was sitting near Pressler in the skybox when the nominations for Convention president were made and later when the tally was announced. When the vote was released, Pressler literally bolted from his seat with astonishment. Adrian Rogers, the man the ruling party feared the most, had won by a whopping 51.36 percent of the vote—meaning no runoff—with five other candidates dividing the rest of the ballots. No contender was anywhere close to Adrian's vote total.

The ruling party's reaction was most obvious behind the scenes. At previous SBC meetings W.C. Fields and his cohorts in Baptist Press quickly surrounded the new president, briefed him for a previously scheduled press conference, then took command of his public persona. That didn't happen this time. Instead, no press conference, no briefing, and no taking charge of Rogers' public persona occurred for the first 24 hours. The frozen silence reminded me of the way the world reacted after the Vatican bells tolled and the new Polish pope appeared on that famous balcony above Vatican square—breathless silence as the reality of the moment sank in and people realized that no Italian insider had won the day.

I also saw these kinds of looks on the faces of opponents in the historic moment in 1976 when the General Convention of the Episcopal Church of the USA meeting in Philadelphia lifted its ban on ordaining women. Though stoic to the core, a hushed, tight-lipped disdain spread across the faces of those who had fought against the move.

However, I happened to be sitting near 81-year-old Jeannette Piccard at the instant the vote results were known. For more than 60 years Jeannette, who had ties to NASA and therefore was of interest to Houston readers, had been lobbying for ordination. I watched the look of rejoicing register on her face when she realized that barriers at last had fallen for those who long had knocked at the door.

At least outwardly, Jeannette Piccard, didn't yell "Woo, pig! Sooie!" when this monumental decision was handed down, but I'm sure her insides felt that kind of exclamation. It was Orwellian to the core—just like the 1945 fable about the power struggles among animals on a farm in an oppressive political order. In each case those who perceived themselves as downtrodden or marginalized summoned the strength to overcome those who had been in charge for a long, long time.

This time, unlike in Rome on that cataclysmic day in 1978, no bells tolled, though moderate conventioners' eyes were beginning to turn upward to Pressler's skybox. The previous ruling party, eventually tagged as the *moderates,* later would affix their disdain on the Summit skybox as a symbol of all that occurred in 1979. I just happened to be at the right place at the right time when the political chill overtook the warm June Houston air surrounding The Summit.

* * * * * * * *

While the party of the establishment tried to collect itself in the wake of the unsettling victory, precious news time was

173

wasted waiting for Rogers' first press conference. I took the initiative and began querying Pressler and Dorothy Patterson about arranging a private interview for me with Rogers. By this point I had observed that Dorothy was much, much more than "the little woman behind the scenes" as some try erroneously to portray the wives of SBC conservative leaders. While Smith College grad Nancy Pressler functioned as the epitome of a well-heeled wife who hostessed in the skybox with the grace and skills of an uppercrust Houston Junior Leaguer, Dorothy Patterson was more of a behind-the-scenes, can-do, take-charge, nuts-and-bolts political strategist. One of my most perplexing memories of the 1979 SBC meeting occurred on Wednesday morning when Paige Patterson slept late—much to the disdain of just about everyone in the skybox—while Dorothy Patterson seemed, in the absence of her husband, to literally function as an equal partner with Pressler.

Several months later Dorothy conveyed some important words to me that made a big difference during times when I felt I was being sifted as wheat (Luke 22:31) because of covering the controversy. She wrote me a letter in which she said she believed God had placed me at the *Chronicle* at that particular time in church history. She quoted the famous passage from the Book of Esther: "*Who knowest whether thou art come to the kingdom for such a time as this?*" (Esth. 4:14 KJV).

* * * * * * * *

Soon I was ushered into a private meeting with Adrian Rogers. He remembered our phone interview and my subsequent story three years earlier when he had been assaulted so severely by the Baptist state newspapers who branded "the rising star from Memphis" unfit for SBC service. I found him extremely courteous, articulate, and firm in his convictions.

Rogers clearly had been briefed thoroughly on Pressler's evaluation of how power flows in the SBC. At the beginning of their movement Pressler had scrutinized the SBC constitution and bylaws and determined the actual pathway to control SBC agencies and seminaries. The key lay in presidential appointments to the Convention's Committee on Nominations. That body chooses the members of the Convention's Committee on Committees, which in turn appoints the Committee on Boards. Factoring in the "good-ole-boys" network that prevailed with the ruling party, the process was clear. It worked like this: The SBC president appoints like-minded friends to the Committee on Nominations. The like-minded friends appoint other like-minded friends to the Committee on Committees, who in turn appoint like-minded friends to the Committee on Boards, which then appoints like-minded friends as trustees of the various SBC agencies and seminaries.

For years the majority party had clearly known the formula but didn't particularly want to circulate it. What Pressler did was make the secret formula available to outsiders. The controversy that ensued then made the formula available to anyone both inside and outside the SBC. Like some kind of clandestine Da Vinci code, the formula had existed for more than a century and been very useful to the incumbents but was a mystery to those outside the ruling party.

* * * * * * * *

Because it was Adrian Rogers' first interview after his election, the *Chronicle* played my story on the front page on

Wednesday morning. In the first edition, my article referred to Rogers, Pressler, and Patterson as *ultraconservatives*, the term Baptist Press requested that the media use for the emerging group of dissidents. In the second and later editions of the paper that morning, the word *fundamentalists* replaced the word *ultraconservatives*. I first learned of the change in a phone call from *Chronicle* News Editor Dan Cobb. "I've been reading your story carefully this morning. I don't think these guys are *ultraconservatives*," he said. "I think they are *fundamentalists*. I've changed your words to reflect that. If you disagree you can come down here (to the *Chronicle* office in downtown Houston) and we can talk about it."

I had learned earlier not to argue with Dan when he got a bee under his bonnet like that. He could be dogmatic and irrational—the way he talked about his own United Methodists bishops being. My sense was it didn't make that much difference and wasn't worth the fight with Dan that I knew would occur. So I told him to just let it go. Years later I wished I had stopped everything and gone to the office for a showdown, because the term *fundamentalist* dogged my coverage of the SBC controversy ever after.

Once my front-page banner headline appeared with the term *fundamentalist*, the Associated Press and other media immediately followed suit; the term stuck. Thus, a very liberal United Methodist layman who fancied himself as an armchair theologian actually named the sides in the Convention controversy!

Pressler, Patterson, Rogers and their supporters disdained the term *fundamentalist* while moderates reveled in it. The *fundamentalists* wanted their enemies to be known as *liberals*, but I recoiled at that term because it seemed not totally accurate. Besides, why call <u>anyone</u> in Baptist life *liberal* when the entire denomination would still line up way to the right of center compared to most other groups in Christendom? To most everyone else, ALL Baptists were *ultraconservatives*.

Years later the rumor spread that W.C. Fields or one of his assistants at Baptist Press had gone over my head to the *Chronicle* executive office suite and lobbied for the paper to change the term to *fundamentalist*. I personally never saw any indication whatsoever of that incident occurring. Later many would allay that attaching these monikers was part of some sort of devious conservative manipulation or plot. What they didn't realize that it was merely an outgrowth of Dan Cobb's pugnacious personality. It occurred just to prove that this editor knew best.

* * * * * * * *

Another sad but compelling development that was all but ignored by most participants at the meeting—conservative as well as moderate as well as secular and denominational media—was the health of Pressler's son, Paul IV, then a teenager. The young Paul appeared to be ill with a headache or some other kind of malady and spent much of the SBC meeting week lying on a couch in the skybox with his mother, Nancy, nearby looking on frantically as any mother in that circumstance would. Pressler, while keeping his eye on the floor, was consumed with Paul's great discomfort on election day as well. Paul's mysterious illness, which seemed to coincide with the uproar in the Convention, puzzled me; I'm sure it must have concerned others, too. Over the years as the Conservative Resurgence progressed, young Paul experienced seizures; his health bobbled precariously. Many wondered whether the family was experiencing severe spiritual warfare because of what else was transpiring. Since this was such an obvious burden on

Paul and Nancy Pressler, I have always been amazed that the parents didn't stop in their tracks, yank up the boy, head home, and tune out what was occurring in The Summit that day. This painful struggle between two majorly competing needs served as a reminder to me how seriously his parents must have taken the events unfurling around them as the Conservative Resurgence began.

On Wednesday morning Adrian held his first press conference. I could see the anger in the eyes of Baptist media members, especially in those of the six state editors who had proclaimed so loudly three years earlier that Adrian should never be allowed to lead the Convention. Now the cauldron was beginning to boil. One could almost sense the temperature rising in the press room. Instead of accepting the new president as the Convention leader, the soon-to-be former ruling-party members appeared to clench their jaws and gird their loins for battle.

Meanwhile, since I had already interviewed Adrian the day before and then heard nothing new in the press conference, I turned my attentions elsewhere. Dorothy Patterson eagerly and politely complied with my request to arrange an exclusive interview with Joyce Rogers, Adrian's wife and new first lady of the Southern Baptist Convention, on her perspective on the role of women. And, of course, plenty of theatrics continued to occur on the floor of the convention as moderate anger began to boil over into the meeting itself.

Late Wednesday afternoon Toby Druin, associate editor of the *Baptist Standard*, approached me in the press room. He demanded, "What exactly is your relationship with Paul Pressler, anyway?" Little did I realize that being in the skybox, snaring the first exclusive interview with Adrian Rogers, breaking all the news angles from the SBC meeting, and having the inside track on SBC developments—simply being a witness to the truth—would spark a streak of professional jealousy that I would scarcely be able to shake.

[1] Elizabeth Goudge, *The Child from the Sea*, (New York: Pyramid, 1971), 630.

Chapter 16

I Just Marvel

Truth No. 16: Playing ostrich can keep you comfy for just so long, and then with a high price tag.

After the 1979 SBC meeting concluded and the janitors had swept up all the debris at The Summit, Southern Baptist moderates seemed to heave a collective sigh of relief. Soon I heard aphorisms such as, "This was all a fluke. This won't last. You and the other newspaper reporters blew this up into something much more than it really was."

Indeed, dire predictions of Houston SBC prognosticators failed to materialize. New moderate-proposed trustee-board slates were elected as planned. Budgets were approved as requested. The 1979 SBC meeting had continued to its appointed end despite a small number of political skirmishes that occurred on the convention floor over the *Baptist Faith and Message* and abortion. Billy Graham spoke at the foreign missionaries' appointment service held at the Houston Astrodome.

When fall 1979 arrived, I was amazed to learn that I would receive the Baptist General Convention of Texas' annual Media Award for my coverage of the Houston SBC meeting. I was a little peeved, however, when James Dunn of the Texas Christian Life Commission reported, "I had to fight off some of your enemies in order to help you get the award." I wasn't sure whether his remarks were a backhanded slap or just his dry-witted way of making sure I knew he had supported me. I did know that "shoot-the-messenger" sentiment was already being advanced big-time about the Baptist controversy. My office mail slot evidenced it daily.

Nevertheless, despite the calm after the storm, the ferociously hated Adrian Rogers was now SBC president. The new Pressler-Patterson coalition was off and running and heady with success. And moderates were divided into two camps: those who comprehended that the "fundamentalists" might eventually succeed if not checked quickly, and those who believed that the whole thing was a media fabrication and would go away quickly.

In the initial flush of reality, Ken Chafin, pastor of Houston's South Main Baptist Church, and brothers Cecil Sherman of Asheville, NC, and Bill Sherman of Nashville, TN, quickly emerged as leaders of the "this-is-serious" moderate faction. Chafin and the Sherman brothers saw themselves as the "watchmen on the wall" who needed to warn Southern Baptists about the impending fundamentalist upheaval that was going to rip the Convention apart and vastly overhaul the direction, style, and political direction of the SBC. Chafin was bent on being the Paul Revere of the controversy, as he spoke, wrote, and networked with the message, "The fundamentalists are coming. The fundamentalists are coming." Instead of being appreciated for his efforts to raise denominational consciousness, he was largely backstabbed.

Most of the Convention's agency and seminary leaders seemed to take the opposite approach. While not fans of Rogers, they mostly discounted his election as an historical accident and predicted a quick return to normalcy. Had these "head-in-the-sand" Baptist leaders locked arms immediately with Chafin and the Sherman brothers, the outcome would have stood a very good chance of being different. The movement, though picking up huge momentum, was still in its embryonic stages. Though powerful people were behind it, it still could have been squelched.

Instead of rallying their troops and fighting back quickly and decisively, moderates squandered the only real opportunity they had to keep from turning over the keys to the denominational agency and seminary doors to the Pressler-Patterson Coalition. In fact, as I wrote in a *Wittenburg Door* article in 1988, moderate agency and seminary leaders misjudged and miscalculated every step along the way to their eventual defeat. They either waited too late to respond, failed to react appropriately, or hatched half-baked, sophomoric political schemes that backfired on them.

From the beginning the Pressler-Patterson coalition proved that its political IQ was far superior to the good-ole-boys' network and political rules by which the Convention had previously operated. In one of the most nonsensical responses I heard expressed, some moderate leaders tried to pretend that the Convention previously had always been above politics. I never could figure out if the people who espoused such opinions truly believed this distortion, were simply lying, or had their heads buried so deeply in the sand that they could not see the light of day. Politics always occur when human beings interact. Before 1979 the SBC has its own peculiar Southern Democratic way of doing things. Politics then were more passive-aggressive, behind closed doors, and publicly polite, but they did exist and always had.

* * * * * * * *

In the spring of 1980 Adrian Rogers made a surprise announcement that threw the moderates a staggering curve ball. He vowed he would not seek and would not accept a second term as Convention president. He gave no explanation as to why. Moderates in the "It'll-all-blow-over" camp were ecstatic. They were in an "I-told-you-so" mood. Moderates in the Chafin-Sherman-Sherman faction were pleased but mystified by Rogers' action. Pressler and Patterson were vaguely noncommital.

In a phone conversation with my colleague, Helen Parmley of *The Dallas Morning News*, the two of us were skeptical and puzzled. We both believed something was afoot that wasn't obvious yet. I made a list of possible scenarios that might be operating. Among them was the notion that Adrian Rogers might be seriously ill; another thought was that this was a political ploy, whereby the Pressler-Patterson coalition yanked its lightning-rod president off the stage and would re-introduce him later at a more strategic moment. My last thought proved to be correct. Adrian eventually was brought back in the limelight for the pivotal moment in 1986 when his leadership skills were necessary to bring the fight to its grand conclusion utilizing the so-called Peace Committee report.

Rogers did, however, send forth a list of nominees to the powerful Committee on Nominations; the list represented just what he had promised—true-blue conservatives to the core.

In retrospect, Rogers' shocker move upended the moderates so severely, they would never recover from it. As Rogers backed off stage, the moderates relaxed and seemed to relax their guard as well. Meanwhile, the Pressler-Patterson coalition worked feverishly to elect Midwest City, OK, pastor Bailey Smith as president. At the 1980 SBC in St. Louis, after Bailey Smith won on the first ballot, I heard Pressler in the meeting hallway effusing not so quietly, "Praise the Lord! Praise the Lord!" Later in St. Louis the discombobulated moderates were too disorganized to oppose Rogers' first slate of solid conservative committee appointments.

Score three points for the new Pressler-Patterson coalition—one point for electing a second presidential candidate, one point for getting Rogers' appointees through the process, and a third point for leaving the moderates reeling and confused.

On things went throughout the early 1980s. Despite Bailey Smith's foot-in-mouth tendencies (i.e., his "God Almighty does not hear the prayer of a Jew," while a Jewish Anti-Defamation League tape recorder was rolling), the Pressler-Patterson coalition just kept on reeling in bigger victories. After Bailey's massively publicized blunder, moderates presumed Smith was dead in the water politically, only to discover at the 1981 SBC meeting in Los Angeles that he was very much alive and electable once again.

* * * * * * * *

In 1981 I was program chairman for the Religion Newswriters Association's annual convention, which we held in conjunction with the SBC in Los Angeles. For one of the programs I invited Paige Patterson to debate Ken Chafin on the issue of whether inerrancy was crucial to the future and survival of the Southern Baptist Convention. Though Chafin firmly believed that he trounced Patterson in the debate, most people in the room left believing Patterson was the winner. Chafin let his anger at the conservatives get the best of him, while Patterson remained logical, controlled, and unflappable. In the midst of the debate, I seriously considered calling a break and hauling Chafin to the men's room to pour a glass of cold water on him to cool him down. From then on I knew that emotions weren't going to win the day against the Pressler-Patterson coalition.

I'll always believe much more could have been accomplished on a one-on-one, interpersonal level if people would have set pride aside and tried to discuss the issues face to face with their protagonists. At one point early on, I suggested to Chafin that he call Pressler and try to have a sympathetic discussion with him about Pressler's ill son, Paul IV. During one point, one of Ken's own young-adult children faced a major health issue. I thought the two foes might benefit from conversing simply as two concerned fathers who were storming heaven's throneroom for their offspring.

A part of Pressler's disappointment concerned the fact that he grew up in and at age 10 made his profession of faith at South Main; his parents were married in that church, but Pressler as an adult did not feel he could be a part of that congregation. The conversation between Ken and Pressler took place by phone. It did nothing to change matters in the Convention, but I believe that for a few minutes the men set aside their differences and ministered to each other.

After 1981 score four more points for the Pressler-Patterson coalition: one for the re-election of Bailey Smith under extremely difficult circumstances for the conservatives, one for getting Bailey's first set of appointees through the process, and one for getting the second wave of Adrian Rogers's appointees (the appointees of his appointees) through the system. And a fourth point for leaving the moderates more divided and confused than ever and with not only their eyeballs spinning but their noses bleeding as well.

In 1982 was the New Orleans SBC meeting already described in "Helping the Cause"—the scene that occurred there over Bailey Smith's presidential address and moderate efforts to undercut it by disbursing it among Bailey foes. Moderates such as Chafin knew Bailey's presidential address symbolized the greatest demonstration they had seen to date to prove to skeptics that the conservative war train was still on track for taking over the Convention's agencies and seminaries. In 1982 the Pressler-Patterson coalition succeeded again by electing James T. Draper Jr., of Euless, TX, as president. Draper promoted themes of peace and love, which earned him a unanimous victory for his second one-year term in 1983. Nevertheless, he continued to make the same type of appointments that Adrian Rogers and Bailey Smith had made.

Meanwhile, Chafin and the Sherman brothers continued to pound away that the tide would soon shift and the Pressler-Patterson appointees would within sight begin to control the boards of trustees of several agencies. I understood the Chafin-Sherman math and concern, because it coincided with the same math and perspective that Pressler was presenting—on opposite ends of the spectrum, of course.

Sadly, Ken's continued high visibility on his Paul Revere Ride began to gall some members of South Main. They became embarrassed at Ken for his continuing stance on and involvement in denominational issues. They wanted their pastor to limit his SBC activities and be more present in the pulpit. Like many denominational leaders of that period, those critics today consider themselves former or moderate Southern Baptists. What Ken tried to tell them became true; eventually they began to see he was a prophet ahead of his time. Like many denominational leaders of that era who ignored his words and shunned him personally, those members today still owe Ken an apology for speaking the truth that they found too difficult to bear at the time.

On April 8, 1984, Ken resigned his pulpit at South Main to take a professorship in preaching at Southern Seminary. Ken vowed that his exit had nothing to do with Baptist politics but reflected his desire to re-enter the academic setting and scale down his hectic pace.

For our family this was a profound personal loss. Ken had been like a surpassingly wise grandfather to our two children; he dedicated our baby daughter, Katie; on one of his last Sundays in the pulpit he baptized our son, Matthew. In the summer of 1982 when our entire family was involved in a serious fire while we vacationed in Colorado, Ken spearheaded the church's effort to get us home from this traumatic event and minister to us while I healed from burns. His inspired preaching on the keystone literal interpretation of God's Word defied all stereotypes of what one might expect from this moderate leader. Though people disagreed politically with this master communicator, no one ever accused him of heresy. We regretted that his political involvement and backbone had not been more greatly respected. As compatriot Cecil Sherman would say at Ken's memorial service when this luminary pastor died of cancer in 2001, "Ken committed the unpardonable sin with Baptists—he was right early."

* * * * * * * * *

I was truly amazed that during this period the moderate agency and seminary leadership was so noncommital and nonplussed. (Ken's successor at South Main, Bill Turner, later would call them "fuzzy minded.") Until Roy Honeycutt, president of Southern Seminary, proclaimed his "Holy War" against the conservatives, these highly paid denominational executives acted like the people who danced on the deck of the *Titanic* and discounted all warnings that the ship was about to sink.

Russell Dilday, president of Southwestern Seminary, had been particularly critical of Ken at the beginning of the conflict and had taken a complacent, ostrich approach for the first few years. "When I think of Russell Dilday, I just marvel,"

187

was the headline of a *Chronicle* column I wrote after the agency and seminary leadership finally awoke to the reality of its *Titanic* sinking. Dilday had suddenly bounded forth on his hypothetical white horse and was now helping Honeycutt lead the charge against the victorious conservatives. I wondered aloud where he had been all along, especially at times when Chafin had tried so desperately and personally (publicly and privately) to get Dilday and the others to envisage the destruction and sally forth in battle.

Truly, I "just marvel[ed]" at all of them. Had Dilday and the others firmly and soberly joined ranks with Chafin and the Sherman brothers as the opening shot was fired across the bow—if they had sat down with their detractors and tried to iron out differences and see what changes could be made in seminary pronouncements that would be more palatable to all sides—I firmly believe they could have turned back the tide that eventually swept every one of the agency heads and seminary presidents out of office.

Midwestern Baptist Seminary in Kansas City, MO, was marked as the first of the SBC agencies or seminaries to fall into conservative hands. When the inevitable was about to happen, its moderate president, Dr. Milton Ferguson, suddenly went on the warpath against the Pressler-Patterson coalition. *Too little, too late,* was all I could say in my bafflement. By this point the others should have merely sent up the white flags because the tide of history had turned so strongly against them. They failed to heed the words of Proverbs 12:15, *The way of a fool seems right to him, but a wise man listens to advice.*

Turning a blind eye backfired in some other denominational situations as well. In recent years several Roman Catholic dioceses have taken bankruptcy in response to large court settlements resulting from sexual-abuse cases involving errant

Catholic priests in their dioceses. Many of the situations that led to the court cases and subsequent financial losses could have been avoided or at least thwarted had the bishops or other top diocesan officials taken seriously immediately the accusations of sexual abuse leveled against their priests. Like the SBC's agency heads and seminary presidents, these diocesan officials first stuck their heads in the sand and denied that a problem existed, then dallied far too long before making the corrections necessary to avert personal tragedies that resulted from them.

When the Lutheran Church-Missouri Synod was caught up in the same theological wrangling that later engulfed the SBC, that denomination's moderate wing doffed off the emerging problem. Long after the optimal time had passed, the moderates believed they still could win the battle. Subsequently, when the LCMS eventually split, its moderate wing was so splintered and fragmented that the resulting breakaway was far, far smaller than it might have been had they separated earlier.

* * * * * * * *

After seven years, the day-in-day-out, week-in-week-out of the wrangling in my personal denomination was starting to grate. My mailbox brimmed with strident letters urging me to take one side or the other. I could have spent my entire work day fending calls from readers who simply wanted to vent— and since I was publicly identified with the controversy, I seemed like a good crying towel.

Throughout the 1980s, I felt a murderous personal tearing between the two factions. Being a graduate of Southern Seminary during its liberal heyday, I knew maybe even better than Pressler and Patterson did that the scent they were picking up was correct. Because of my roots at Capitol Hill Baptist Church in Oklahoma City, I knew what conservative Southern Baptist theology was; it didn't comprise the bulk of what I was taught at the Baptists' mother seminary.

I also was appalled that the Convention leadership tried to deny liberalism on the seminary's campus and in other aspects of Southern Baptist life. *Why don't they just admit this is what they are teaching and let the chips fall where they may?* I would ask myself every time I would hear or read a Convention leader denying that liberalism in any form existed within the Convention. I saw much of the moderate defense as semantical word games designed to camouflage rather than clarify. It also struck me as untruthful.

At the same time, I wasn't convinced that a return to Southern Baptist traditional theology was necessarily the best approach either. I liked the fact that Southern Baptist scholars were studying at some of the finest institutions of higher education in the world—Oxford, Cambridge, Harvard, to name a few. *So, what's wrong with students learning what's best taught in the classrooms of the top echelon of theological education?* I asked myself.

I saw clearly a cultural and class divide between the moderates and the conservatives. Except for Pressler, whose patrician background set him apart from most Southern Baptists, and Pressler's protégé, Richard Land, whose working-class background had been upgraded by his Princeton and Oxford degrees, most of the emerging conservative leadership and followers were from a different socio-economic world than were the more urbane, more literate, more culturally refined moderates, many of whom were graduates of Baylor, Mercer, Samford and other top-tier Southern Baptist colleges and universities. Conservatives struck me as more likely to have gone to Bible colleges, smaller state universities, and non-mainstream (that is, non-union-card) seminaries.

As the Conservative Resurgence moved forward, it also appeared more and more to be an eclectic grouping of disgruntled Southern Baptists. The moderates had done a marvelous job of alienating and separating the academically bright from the academically pedestrian, the cultured from the primitive, the politically correct from the politically incorrect. Doing so, they had created a vast wasteland of disenfranchised people across the South. Rejecting candidates for doctoral programs, for missionary appointment, for denominational bureaucracy jobs, for Convention appointments, and for basic self-esteem eventually takes a toll on any organization, as the number of disenfranchised grows with each passing year. The moderates had quite a legacy of "rejects" who were ready and willing to see the incumbents' reign end.

My educational and professional background cast me as one of the moderates, yet my heart ached for the conservatives whom I saw as more akin to my upbringing. At the same time most of my friends and close acquaintances within the SBC were moderates. I found relating on a personal level to many of the early conservatives to be difficult. Some seemed more interested in advancing opinions than in exploring options and ideas.

As a journalist whose curiosity led me to explore every possibility and as a "thinker" on psychological profiles, which left me more interested in the processes than the final decisions, I found the whole mess in the SBC quite disheartening, once it moved from academic discussion to a truly hardball political tussle and emotional wrestling match. Day by day people were becoming edgy, angry, unfriendly, and in many cases downright mean to each other—and, because I was the bearer of bad tidings, to me. I found none of that appealing.

As the fight continued and strengthened, my discomfort intensified. Had this been the Roman Catholic Church instead of my own denomination, I could have retreated back to the "convent" of the SBC for comfort, nurture, and refreshment. Instead, my own people were the ones who fought; year by year the opportunities to escape it seemed to evaporate.

No wonder that Baptist churches ultimately began seeing an increase in congregations that wanted to call themselves "First Family", "House of Hope" and other names that left *Baptist* out of their titles. Part of this stemmed from a genuine desire to reach out to those who normally ran from a traditional church label; others simply wanted to distance themselves from the brouhaha.

* * * * * * * *

In the thick of the battle, being able to attend worship as an average parishioner at South Main became impossible.

Any time I arrived at church and took a few introductory footfalls down the church hallway, fellow members seized me. Naturally, while Ken, the identified fall guy, was still pastor, feelings ran higher than the church steeple. Fellow members would pull and tug at me. *What did I think about it? What could be done about it? Why did I write about it? Why couldn't I put a stop to it?* But things didn't subside much after Bill Turner was in place. The subject was still in the headlines; stories with my name on them appeared under those headlines. So curiosity—sometimes morbid curiosity—followed.

Attending Sunday-morning Bible study was tortuous. Instead of focusing on our lesson, fellow class members wanted to involve themselves in the SBC debate—and wanted whatever my most recent column was to be their subject matter. With me in the room, diverting to that topic was irresistible.

The only time I was at peace was during the actual worship period. If I could time my late arrival at my seat with the start of the choral prelude, I was safe. Before and after the service I was being buttonholed and arm-wrenched—all on the same nauseating theme.

Finally I began cocooning at home on Sunday mornings and watching the televised service. Kay drove the kids to their Sunday-morning activities. At first she tried attending Sunday school and making excuses for me. Finally she dropped the kids off and sat in the car in the parking lot or meditated on her Bible in a nearby hotel coffee shop until time to retrieve the children to sit with her in "big church." My absence was always noted with "Where's Louis? I wanted to talk with him about the _____ (fill in the blank about my most recent SBC column topic)." Courteously but firmly she segued herself, Matthew, and Katie to the car and tried to avoid engaging.

The last straw occurred one Wednesday night in the church supper line as we rushed to get Matthew and Katie fed before their choir and missions activities. Though we were by then both avoiding most everything at church, we still tried to make the Wednesday supper time because, quite frankly, it was physical nourishment for our family of four—inexpensively and expeditiously.

A fellow church member spotted me and considered that since I was standing in line waiting for my tray, I was surely fair game. "Let me tell you what I think about these feuding Baptists . . .," he began. The three people who separated me from sidling up to the salad bar seemed to move inexorably slowly. I thought once I reached the cutlery and trays, I could shake the insensitive chatterbox, but he never stopped his stream of opinions, even when he was directing the server about whether he wanted potatoes or white rice with his beef tips.

I stuck it out through the serving line and then steered our family to a table where I recognized the usually calm heads that were seated there. I thought we were safe with some folks who typically respected our boundaries and left us alone when we were off-duty from the *Chronicle*.

But as soon as our trays touched the tablecloth, another set of opinions spewed forth again. One of the usually calm heads at the table *just had* to know . . ..

I ate, smiled, nodded, ate, nodded, smiled, nodded, and murmured as little as possible until my food was inhaled. Though my head might have been bobbing mechanically at whatever prattle was directed my way, I by that point was tuned in to only one thing—the two words that at some point, almost without my realizing it, had begun forming in my head and at that point were chasing themselves round and round and round in a silent mental conundrum.

My saturation point was reached, my patience was spent.

My tolerance for covering the SBC controversy had just, unalterably, dried up. I could take this assignment no longer.

When I finally put away my tray and broke loose from the stifling dining hall to the freeing, fresh air outside, I said those two words aloud.

"No more!"

And I meant them.

Chapter 17

For the Pharaoh
Who Knew Not Joseph

**Truth No. 17: God doesn't drop you from His plans
even when you drop Him from yours.**

When I said "No more!" to covering the Baptist controversy, these determined words were certainly not uttered without strategy aforethought.

Obviously I couldn't cope with my frustration by simply ignoring the SBC for a year or so as I had the Catholics during the my early tenure. I couldn't merely concentrate on other denominations until things settled down. *Settling down* wasn't going to happen with the Baptists any time in the near future.

I also would never be able to get away with simply dumping SBC coverage on another reporter. As long as I was in the job, readers (though they might criticize) would expect me to be the one interpreting and columnizing on these topics. I couldn't pass this chore off to someone else. My sources, the *Chronicle* management, the religion section's faithful readership—no one would let me off the hook for many days. As long as Baptist news was being made (and I saw no sign of it stopping any time soon), people would look to my byline to keep walking them through it.

As I mentioned earlier, by the time I had achieved the top office in Religion Newswriters Association in 1984, I had already begun to ask myself, "What now?" I understood my personality well enough to know that I would continue to look for new hills to climb—and I simply wasn't sure what they would be. Approaching my 40th birthday represented the first time in my life that I could not identify any specific big dreams that were still ahead for me. At a very early age, comparatively speaking, I had been phenomenally blessed to accomplish all my professional goals. Few people can ever make that statement so early in their lives. Some never can.

The extreme discomfort that covering the SBC was bringing on was only part of the problem. Kay and I had now been at the *Chronicle* for nearly a decade and a half. Quite frankly, I was becoming bored.

Early in his new administration, editor Jack Loftis made some initial forays about whether I would be interested in joining his *Chronicle* management team. He told me he had seen good leadership characteristics in my personality and style.

Shortly after that time, however, other reporters began reacting negatively to what they called the growing "Baylor mafia." They saw an unhealthy alliance emerging with too many Baylor grads in key *Chronicle* management slots all at the same time. One couldn't be in the *Chronicle* lunchroom or at the water fountain without picking up on the negative aspersions.

Given that environment, neither Kay nor I could foresee a future beyond our current jobs. When I tried to talk with Jack and his associates further about moving into management as he once mentioned, they now simply responded with effusive praise for my work as religion editor and gave me large pay raises and other inducements. They meant this to be affirming; these perks were, of course, welcome, and satisfied for a while, but they did not scratch the itch that existed deep down inside. I wanted to do something different. Management seemed the best alternative, but the answer I continued to receive was, "Oh, but you're just too good at what you do." In so many words, they communicated to me that I held a job I could have for the rest of my life and that I needed to be content with that. Job security was something no one thought I had any worry about—as long as I remained religion editor.

During December 1985 the *Chronicle* took out a huge billboard on a high-visibility spot on one of the major freeways in town. In promoting a series I had done on the topic of Christmas, they ran my photo, larger than life, with an advertisement that read, "Religion: Coverage and Insights from Louis Moore in Houston's Leading Information Source, the *Chronicle.*" It was but another crumb the *Chronicle* tossed to me in an effort to keep me happy. At almost 40-years old I was the toast of town—and I had wanderlust like crazy. I had the "quarterback syndrome"; Troy Aikman would have identified with me thoroughly. In a young person's profession, the best years of my career already were behind me, or so things seemed. What does an aging quarterback—or religion editor—do after the world has been his oyster?

Yet another thing bothered me even more. I feared I needed to prepare for the Pharaoh *who knew not Joseph* (Ex. 1:8). Because of legislation directly impacting the *Chronicle*, I knew that newspaper someday would have different ownership—new bosses from another newspaper chain who might want heads to roll. What kind of job security would I have when the *Chronicle* was run by someone who didn't have a frame of reference with Louis Moore—a *pharaoh* who didn't know my history on the beat, how I had entered this job under the most dreadful of circumstances, how I had painstakingly courted sources and developed the religion section into one that was nationally acclaimed and mightily respected in the community? Would I be swept aside in the kind of newspaper-wide housecleaning that often accompanies a takeover? What if that occurred, maybe not now but as I approached my 50s, when I would be less employable and considered "over the hill" and "shipwrecked"? What if I didn't plan ahead by having some escape hatch? Would I live to regret it?

At first I tried to channel my malaise into a frenzied focus on hobbies—my farm, my freelance writing, a boomlet spurt of camping, a seat on the board of the *Houston Chronicle* Credit Union—to try to carry me over the hump. Kay and I even ill-advisedly bought a new house—our dream house, as a matter of fact—our actual favorite of all the dwellings we've lived in before or since. We thought that pouring ourselves into fixing it up might be a new trapeze on which to swing. It bandaged things for a short time.

But Kay was starting to realize she, as a feature writer, was in essentially the same boat as I was careerwise. She admittedly had the best job anyone could wish for, with an adoring public that was on par with mine, yet she could see no room for advancement. The "Baylor-mafia" paranoia that had developed because of the *Chronicle* management team was limiting her, too. We wondered whether, after 14 years, the time had arrived to move on.

We could hardly imagine living anywhere but Houston. Our children were comfortable with their schools and friends. I toyed only briefly with moving to another newspaper as religion editor. I knew that would not distance me from the fistfight under way in the SBC.

The solution I hit on was to purchase a small-town newspaper somewhere in the Texas Hill Country, preferably near our farm at Round Top. Several years earlier I had been enthralled by the TV sitcom *Apple's Way*, about a man who had done just that sort of thing. Between 1982 and 1986 I became an expert on every small-town or county newspaper in Texas that was for sale. I began focusing in on the *La Grange Journal*, about 15 miles from our farm.

In my fantasies I could envision escaping from big-city traffic, big-newspaper politics, and the developing inferno of SBC infighting. My family and I would live in paradise—in an idyllic, stress-free, semi-rural but exciting, independent lifestyle, I thought.

In the midst of my research about buying, financing, and operating a small-town newspaper, I learned about the sale of a group of nine suburban newspapers in the Dallas area to the Harte-Hanks newspaper chain. I traveled to Bryan-College Station, TX, to talk with a fellow Baylor graduate—John Williams—who had been instrumental in the Harte-Hanks purchase and had just been named as publisher of those newspapers. John, a contemporary of ours at Baylor, had until recently published the Bryan-College Station *Eagle*. I wanted to seek John's counsel about whether he thought buying a paper such as the *La Grange Journal* was a good idea.

During our conversation, the discussion at some point turned from the merits of my buying the *La Grange Journal* to the lure of my becoming editor of the *Plano Star Courier*, a daily small-town newspaper and the largest of the nine papers in the recent Harte-Hanks acquisition. I can still hear John proposing to me, "Instead of losing $100,000 when you buy the *La Grange Journal*, wouldn't you rather make that kind of money editing the Plano paper for Harte-Hanks?"

Ultimately John made us an offer we couldn't refuse. To sweeten the deal, he offered to hire Kay for another lucrative sum. He would make her city editor of the Plano newspaper; she would manage the staff of reporters. Harte-Hanks would buy our house in Houston so we could immediately purchase a new home in Plano and wouldn't have to wait behind to sell it.

Furthermore, the move would put us in suburban Dallas near Kay's parents, who were now retired and would be over the moon with joy in having their grandchildren only 30 minutes away. This would be the closest to Garland and her extended family that Kay would ever have lived during our married life. She was awash with excitement about the prospect of hosting big family Christmas dinners in our own home.

We were intrigued with the idea of re-making a publication—literally starting from scratch—and helping the lackluster Plano paper reflect the dynamic, prosperous North Dallas suburb the city was becoming. Doing this would scratch the management itch that both of us thought we were feeling. And we'd be able to tackle it together—combining all our professional skills into a true partnership, instead of heading separate directions on two different newspaper beats as we had for years now. We'd be able to capitalize on the best of all our training—from McHam's guidance during Baylor days to all we'd learned from working under Don Pickels and later Tony Pederson, who became managing editor on Don's retirement, and Tony's assistant, Tommy Miller.

Though we knew about it from news reports and also from my being on the board and credit committee of the *Houston Chronicle* Credit Union, we failed to pay careful attention to the extent of the economic storm clouds gathering over Houston. The price of oil during the early 1980s had shot skyward (much like today), then plummeted severely. This set off a serious economic collapse in the city and region. The savings-and-loan debacle was only beginning to unfurl; most people thought the economic upheaval would be confined to the Houston area. They thought it would reach only into certain Texas oilfields and avoid the Dallas area altogether.

Harte-Hanks' offer to buy our house immediately at full price seemed like the right antidote to the local situation. The gloom and doom we saw on the people's faces in Houston was vastly different from the cheery smiles and positive outlooks that still prevailed in Dallas. Nobody seemed to have a crystal ball telling them the future.

We mapped out our strategies for departure—how we'd wind things up in Houston at the close of the kids' school years and transfer during the summer, so they could start new schools in the fall. We mapped out how we'd say goodbye to our news sources and contacts that we'd developed throughout 14 years. I could see that in Kay's mind, she was already decorating the rooms in our new Plano home, with its fabulous swimming pool and stunning backyard.

Only one base had we not covered: praying about the decision. Unlike any other time in our careers, then or now, we never stopped to ask God whether He thought we were doing the right thing. We were certain we knew. The Bible admonition, *Commit to the Lord whatever you do, and your plans will succeed* (Pr. 16:3), wasn't even a flicker in our thought processes. We were like the Old Testament character Joshua and the men of Israel (Josh. 9:14) who *did not inquire of the Lord* on a crucial decision involving the Gibeonites and made an ill-advised treaty.

Even if we had heard God say a reverberating "No!" it probably wouldn't have stopped us.

* * * * * * * *

Neither Kay nor I could have predicted the responses we would receive when we began to break the news that our time in Houston was ending.

Our bosses gave us their good wishes but did so through tight-lipped smiles. Looking back, we now realize they thought we were absolutely wacko to leave behind all we'd worked to achieve—how someone at the top of his game like I was could turn his back on such success. I'm sure we seemed utterly profligate in our decisions, but no one wanted to thwart our blind euphoria and beg us to stay. One said he hoped the Houston's economic downturn wouldn't follow us there but that no one could be sure. In our fantasy world, we dismissed any naysaying. In a few years all would look up and see that we'd really put the Plano paper on the map, we felt certain.

The news sources we'd spent years developing, however, were a different matter. Genuine sorrow and pleas to reconsider poured forth from corners of the community we never expected. My Jewish readership, the United Methodists, the Churches of Christ, the Catholics—yes, the Catholics who rued my arrival in 1972—tried to outdo themselves to see who could throw the biggest and most mournful goodbye parties. The farewells went on for days; they were sincere and filled with profound gratitude. The people who were devoted to Kay and her special brand of warmhearted feature stories were equally traumatized. We had no idea that our writings had touched so many lives. The collection of parting letters, which still sits on our shelf, remains a jaw-dropping keepsake testimony of ways in which Houstonians reflected the contributions we'd made through the written word.

Our eyes misted at their thoughtful outpourings, but nothing could rob us of our ebullience about the opportunities in North Texas that we thought lay in wait for us. While we knew we would forever treasure past associations in the Bayou City, we were astir with the optimistic (and blessedly, Baptist-less) future we believed was ahead. In my goodbye column, entitled "Goodbye, God Bless, and Keep Reading About Religion," I asserted that I would happily take squabbling Plano city fathers any day over a bunch of feuding Southern Baptist pastors.

"After all, none of the members of Plano's city council were ever my teachers, my pastors, my friends and my peers

in college and seminary," I wrote. I believed I was washing
my hands of the whole repugnant deal.

* * * * * * *

So with a U-Haul trailing behind us and most of our
belongings already on a large moving van headed north, we
pulled out of our beloved Memorial-area cul-de-sac and away
from our dream home we'd occupied only 15 months. In our
rearview mirror we spotted our neighbors clustering at their
curbs, tearfully waving and wishing us well.

As we headed up Interstate 45, we passed skyscrapers,
shopping centers, and suburbs in which at least one of us had
visited to report some news event. We breezed by spires representing vast scores of church announcements I'd written during the past 14 years. We drove away from the city of our
early marriage—the city where our children had been born—
the city where we had known deep friendships, memorable
church experiences, and jobs that had given us more rewards
than most people get to have in 10 careers.

The incredible thing is—we did so with spirits high.

* * * * * * *

God hadn't given up on us for not consulting Him about
the North Dallas move, although years would pass before we
would fully grasp His heavenly perspective on the whole matter. Our moving crates had hardly touched the floor in our new
Plano home before we began to realize that we had just made
a giant wallapalooza of a mistake.

Chapter 18

Learning Curve

Truth No. 18: Don't expect church people to look out for their own.

The *Plano Star Courier* was in desperate need of a makeover. It got one.

John Williams, with his pronounced champagne tastes, wanted things to be first-class down to the last jot and tittle. In us, he already had hired first-class editors to kick off the transformation, he reasoned. The image-boosting he envisioned needed trendier offices, so he sold the dank, bedraggled newspaper building in the downtown area and moved into swanky new leased quarters on Plano Parkway.

John wanted the look and quality of the paper overhauled. We crafted a new, sleek four-color design but also began hiring new staff and filling vacancies with inexperienced but promising J-school graduates to improve the kind of reporting that was done. Quickly the paper experienced a dramatic turnaround in looks and depth of reporting.

John also hired veteran advertising execs, brought in an experienced circulation manager, and even secured a new press and crew to operate it.

Money flowed freely. Under the old owners the paper had produced a profit of more than $2 million annually. For a small daily newspaper in a suburban setting Harte-Hanks thought it had found another of its famed "cash cows."

We imported our former news editor, Dan Cobb, by then

retired from the *Chronicle,* to train reporters and copy editors on hard-hitting news-production techniques.

We even twisted the arm of David McHam, by then a journalism professor at nearby Southern Methodist University, to help us toughen up these youngsters to become the best of the best, just as he had drilled excellence into us in *The Lariat's* heyday.

Soon *The Dallas Morning News* took notice and instituted its own suburban competition—the Plano section of *The Dallas Morning News.* The Plano section attempted to siphon away our advertising revenue. We constantly scooped the Plano section on story after story, including the blockbuster news that J.C. Penney was moving its corporate headquarters from New York to Plano.

We brought retired *Chronicle* graphic artist Bob Chen up from Houston to join the staff to create an upscale, streamlined design that gave it a "take-us-seriously" look.

Instead of having to cover religion for a daily newspaper, I now could step aside and supervise our own reporters in religion coverage of the community. It was a break I convinced myself I was ready for.

Soon the Dallas Press Club named the *Plano Star-Courier* as one of the three best daily suburban newspapers in the Dallas-Fort Worth Metroplex. Our coverage of the J.C. Penney relocation also took top honors in the nationwide Harte-Hanks Writing and Photography Contest.

Our efforts were reaping rewards.

* * * * * * *

Though Plano in those days was fueled by new money and lacked the genteel sophistication of Houston, life in the suburbs had a certain appeal. We joined First Baptist Church of Plano; our daughter, Katie, made her profession of faith there and was baptized by Dr. Michael Riley, the pastor. For once family members were close enough to attend events and activities for our children.

Living close to Kay's parents was especially poignant, because it represented the last few clear-minded years for Kay's dad before he succumbed to the fog of Alzheimer's. We'll always thank God for providing this narrow window of time for J.D. to exult over a precious granddaughter in a ballet recital or the companionship of a growing grandson to watch ball games with him.

* * * * * * * *

Although I told myself the break from the Baptists was restoring me to sanity, I never strayed very far from the periphery of SBC news.

One day our last Houston Sunday-school teacher, attorney Howard Lee Sr., called to ask whether he could bring a friend to Plano to dine with me. He didn't mention the mystery guest's identity but said the two of them and Lee's wife, Sarah, would fly there in a private plane. Since I looked forward to seeing Howard and Sarah again, I agreed to meet them the next week at a Chinese restaurant on Central Expressway in Plano.

When time for the lunch arrived, I was introduced to John Baugh, founder of the SYSCO Corp. restaurant-supply business and an arch-foe of Paul Pressler. I had never met the man, but I knew him by reputation.

I had heard the peculiar story of John Baugh and Paul Pressler's alleged clash while they were Sunday-school teachers at Second Baptist Church of Houston—years before most people in the SBC had ever heard of either man. This occurred in the era before Ed Young Sr. became pastor of Second Baptist, Houston, and totally transformed the congregation into one of the emerging megachurches. At that time Second Baptist was a small enclave for mostly wealthy Houstonians living in the affluent Memorial area of town. The Baughs and the Presslers certainly fit the stereotype of wealthy success stories populating the church.

At the luncheon, John laid out for me his concerns about the Conservative Resurgence in the SBC and his determination to do something about it. He told me that he and Dallas lawyer Dewey Pressley, a former chair of the Baylor trustees, were organizing a counter-resurgence to reclaim moderate control. He said they needed a younger, media-savvy person—me—to join them in a triumvirate. I was flattered but very reluctant.

After listening to John Baugh for nearly an hour, I said to him, "I want to ask you one question. The answer is very important to me, so I want you to think carefully before you answer. I also hope you will not get angry, because I must know in order to give you an honest answer."

Now that I had his attention, I said, "John, people say the conflict between you and Paul Pressler has nothing to do with moderate or conservative theology nor anything to do with the fundamentalist takeover of the SBC. Instead, many people I know say it is all about some issues between the two of you that dates back to the days when the two of you were teaching Sunday-school at Second Baptist and mushroomed into a major personal conflict. If that is the case, then certainly you would understand why I would be reluctant to get involved in an old dispute between the two of you. On the other hand, if that is not the case and you can give me your personal assurance that this is strictly a theological and political conflict, then I will consider seriously what you have offered."

Before I could complete my last sentence, I had my answer. John Baugh's face fired red with anger. His voice strengthened. His body language communicated he was furious at what I had said. Though he denied his roots with Pressler had any influence over his current moderate cause, Baugh's words said one thing; his body language and tone conveyed another. I was not convinced.

Still, I promised John that I would pray over the matter and talk it over with Kay. Ever the precise businessman, he pinpointed a time that I would give him my final answer. The next week when he called me at home in the evening and I declined his gracious invitation to join him and Dewey Pressley in their campaign, the frost in his voice again reassured me that I had made the right decision.

I was grateful that my friendship with Howard and Sarah Lee was secure and not affected by my encounter with John Baugh.

* * * * * * * *

I was amazed at some others in the Houston religious community who wanted to keep up with us though we were history there. One such group—amazingly—was the Church of Jesus Christ of Latter-day Saints (Mormons). When their Salt Lake City headquarters decided to create a special video for local churches on "How to Work with the Media," its public-relations office asked whether it could film a segment interviewing me in my new office in Plano. Though I clearly found Mormons' theology offbeat and troublesome, I also found their individual wholesomeness and family orientation a welcome relief from some attitudes and behaviors I saw around me in the world and in the church.

In 1984, when I was RNA president, the Mormons had invited me to Salt Lake City to speak to their top church brass about the Mormon public persona. They had been extremely candid and gracious with me then, including a private dinner at the home of Gordon B. Hinckley, then the youngest and most vigorous of the Mormon leaders. As I finished writing this book, Hinckley had just died at age 97. He lived to become the oldest Mormon president ever.

My Salt Lake experience had brought me a singular distinction. Few if any other Southern Baptists have ever addressed the top Mormon church leadership.

* * * * * * * *

Our success in Plano had one major drawback. Kay and I soon found ourselves working more than 70 hours a week making and overseeing the changes and leading the newspaper. We thought this intrusion into our lives was temporary; "Tomorrow"—the day everything would be in place and we could cut back to 40-hour work weeks like we had at the *Chronicle*—was always just around the corner. *Tomorrow* never occurred.

John kept raising the bar and expectations higher and higher. The psychologist John kept on retainer to help manage the transition maintained that John was a "bottom-line manager." At first I thought that meant he liked to see results. Then I began to realize *results* meant only one thing: *dough-re-mi.* The plan was not to create a quality newspaper and let it continue to bring in $2 million in profits each year. The plan was to create a quality newspaper and increase the profit margin higher and higher.

That was a great dream and vision except for one major flaw: During that time the Texas economy tumbled into its worst recession since the Great Depression. Oil prices fell dramatically. Bankruptcies skyrocketed. Unemployment rates doubled to more than 11 percent, meaning more than one in 10 Texans was out of work. The savings-and-loan scandal forced savings-and-loans and banks to collapse and sent a record number of public officials and bankers to jail. Housing foreclosures rose to unprecedented peaks. The price of housing fell dramatically, bringing down real-estate tax appraisals and lowering tax monies available to cities, counties, and the state. All in all, it was a horrible mess. Surely the Great Depression in the 1930s could have been no worse. Some say the 1980s debacle was actually worse for Texas than the Great Depression had been. (For more on this tragic era in Texas history, read M. Ray Perryman's *Survive and Conquer: Texas in the '80s: Money—Power—Tragedy—Hope!*)

By the time that era ended, dozens of newspapers across the state and region closed their doors or were bought out by their competitors and then shut down. This included such large papers as the *Dallas Times Herald, Houston Post,* and *San Antonio Light* but also a large number of smaller ones. Even the financially stable *Houston Chronicle* posted a hiring freeze and eventually laid off employees—something longtime, legendary owner Jesse Jones refused to do during the Great Depression. During that '80s era the owners of the *La Grange Journal*—the paper we had contemplated owning before we were hired in Plano—shut down there, too.

The *Plano Star Courier* went from being a "cash cow" to a financial deficit for Harte-Hanks. Frantically John began dismissing staff, including his prized "directors" whom he had recruited from other papers at great cost.

I was one of the victims. Everything happened with such lightning speed. In October 1987 the Harte-Hanks board had awarded me a major stock option for meritorious service. John Williams wrote me a glowing note about my value to the *Plano Star Courier*. By February 1988 Kay and I were both gone from the paper.

Delivering the cup of hemlock to us was our Baylor contemporary and fellow Southern Baptist, publisher John Williams. For the next six months, departing directors and other staff called weekly to tell us of the continued upheaval that was occurring at the newspaper.

As the months rolled by, we called friends and professional contacts everywhere to seek help in finding employment. Most seemed to turn a deaf ear or dismiss us with some sort of religious platitude. Our Baylor contacts most disappointed us. At a journalism alumni meeting in the *Star Courier*'s wake, one arrogant and heartless Baptist alum had the nerve to introduce Kay as a freelancer, then turn to the audience and say, "That means she can't get a job." Today that same alum loves to tout his moderate Baptist affiliations; his wife once was a Cooperative Baptist Fellowship moderator.

Another friend who was in a major position to help visited us in Plano and promised he would try to help, but we never heard another word from him again until years later.

Attending our local Baptist church on Sundays was agonizing. Our "parting of the ways," as a front-page *Plano Star Courier* article called it, was widely known in the community. The responses of most fellow churchgoers merely took the form of boorish, curious stares. As a converse to truth #6, the church may perform splendidly when people die or sicken, but its response in times of emotional travail is abysmal.

Through it all, we learned a sad but valuable lesson: When the chips are down, don't expect your fellow church people to care for their own. To us they represented anything but the biblical *friend who sticks closer than a brother* (Prov. 18:24).

* * * * * * *

Since Baptist brethren clearly let us down, who did serve as the body of Christ to us in this dark night of our souls?

The hands and feet of the Savior arrived in the form of Bill and Peggy Oades, our Roman Catholic neighbors who appeared at our door the morning after our "parting of the ways." They bore steaming mugs of coffee and fresh-baked muffins. Compassion poured from their faces like light.

In absolutely no rush on this weekday work day, this couple, whose ample houseful of kids spoke to their Catholic literalness, sat at our kitchen table and prayed with us as we poured out our hearts to them in our despair. They imparted comforting Scripture and assured us that Jesus who died for us was holding us in his protecting arms. This from Catholics!

It arrived in the form of Mary Anne Seale, a Presbyterian, and Nancy McClune, a United Methodist, who unfailingly called Kay to check on her well-being. They then invited her to join them in the Junior League of Plano to demonstrate that the community in which she had invested a portion of her professional life still cared about us.

It arrived in the form of our former *Chronicle* managing editor Tony Pederson, a United Methodist layman, who visited us in Plano to convey concern and relay to us the *Chronicle*'s genuine collective horror at our Plano misadventure. Tony, a personal friend and peer long before he had become our boss, explained that he regretfully could not re-employ us because he had only months earlier hired my replacement and now faced a hiring freeze. Though thoughts of returning to the familiar bosom of Houston at that moment seemed like paradise on earth, we knew that was not to be. Twenty months beforehand, accepting the full consequences of our actions, we had consciously set aside that life. We were touched that anyone there even cared. It was way more than we experienced out of some others.

* * * * * * * *

Totally knocked to our knees during this Texas carnage, we had never depended on God so desperately. In less than two years we had gone from the top of the mountain financially, spiritually, professionally, and in just about every other way down into the abyss of financial and career uncertainty. Miraculously our faith, health, marriage and family held together. In early 1986 we had substantial assets, including sizable equity in both our home and farm and significant savings. By mid-1988, the equity was gone; we owed more on our home and farm than they were worth (that is, if you could find a buyer in that day and time). During most of 1988 we used our savings to pay for food and to make the mortgage payments.

God immediately prompted Kay and me to become infinitely creative in putting together a patchwork of freelance assignments to keep some income streams flowing.We turned the gameroom in our home into an office for both of us.

Even though they faced hiring freezes and staff layoffs, the *San Antonio Light* and *The Dallas Morning News* hired me on a contract freelance basis. *The Dallas Morning News* and *Fort Worth Star-Telegram* did the same with Kay. (Ironically, the *San Antonio Light* hired me specifically to cover the 1988 Southern Baptist Convention in San Antonio. Suddenly reporting on the Baptists again—*it's just for a few days*, I told myself—didn't look so stultifying.)

I also arranged freelance writing contracts with the Roman Catholic newspaper, *Our Sunday Visitor*, and the Evangelical magazine, *Moody Monthly*, as well as with other publications. Word Books, which had published our first three books, immediately offered freelance editing contracts for several projects. Our pastor, Michael Riley, created a temporary, one-day-a week job for me producing the church's weekly newsletter. To augment all this, I also worked two days a week as an adjunct professor of journalism and student-newspaper adviser at Collin County Community College.

A true silver lining was being home with the children, who had suffered plentifully with our 70-hour workweeks at the *Plano Star Courier*. Strangely, the four of us today would probably vote unanimously that this odd period of our lives (though the poorest) was hands-down the best family time we ever experienced. At night we read aloud, played board games, went on picnics, and rediscovered the sheer enjoyment of being together. God had certainly gotten our attention about putting family priorities back in place.

Kay kept the sewing machine spinning to make clothes for the kids. She practically memorized a Mormon cookbook, *A Family Raised on Sunshine,* and its from-scratch recipes for inexpensive meals and other great ideas for home maintenance on a painfully limited budget. I cancelled the pool service, the yard service, the maid service, and other trappings of our North Dallas lifestyle and started doing everything myself. I even turned off the sprinkler system to save water and electricity and planted a garden in our backyard. (Working outdoors also provided a weird form of entertainment. I had a physical ringside seat as one by one, every house surrounding ours in our West Plano neighborhood went into foreclosure. I vowed that ours would never be one of them. It didn't!)

For all the freelancing success, however, we knew that ultimately we needed full-time employment again.

That opportunity arose in an odd place—my home state of Oklahoma. Though he faced a hiring freeze, Bob Mong, deputy managing editor of *The Dallas Morning News* (now the paper's top editor), asked me to be chief of the newspaper's Oklahoma Bureau. This would have meant general news coverage—prison breakouts, murders, the legislature, the like. As much as I was eager for regular sustenance, I was reluctant to go in this direction.

By this point, I was convinced that I needed not to depart again from my original calling to Christian journalism. (I wasn't fond of lightning bolts; I didn't want to invite one.) Bob tried to convince me that the Oklahoma job could be a holding station for me until Helen Parmley retired as religion editor. That date had not been set. Helen might continue on for years. I couldn't get a sense of peace that the move to Oklahoma was right. I wasn't about to stray again from God's original direction. Clearly I had forgotten it when I moved to Plano.

We settled in for a long, dry spell. Christmas was approaching; it would be lean. When our dear friends, Reg and Caroline Hancock, drove from Houston to Plano one December weekend just to indulge our children with a lavish Christmas-shopping adventure (and a meal at McDonald's, where they hadn't been for months), we cried with thankfulness.

* * * * * *

In November 1988 I wrote Dr. Richard Land, who had just been elected leader of the SBC's Christian Life Commission, and offered my services as a freelance writer/editor. I knew Richard had a need; I knew I had skills to offer. Richard was the first duly-elected conservative to head one of the SBC agencies in Nashville. Reading between the lines, I could tell he hadn't received a warm welcome. From the time his predecessor had resigned abruptly, moderate staff members had fled and took with them important files and other information necessary to run the agency. His media office was particularly hard-hit by the departures and "scorched-earth" turmoil. Within a few weeks Richard and I signed a freelance contract that required my presence in the Baptist headquarters in Nashville several days each month. I added the CLC to my juggling act of assignments. I knew I was walking right back toward the dreaded *B-word*—the subject that I had moved heaven and earth to avoid. But, I reasoned, the assignment was for only a few days a month; I had many other freelance tasks on my plate to provide diversion.

Kay and I continued to piece together our upended livelihood. Day after day God miraculously supplied.

He really shouldn't have, since we totally ignored Him in our decision to move to Plano in the first place. *Serves you right* is the only response we should have heard out of Him for spurning His will so treacherously. Instead His infinite mercy carried us along and met every need (a few pure "wants" sometimes, too!). He didn't see *the righteous forsaken or their children begging bread* (Ps. 37:25).

We felt confident He ultimately would provide a full-time job also. We just didn't know where or when.

Probably best that we didn't. If we had realized that our dry spell would last for 18 long, torture-chamber months—and if we had realized where He ultimately would take us—we probably would have been scared to death.

Chapter 19

Leaving the Lights Off

Truth No. 19: For something that's supposed to be a *city set on a hill**, **the church operates in darkness a large percentage of the time.**

(*Matthew 5:14)

What began as a part-time, few-days-a-month contract project was becoming all-consuming. By the spring of 1989, my freelance work for the Christian Life Commission— Southern Baptists' public policy entity—was requiring more and more of my efforts. I no longer had the luxury of time to develop new clients for the rest of my freelance business. The moderates who fled the CLC's media office had left things in a disaster. Increasingly Richard Land looked to me to help him get the place functioning again.

Soon I was in Nashville every other week. I could see the outline of where this arrangement was headed. Richard wanted me to move to Nashville by June 1 and become an official part of Southern Baptist Convention life again. My job title would be Director of Media and Products for the CLC. I would be dealing with topics such as race relations, the environment, and pro-life issues—all things that interested me.

Kay and I prayed earnestly for a way around having to make this drastic decision to relocate our family to another state. With Kay's father now officially diagnosed with Alzheimer's, her mother was attempting to care for him at their home. Instead of being 30 minutes away from this increasingly stressful situation in Kay's family, we would be moving 12-hours away from Garland. Naturally we had urgently hoped that things would work out for us in Texas.

But when we took our family to Nashville for a look-see visit, we were surprised at how much we liked Music City and the charming, historic community of Franklin, where many SBC employees lived. The school system was superior yet far less pressurized than Plano's sometimes manic, obsessive educational structure. Other than the uncomfortable distance from Texas, we could find few drawbacks to starting a new life in this family-friendly place.

No dummies this time, we prayed fervently that God would make His will directly known to us as to whether we should take this life-altering step.

One of the main answers that propelled us to say *yes* to joining the conservatives emanated, interestingly enough, from a most unexpected source: through God's human instrument— a moderate supporter.

As we shared our concerns with Kay's mother's pastor, Roger McDonald, who later majorly affiliated with the moderate Cooperative Baptist Fellowship, his wife, Dorothy, spoke some highly reassuring and insightful words. She reminded Kay that if God willed for us to move to Nashville, He would certainly provide the right resources back home to sustain her mother through the difficulties of caregiving.

After that well-placed, God-anointed reminder from this long-time family friend, we both began feeling the freedom to take this high-stakes step. Even as we deliberated, various support systems for Kay's mother began to arise. We believed that God definitely was propelling us toward this assignment in the Southern Baptist nerve center.

Our personal finances still were not stabilized after 18 months of erratic income, so we planned that Kay would find employment there soon as well. In time we believed that we would be back on solid economic footing again.

I would be finding myself at a very curious moment in history—at the vanguard of the first wave of new employees, as the SBC conservative takeover by now had been in effect long enough that it was threading its way down through the individual agencies of the massive SBC bureaucracy. I literally would be in place to witness the changing of a deeply entrenched old guard. The CLC had been the first to fall into conservative hands, but throughout the next decade, office by office and even desk by desk would begin to be intricately affected by the switchout.

Amazingly enough, in trying to decide about the Nashville move, I never thought of myself as "going to work for the conservatives," as many would brand me later. As I mentioned in my chapter on leaving the *Chronicle*, I still didn't consider that I had a "side" in the controversy. As a journalist I tried to be a *witness to the truth* and tell the SBC story from a balanced perspective. I had friends, connections, and news sources in both camps. My independent streak would never let me sell out thoroughly to a cause.

When the chips were down in our professional lives, bottom line was—the conservatives delivered the goods, while the moderates ran and hid. At the time of the *Plano Star Courier* debacle I recalled a conversation with Judge Pressler. When I confessed to Pressler about my life transition, he merely disclosed, "I'll be interested in seeing how God works this out for you."

That's when Richard Land's professional need surfaced. I believed God's way of working things out was for me to present myself to Richard as a professional with a certain skill set that could get him—and me—through a rough patch. And I <u>did</u> know Southern Baptists.

* * * * * * * *

Though I had known my new boss briefly through news stories, I learned more about him when I assigned a *Star Courier* reporter to write about a Southern Baptist pastor who was then on the staff of Texas Gov. Bill Clements and was dealing with moral and religious-liberty concerns. The pastor, Richard Land, who was just a year younger than I, also had been vice president of Criswell College. I was fascinated with his undergraduate degree from Princeton and his doctorate from Oxford. Like Pressler, he represented a rare strand of hypereducated clergy among the conservative movement. His wife, Becky, hardly fit the conservative-wife stereotype either. She had her doctorate and her own life as a marriage-and-family therapist.

Before we made the move, a student at Criswell College who was enrolled in one of my media classes at Collin County Community College asked to talk with me privately about my decision to move to Nashville. In our conference the young man said he was familiar with Richard Land and wanted to know how well I knew him. He asked specifically whether I knew how "self-centered and egotistical" Richard was. He said he knew Richard from his work at Criswell College. He said Richard's self-absorption and imposing his will on others was legendary at the college. The young man, who identified himself as a friend of the Conservative Resurgence, said he had observed that I was an independent thinker and personality. He said he wondered whether I realized what I was getting myself into. I assured him that I was accustomed to being around strong-willed, self-assured religious figures. I told him about my *Houston Chronicle* column titled "Ego pos-I-tively" about the self-centered nature (often necessary for what they do) I had observed in many highly successful Christian leaders.

That conversation aided me in many ways. It alerted me to Richard's tendencies—I had suspected some of this but not to the degree that the student described. By making the covert overt, the student's words also helped me to quickly look beyond Richard's advancement of himself and find a healthy way to cope with this very strong personality.

I basically look back on Richard Land as an excellent boss and a good friend. Once I accepted that Richard was a high-profile supervisor who had an incredible desire to be in the limelight, then working with him was fine. He really had no other hidden agendas. Unlike some people who run from controversy, Richard ran toward it. To his credit, he was not shy about taking strong stands that would make him the lightning-rod in tense situations. He knew that the powerful stances he would take on public policy and ethical and moral issues would attract attention. I understood that part of my job was to help draw that attention to him so Richard would have the platform he needed to speak his (and what he believed was the collective Southern Baptist) mind. As the person in charge of media for the office, I needed to look for ways for Richard to do what he does best. Those were easy rules to figure out and follow.

Another factor of life about Richard was his undying devotion to the Republican Party. He never tried to hide the fact that he was, had been, and always would be a Republican. Equally obvious was his determination to shift the SBC into that political camp.

While I personally believe Jesus Christ was neither a Republican nor a Democrat and expects His followers to independently follow His leadership on an issue-by-issue basis, not a party basis, I never was overly bothered by Richard's flamboyant "I'm-a-Republican" demeanor, his suspenders bearing that message, or his many mementoes that cried out "GOP." I saw it more as his "What-you-see-is-what-you-get" approach to life. I certainly preferred his honesty to that of those in the moderate camp who cozied up to the Southern Wing of the Democratic Party, including President Jimmy Carter (and later Vice President Al Gore) and then denied they were doing so.

I also never found Richard to be quite as conservative as his reputation. Becky Land—Dr. Rebekah Land—became a highly regarded sex therapist in Nashville and a person in her own right—as well as a devoted mother to the couple's three children. While he opposed women as senior pastors, Richard on numerous occasions told me he could envision a woman as a seminary president or head of a Southern Baptist Convention agency. He told me that he believed the Bible does not forbid women from being ordained as deacons but said he opposed it because ordaining women as deacons was too difficult for rank-and-file Southern Baptist pastors to face.

However, I often wished someone had warned me—as the young man had about Richard Land's high level of self-confidence—about the overflowing hatred among the moderate Southern Baptist bureaucracy toward the Conservative Resurgence. Perhaps some people tried. But when they did, their anger got in the way of a clear, coherent, concise explanation like the one my student friend had used.

As we were on our way out of town, our pastor, Michael Riley at First Baptist, Plano, who had helped bolster our income during our family's financial crisis, unleashed verbal fireworks at me that I would even think of such an alliance. Our Baylor professor and mentor, Dr. Glenn Hilburn, who had performed our wedding ceremony at First Baptist Church of Garland, was another who expressed profound puzzlement about our taking this step.

Had we known the full story of what we were about to encounter, we absolutely would never have budged from Plano. We also would have missed being eyewitnesses to one of the most significant shifts in American Christianity in the late 20th century.

* * * * * * * *

We arrived in Nashville just as the first wave of the Conservative Resurgence was making its impact on the Southern Baptist bureaucracy there. After a decade of ferocious fighting, the conservative leadership was ready to lay siege to the capital of Southern Baptist life—Nashville. We found the city's Baptist bureaucracy to be in an open state of rebellion. Because I was one of the first new-wave employees on the scene there, I was quickly targeted.

To understand this situation, one needs to understand the size and strength of that SBC bureaucracy. If the Southern Baptist Convention was a regular secular business, it would probably rate as a Fortune 500 company because of the number of people it employs and the money it brings in. Because it is a church, people often miss the economic, political, and social dimensions of the church's culture.

In addition, Southern Baptists had for decades prided themselves as being non-Catholic. This translated itself into almost a phobia of all things Roman Catholic. Catholics were presented in Southern Baptist stereotypes as being hierarchical, bureaucratic, and controlling. In light of Roman Catholics, Southern Baptists saw themselves as democratic, loosely organized, and freedom-loving. As Dan Cobb at the *Houston Chronicle* often said, "It's dangerous when leaders, both religious and secular, start believing their own press releases." Southern Baptists, indeed, for the most part, believed their press releases—that they were truly democratic, truly loosely affiliated, and truly free people. As with all stereotypes, some truth existed to these self-images. In reality many of their self-images were far, far from the truth.

These myths, however, camouflaged the reality that the Southern Baptist bureaucracy then as well as today can stand toe-to-toe with the Roman Catholic bureaucracy in the United States in size, scope, and power. In fact, a solid argument could be put forward that Roman Catholics are less bureaucratic in many ways than Southern Baptists. Nashville was the prime example.

With more than 2,000 people employed by the assorted SBC agencies in Nashville in 1989, the SBC bureaucracy was self-evident. Counting spouses, children, parents, etc., the Nashville SBC bureaucracy was more realistically 7,500 to 10,000 strong. A tight, cohesive, inner-focused community with its own set of rules, pecking orders, and social customs, Nashville's Convention bureaucracy was truly a "world unto itself." Certainly it was far, far different from life as we had known it in Houston. Our watchword in Houston was *variety*. We knew and interacted with many people of different races, creeds, religious views, and lifestyles on a daily basis.

From a secular journalism background where my days revolved around people representing a potpourri of religious and cultural backgrounds, I was stunned at the lily-white uniformity and monofocused single-culture nature of Nashville's SBC bureaucracy. Little contact existed between the SBC and the city's secular or religious leadership. I was accustomed to having lunch or dinner with Roman Catholic, United Methodist, Episcopal, Mormon, and Jewish leaders either in restaurants or in my or their homes. I was accustomed to having friends of various cultural and ethnic backgrounds. I wasn't accustomed to such provincialism and isolation.

Within weeks of arriving to live in Nashville, I realized with sadness that I would have to acclimate myself to a truly narrowed lifestyle and focus within an SBC community that was more like a small, inward-looking town than a "city set on a hill" to be a light to the rest of the world.

This narrow culture characterized both the moderates, who dominated when we first arrived in Nashville, as well as the conservatives who dominated during our last years in the city. The moderates lambasted the conservatives for being too narrow and closed, yet they seemed to miss the point that their words were often like the proverbial "kettle calling the skillet black." Neither group was particularly open and integrated into the wider Nashville society.

My sadness over this narrow outlook was nothing compared to my shock and horror at the seething anger within the moderate bureaucracy at the Conservative Resurgence. The moderates who ruled Nashville's SBC community in 1989 saw the conservatives as something akin to the Barbarian hordes who overran Europe in the Middle Ages. Conservatives were seen as multi-headed, wart-nosed conquerors to be feared and hated instead of people who had won elections like what happens with the changing of the guard in Washington, D.C., from Democratic to Republican or Republican to Democratic after national elections.

* * * * * * *

Within days of moving my family from Plano to Franklin, I received my first horrific baptism into this angry cesspool. The episode occurred in Las Vegas, NV, in mid-June 1989 where the annual Southern Baptist Convention was under way—my first SBC to attend after I joined the Convention's employ. This SBC meeting marked the moment at which Convention moderates realized fully that they had lost the

Convention to the new conservative majority. After my brief hiatus in Plano, I once again was there as a witness to this important moment in modern religious history.

After the election and the outpouring of emotion that week, I naively opted to attend the annual Baylor University alumni get-together in a local Las Vegas hotel. The Baylor pie supper always was a large, elaborate, annual gathering at the SBC meeting. I tried never to miss it so I could renew old ties.

As I headed in the direction of that fellowship, I never realized who was going to be the "pie" at the 1989 event.

After I signed in at the door, one friend after the next spotted me and wasted no time in upbraiding me for going to work for the hated Richard Land and his ugly conservative cohorts. Unbelievably, two of those critics were Dr. Ralph Langley, our first pastor in Houston when we were members at Willow Meadows Baptist Church, and his wife, Grace, our first Sunday-school teacher! They both expressed their profound disappointment that I would "turncoat." At first I thought this merely represented friendly banter among colleagues and that the ungracious behavior would die down after a few minutes of good-natured ribbing.

Other friends who weren't castigating me were cutting wide berths to go out of their way to avoid me, I noticed.

About 45 minutes later, when the "banter" did not let up, I determined that the talk was lethal and had acquired an incisively personal dimension. Instead of seeing me as an ally who could help them understand, make peace with, and even be a bridge to the new Convention leadership, I somehow was seen as "one of them"—those evil fundamentalist victors. That caught me completely by surprise. I remembered Barbra Streisand's line from a song in *Funny Girl*, "*A bit of dinner never hurt, but guess who is gonna be dessert?*" The Baylorites may have been serving pie at its dessert event and not dinner per se, but I saw who was being "sliced and diced" for general dessert consumption.

I presumed that anyone who loved and cared for Kay and me would have understood our circumstances: given the economic upheaval in my home state of Texas and in the secular newspaper world of which I was a part, God was using those circumstances to point me to a career inside the SBC. My Baylor friends comprehended none of this. They immediately accused me of being a part of some undermining plot to overthrow them. No one asked me to shed any light on why I had made the decision I had made; no one asked how Kay and I were doing and what might have led us to move to Nashville. They just lectured and screamed, then lectured and scolded some more. I was stunned by their histrionics and out-of-control rage.

About 20 progressively bitter conversations into the evening, I headed toward the exit. I encountered Lee Berg, a young pastor and the son-in-law of Foy Valentine, for many years the head of the Christian Life Commission (which Richard Land now led). With eyes blazing fire, Lee heaped on me his frustration and anger with the loss he personally was sustaining with the conservative triumph. (Then, as now, having a father or father-in-law in high places in the SBC was/is an asset for young preacher boys. The cronyism that characterized the SBC then and still characterizes it today can be quite helpful for a young man marrying into one of the leading families.)

Lee's diatribe was the last straw. With tears now unabashedly streaming down my face, I walked away from the conversation. "Why, oh why, oh why, are you people being so mean, so cruel, and so ugly?" I asked aloud as I left the meeting.

Back in my hotel room, I alternated between tears and

227

iron-willed determination to flee Las Vegas immediately, return to Nashville, pack up my family, and whisk us all back to Texas.

First the heartache of Plano, and now this! I mourned on my knees in a desperate petition. *God, have you forgotten us?*

He hadn't, of course. In my life already full of "God-incidences" He was simply delivering to me yet another window where I was to be a *witness to the truth.* I was getting to walk within the capillaries of those who believed their lifeblood was about to be sucked out by a circumstance they felt was beyond their control. The Baylor pie supper was a tip of the iceberg to what I would see out of the moderate establishment over the next few years.

The next morning, I found an envelope under my hotel door. The envelope contained an apologetic note from Lee. After I read and studied the letter, I chose to forgive him of his uncouth behavior the previous night. I decided to move on without remorse.

In ensuing years, I became grateful for that disastrous night. What Lee and the others might have meant for ill, God used for my all-surpassing good.

* * * * * * * *

When we arrived in Nashville, I would have estimated the ratio of my moderate friends and acquaintances to my conservative friends and acquaintances to have been a generous 20-to-1 in favor of the moderates. During the next seven years I would see that gap close, then widen in the other direction in favor of the conservatives. I never intended for this to happen. I sincerely believed that I could help my moderate friends understand and relate in healthy ways to their new conservative peers. I often told friends, "I want to help bridge the gap. I know both of you; I can help." People seldom let me. The chasm was too wide and too deep. It indeed was a sad, regrettable situation.

Back in Nashville, during the months after the SBC in Las Vegas, we did our best to settle into life in this very unusual era of Baptist history. The feud aside, we had much to learn about Southern Baptists and their peculiar ways!

Needing a new church home, we decided to join First Baptist Church of Franklin, about two miles from our house. Before we took that step, Richard and Becky Land (now also our neighbors on our new cul-de-sac in Franklin) claimed that one of that church's staff members had once engaged in immoral behavior. By the time the Lands finished their stories, we opted to look elsewhere to move our membership.

Several months later, after we had joined First Baptist Church in downtown Nashville—more than a 50-mile, arduous, round-trip commute from our home—the Lands joined First Baptist, Franklin—the very church they warned us against! We were speechless. How could they be so negative about a church that they dissuaded us from joining, then turn around and affiliate with the same fellowship? From that experience we learned that personal opinions flow freely in Nashville's Baptist kingdom and that casual gossip about others is a way of life among the conservatives and moderates alike.

Nevertheless, we loved being members of First Baptist Church of Nashville. The *persona* of Southern Baptists' best, the church as a whole was an amazing oasis of life for us. We couldn't believe we were actually fellow church members with such people as Reuben Herring, the longtime editor of *HomeLife* magazine, and Dr. James L. Sullivan, whose name Kay had memorized as part of her childhood missions organization's homework. The church membership was a Who's Who of Baptist notables. Our children were enrolled in classes taught by the *crème de la crème* in Southern Baptist Christian education. We thought that was a fabulous bonus. (Even today, our children, now grown, look back on First Baptist, Nashville with a warm and abiding appreciation for the rich depth of their religious upbringing there.) The church was populated by a large number of families in which at least one individual was employed by one of the SBC agencies.

This, of course, was a two-edged sword. For all the fine qualities the church had, many of the SBC-employed bureaucrats were angry at the conservatives. But they faced a real dilemma: They knew change was inevitable. They enjoyed the perks associated with being on the top of the SBC mountain. To alienate the new leadership too severely would deny the church and its members access to the halls of power and the prestige that it had long enjoyed.

In later years, the church's pastor, Dr. Charles Page, would identify himself fully with the Conservative Resurgence. For the moment he tried to balance the needs of his congregation with the reality outside its walls and to guide the church through the difficult transition that awaited it. A magnificent pulpiteer and selfless pastor, Charles, and his wife, Sandra, instantly became our close friends. They, more than anyone, loved us, ministered to us, mentored us, and helped steer us through those difficult days of 1989 through 1991.

Charles, in fact, warned us of some of the troubles he feared we soon would face. He told us about his first staff meeting after we joined the church, in which one staff member made the covert overt. Charles said the staff member advised others on the staff that the rumors were spreading like wildfire at the Sunday School Board that I was a "spy" for Judge Paul Pressler and that his ultimate goal was to topple the current leadership at Baptist Press and place me at the helm of that institution. Charles told us he had termed *ludicrous* the "spy" rumors in Baptistdom and said he thought speculation on my future was nothing more than political gossip perpetrated by people with their own political agendas.

We were stunned by Charles' revelation, but once we got over the shock, were grateful for his candor with us. His words prepared us for what felt like our own personal "Battle of Franklin." (Franklin, our hometown in Tennessee, was the site of a significant Civil War battle.)

* * * * * * * *

Friends Wayne and Carolyn Jenkins also helped us interpret the turmoil. Wayne and Carolyn had moved to Louisville to attend Southern Seminary about the same time we did in 1969. We had not known each other well then, but on our arrival in Nashville, the Jenkinses sought us out. Wayne worked at the Baptist Sunday School Board; Carolyn was the youth minister at our church.

Within days after we joined First Baptist, Nashville, Wayne and Carolyn convinced us to become teachers in the college Sunday-school department there.

Wayne and Carolyn, though clearly identifying themselves as moderates, tried their best to interpret for us the ways of what I began calling *Baptistdom*—my label for the highly unusual Southern Baptist way of life we encountered there. Baptistdom was like a peculiar and alien culture. This wasn't because of its theological orientation so much as because of its unique small-town, Southern, bureaucratic, passive-aggressive style. Over the years I realized how much Baptistdom was like the notorious Roman Catholic "Curia." Both are bureaucracies with their own social codes, political agendas, and unusual way of conducting business.

Months later Wayne confessed that some of his co-workers at the Sunday School Board had chided him for his friendship with me. By this point I no longer expressed surprise at anything people in Baptistdom said or did. Gossip and behind-your-back, cutting remarks seemed to be written into that culture's genetic code.

Wayne also disclosed that when he first announced that Kay and I had joined on as teachers in the college department, a fellow teacher, Martin Bradley, expressed concern about "what kind of theology" the two of us might espouse.

Martin and his wife, Ruth, eventually became good friends of ours, even though Martin, as a moderate incumbent, was later deposed in his role as recording secretary of the SBC.

This case stands out to me as a clear example in which Nashville's establishment moderates continued to make strategic blunders and failed to "live in the light." Easily, people who feared for their jobs could have utilized our contacts and offers to build bridges. A rare few street-smart ones ultimately said, "Look, I'm just here to serve the Lord. I can work with anyone. Can you introduce me to some of the new conservative leaders so I can offer my services and explain who I am?"

Most, however, rebelled angrily, acted impractically, and in the end, succumbed.

I will always be grateful to Wayne and Carolyn for being willing to take some "black eyes" of their own to help shed light on Baptistdom's unusual ways in the transitional early 1990s.

* * * * * * *

Another teacher in that Sunday-school department, Howard Bramlette, personified the paranoia that ran amok in in that day. At the time Howard had recently retired from his long tenure at the Baptist Sunday School Board. Never married, he was in so many ways like a Roman Catholic monk— in his own eccentric way, affable but most unusual. Realizing that sometimes the "best defense is a good offense," I began the strategy of making luncheon appointments with select people in Baptistdom I suspected of being highly suspicious and antagonistic toward us. (Nothing like looking your enemy square in the eye and buying him lunch!) Howard was near the top of my list of those invited to dine. I still believed that people who would allow themselves to get to know me would like me. My life was an open book; I lived in the light, with nothing to hide.

About an hour before our luncheon, Howard called and asked me to meet him in one of the reception rooms on the SBC Building's third floor. When I arrived at the room at the designated time, the lights were off, but I could see a silhouetted figure about 25-feet away. The figure was seated in one of the room's many wingback chairs. I started looking for the light switch but stopped when I heard a voice quietly instruct me to keep all the lights off. The voice directed me to sit in another chair near him. By this point, my eyes had adjusted enough to see Howard's dim outline and some of the room's furniture. I spotted the room's exit light in case I needed to leave quickly.

After I took my seat about five-feet away from him, Howard softly began, "Louis, I know this has been tough for you. I know this has not been easy. You're an OK person. Given enough time, people here are going to begin to realize that. But you are going to have to be patient. People are angry [about the Conservative Resurgence]. You are just going to

233

have to give them enough time to see you for who you really are."

I wasn't sure whether to be complimented or wounded by his words. I felt troubled by this surreal setting. *Why have we met in the darkness?* I wondered. We continued to converse about three more minutes; then Howard directed me, "Louis, you need to leave now. After you have been gone for about five minutes, I will leave. I can't be seen with you right now. I have my reputation to protect."

My jaw clunked to my chest.

"Are we NOT going to go to lunch together as planned?" I asked in total disbelief.

"We will sometime," Howard replied, still in hushed, covert tones. "But not now." (We never did!)

I exited the room quickly. Back in my office, I first called Kay to report this berserk encounter. She expressed surprise and disappointment. Kay is an excellent reader of people's personalities. She usually hits right on the money. She hadn't expected this of Howard, who seemed to her like someone's well-meaning but slightly quirky great uncle.

Next I called Charles Page, our pastor, to relate the incident. He said everyone knew Howard to be a strange bird but harmless. In the years after that, Charles loved to prompt me to re-tell my "Leaving-the-Lights-Off" anecdote. We always concluded the re-telling with Charles assuring me that I was not the one who was off base.

I was reminded that Baptists were not the only ones who pulled such freakish stunts. I once interviewed a United Methodist pastor about divorce among this denomination's clergy. The pastor had been eager to be my source for Methodist news in Houston, so I curiously picked his brain to see if he knew of any Methodist clergy who had been divorced and remarried but were still pastors. His eyes widened; his countenance fell.

This pastor asked me to follow him to the church's basement; mystified, I accompanied him. Down below, with numerous, intervening doors along the way shut tightly, he turned to me and asked, with breathless paranoia, "How did you know?" He then explained about his previous marriage and divorce but frantically begged me not to report it. My jaw dropped in astonishment, since I was merely asking him for names and had no idea he perfectly fit the profile I was seeking.

U.S. Roman Catholic bishops often battled with religion reporters in the late 1960s and early 1970s over business conducted away from the light. I knew reporters who attempted to hide behind meeting-room curtains to try to gain knowledge of these clandestine gatherings. Without the light of openness, these meetings spawned rumors and stories of political misconduct. Reluctantly the bishops eventually "saw the light" and opened their meetings to the press and public, thus saving themselves the problems such secrecy naturally generates.

* * * * * * * *

A short time later, another bizarro situation occurred involving Lynn Davis' wife, Karen. Lynn, my former boss at Ridgecrest, is the one who so aptly taught me about Baptists' union cards. When we first moved to Nashville, I looked forward to having Lynn around as a good friend. Karen worked for another SBC agency in my same building.

One day in my office mail cubby appeared a handwritten letter from Karen.

Her letter was similar in content to Howard's conversation. She wanted me to know that people in the building were gossiping about me, criticizing my relationship with the Conservative Resurgence, and stating as an undisputed fact that Judge Pressler had placed me in the SBC Building as part of a sinister plot to overthrow the leadership at Baptist Press.

I called Karen and told her I was shocked by her letter. I asked why she had written it and not talked to me privately in person. After all, I told her, she was the wife of my former boss whom I had appreciated very much. She said she felt she needed to be clear and wanted me to know of her concern for me and my family.

I invited Karen and Lynn to our home for dinner the next Friday night. After eating our meal, we talked candidly for about three hours. Lynn commented that people in Baptistdom (word choice mine) were scared, that people knew my credentials would easily qualify me for the leadership at Baptist Press, and people (moderates) were jumping to false and speculative assumptions about the future.

When the Davises left, something between disgust and cold terror clutched me once again—as did the unrelenting temptation to pack our belongings and head back to Texas and the clearly less-political life of being secular freelance writers.

I called Charles Page, my friend and pastor, who advised me that some FBC Nashville members had taken similar "helpful" steps with him and that I should ignore them. I needed Charles' wise counsel to determine where the land mines were strewn, for they seemed to be plentiful.

Charles made an interesting comment about the number of anonymous letters he had received since arriving at First Baptist, Nashville—a number far exceeding anything he had gotten in previous pastorates. Because of their content, he was sure that all the anonymous letters were from church members. I thought that was a strange way—hidden from the light—for members of a congregation to interact with their pastor.

Charles said that on occasions in which he ultimately was able to track down the source, "You'll find that they're from the people you least suspect would do a thing like that."

Eventually we got our own, personal, unsigned hate letter, too; in its aftermath, you could have knocked me off my Christmas tree! This anonymous missal reported some gossip involving two fellow FBC Nashville church members, whom the letter identified. Since the letter also mentioned one of our children by name, I immediately rushed it and its envelope to the main U.S. Post Office in Nashville and asked for an investigation into its origins.

Just as Charles had shared, the letter writer that the post office identified from the barcode was someone I knew well. In a trillion years I couldn't have fathomed that I would be on this man's hit list. This letter-sender had been supremely helpful when we first arrived and had actually used his networks to help Kay try to locate a job. Since the letter did not specifically threaten physical harm to either of us or either of our children, we decided not to press criminal charges and to let the matter drop, although we did keep a wary eye on the person who sent the letter.

The letter had done its work. I now realized that in this bewildering church bureaucracy, I could trust absolutely *no one*.

* * * * * * * *

Never was life at the secular *Houston Chronicle* as mean-spirited, confusing, and downright harrowing as things were becoming in the headquarters of Southern Baptists.

I longed for the days when I had been in Houston and at the *Chronicle* working alongside people who were openly alcoholics, womanizers, drug users, homosexuals, and people who smoked marijuana in the very halls of our workplace. Despite what I considered to be their wrong lifestyle choices, they were people who all treated me and Kay with love and respect.

Yet I remembered that Kay and I somehow were in Nashville on God's assignment. Whatever He was trying to teach me by being around these highly alien beings populating Baptistdom, it surely must be something very important.

Chapter 20

The Big Flush

Truth No. 20: Truth always wins.

No matter whom I met in Baptistdom, the person usually soon confronted me about Baptist Press. Again and again I was told that *everyone* knew for *absolute certain* that Judge Pressler was plotting to run off the top Baptist Press leadership and catapult me into the office.

Only one thing was wrong with this story: If these plans were true, no one in any position of authority had bothered to tell me.

During my job-hunting days in Plano, Judge Pressler had been spiritually encouraging, but he never promised to create a job for me at Baptist Press—nor did I expect him to do so.

I was hired for the sole purpose of being director of media and products at the Christian Life Commission. I was happy to be there because I believed that was what God called me to do at that juncture in my life. Also, as my job evolved, I could see it coinciding with some of my long-term goals. Plano had whetted my appetite for the day when I could be an independent entrepreneur journalist/publisher.

Since Baptistdom appeared hell-bent to advance its rumor, I often wondered how much of the rumor would turn out to be a self-fulfilling prophecy. Baptistdom by now was ablaze in anger over the Conservative Resurgence. Baptist Press, in particular, seemed to be growing daily in its hostility toward the Conservative Resurgence and especially toward Judge Pressler, whom moderates pinpointed as the "brains" behind the "Fundamentalist Takeover," as they called it. No rocket scientist was necessary to see the temperature among the moderate bureaucrats rising and the inevitable likely to happen.

The conservatives were continuing to win elections and were set to gain majorities on the various boards of trustees of SBC seminaries and agencies. SBC history seemed to be moving toward a dramatic, eschatological moment. The days of the moderate reign were clearly numbered. A new day was dawning in the SBC, with the new conservative tentacles reaching down to the last detail.

Sadly I continued to encounter few moderates who seemed interested in working out some sort of quiet peace treaty regarding the inevitable. Baptistdom was marching headlong toward its own Armageddon.

I saw that the very mention of Judge Pressler's name sent apoplexic ripples of dread through the bodies of every moderate around. Defending him or attempting to explain about his background and his motivation for change was like trying to defend Hitler. People much preferred their gossip, rumors, and stereotypes.

Since the judge had always treated Kay and me with utmost respect and decency, we refused to take the easy route and join in the dissing. The only viable option seemed to try to ignore Baptistdom's hysteria and live our lives as best we could, despite the turbulence all around us.

I also realized that my denials about Baptist Press were being greeted with skepticism or outright refutation. Whoever was spreading this scuttlebutt had done a marvelous job of making it sound thoroughly convincing to an awful lot of people. Eventually I decided to let the gossips have their say without trying to respond back, since my denials seemed to be as ineffective as trying to heat up an auditorium with a hairdryer.

Despite dealing with the predictable byproducts of a lime-light-seeking boss—no trouble for me since I was forewarned—and despite the antics of a couple of holdover moderates on the CLC staff who seemed more interested in keeping the pot boiling in our office, I basically liked my job at the Christian Life Commission. I found it challenging—exactly what I had been seeking when I left the *Chronicle* desiring training in media management and new horizons. My first opportunity in Plano had been cut short. Now I had another chance to learn to do more than just write news stories and columns. Managing the Christian Life Commission's publications department was solid, on-the-job training for my long-term goal—to become involved in publishing in broader ways—perhaps even to eventually own my own publishing company.

No member of Baptistdom—neither moderate nor conservative—bothered to discuss with me my work history or my career goals. One thing I learned quickly about Baptistdom bureaucrats was that they spouted opinions first, then asked questions long after their opinions proved to be wrong. If instead of telling me that they were *sure* they knew what was in my heart and mind, they had listened and asked appropriate, non-judgmental queries, they would have learned that I felt burned out as a newspaper reporter and wanted to spend the rest of my professional career in publishing management or perhaps as a book author—definitely not on the frontline reporting the news. The last thing in the world I wanted to do was to continue to be involved in cutting-edge, day-to-day reporting of the Southern Baptist Convention controversy. As the expression goes, "Been there, done that"; I had had it! At the *Houston Chronicle* I had been in the best situation in the entire U.S. for covering that story. I left that behind. I couldn't imagine covering it from some other media outlet, especially self-serving Baptist Press itself.

Early in my career I held Baptist Press in great esteem. I thought the news organization did a credible job and was deserving of praise. I thought Jim Newton and Robert O'Brien were excellent reporters and managed Baptist Press well. In the days before the Conservative Resurgence, I believed BP did an extremely good job of balancing its coverage. After the Resurgence began, I observed that slowly but surely its coverage seemed to tilt more and more in favor of the moderates.

During my last years in Houston I was amazed at Baptist Press and felt the organization had become too busy defending the Baptist establishment (moderates) and attacking the victorious conservatives. The episode involving Bailey Smith's convention sermon in 1981 and W.C. Fields' cloak-and-dagger affirmation had caused me to look on Baptist Press suspiciously.

Also, the two top editors at Baptist Press during the 1980s and early 1990s were not in my circle of friends. Al Shackleford, W.C. Fields' successor as the top leader in BP, had been editor of the Indiana Baptist newspaper when my former boss, Pat Pattillo, quoted him as being highly critical of my decision in 1972 to go to work for the *Houston Chronicle* instead of some denominational agency. Since Shackleford never spoke to me directly about the matter, and since I never knew Pat to lie, I was wary of any contact with Shackleford. I never found Dan Martin, BP's news editor and a former *Dallas Times Herald* reporter, to be particularly friendly or helpful. I always had a sense when I was around him that he saw me more as a competitor than a potential friend or colleague.

On our arrival in Nashville neither Shackleford nor Martin was welcoming toward me. I dutifully paid visits to their offices to try to become better acquainted. They were polite and cautiously hospitable. But they did not reciprocate and visit my office two floors below theirs. Suggestions about lunches together were always made by me and greeted with the same message—"Someday," which never arrived. I was puzzled by the aloofness. I eventually decided their behavior probably was impacted by the rumor about Judge Pressler, Baptist Press, and me. I also wondered how much each man was contributing to the rumor.

Nevertheless, I determined to reach out and try to be friendly with both Al and Dan. I tried to make regular, courtesy visits to their offices.

Those visits mostly ceased after one incident in Dan's office. That occurred the day I had learned that Marv Knox, then third-in-command at Baptist Press, was leaving to become editor of the state Baptist newspaper in Kentucky, the *Western Recorder*. I liked Marv; early in his career I had tried to hire him as my assistant at the *Houston Chronicle*. I was happy for Marv's new opportunity at the Kentucky paper, so I went to Baptist Press' office to congratulate him.

After speaking with Marv, I went to Dan's office to chat. Dan caustically told me that I should go home immediately and tell Kay to visit the Baptist Press offices to measure Marv's desk, since she was clearly going to occupy it very soon. His tone was not affirmative of Kay. He was not the least bit pleasant.

I was stunned by the attitude in his voice and his insinuations against my wife. For the gossips in the SBC to badger me was one thing, but to make caustic remarks about my wife was another matter. From my perspective, Kay, of course, was far more proficient journalistically than any of the three men (Shackleford, Martin, and Knox) there at the time. But she had absolutely no ambition or interest in that institution.

I've never known what possessed Dan to make the remark or to say it with the sneer that he had. Kay was never contacted by anyone in or out of authority in the SBC about joining the staff at Baptist Press. Had she been approached about the job, she would have politely declined. Covering denominational politics was never her "cup of tea."

Nevertheless, I didn't like the attitude that Dan expressed. I found it very off-putting and troubling. Afterward I decided to avoid visiting people at Baptist Press except when absolutely necessary. BP clearly was becoming enemy territory—not by my choice but by theirs.

Over the next months, the tension between Baptist Press and the conservative leadership escalated dramatically. It culminated in a specially called meeting of the SBC Executive Committee in which Shackleford and Martin were fired. Moderate SBC journalists tried to frame the firings as a moral crusade somehow tied to freedom of the press. I felt sorry for Al, who seemed to be a nice guy but also a dedicated Baptistdom bureaucrat. I could never muster much sympathy for Dan. I saw neither man as a symbol of press freedom but instead victims of their moderate bosses and colleagues in Baptistdom. I know of few newspapers in the country that would allow their reporters or editors publicly to thumb their noses at senior management or the company's board of directors. To me Al and Dan were doing exactly that—thumbing their noses at their own incoming board of directors. I knew the *Houston Chronicle* wouldn't tolerate that. I knew neither *The Dallas Morning News*, *The New York Times,* nor *The Washington Post* would tolerate it. I could not figure out why staff at Baptist Press should be allowed to do what others would be fired for doing.

* * * * * * * *

Being in the SBC Building and an eyewitness to these

events provided some interesting and at one point humorous insights.

In the weeks before Al and Dan were fired, the moderates occupying most of the offices in the seven-story building in downtown Nashville appeared to be one nervous bunch of horses. People lost their pleasant demeanors and outlooks— even their smiles. For months before, just a mere few seconds in the lunchroom, with its huddled klatches that suddenly went silent when any of the new conservatives entered, gave me a sick headache. I finally decided to eat lunch in my office alone and only make occasional forays there to pick up a free cup of coffee.

I started to appreciate Karen Davis' and Howard Bramlette's cryptic, advance warnings to me. Thanks to both of them as well as some others, at least I knew what the rumors were and how hysterical people in Baptistdom were becoming. Karen's and Howard's actions alerted me to stay out of the way as much as possible so as not to become a target for all the free-floating anger engulfing the epicenter of Southern Baptist life.

One humorous incident occurred late one afternoon as I was leaving the building. Near the entrance to the parking garage in the SBC Building's basement was a tiny, one-seater men's room (toilet and wash basin with barely enough room to move between the two). On this particular evening as I left the building, the door to the restroom popped open. Two well-known moderates (both of them men) emerged from having been squeezed together in this minuscule bathroom. They saw me, ducked their heads, and were awash in guilty looks.

In any other setting I might have suspected that I had stumbled into two guys emerging from a homosexual tryst. In this case, I knew that sex had nothing to do with this curious scene. Throughout the weeks of tension, moderates in the SBC

Building had been clustered in small groups of two or three. They nervously watched over their shoulders to see who was looking and murmured to each other what I presumed to be their latest juicy morsel about the state of the Convention. I concluded that one member of the restroom duo probably had learned some delectable tidbit that was too important to share with his friend in an open hallway or even an office!

Had it not been so serious, the behavior in the SBC Building during this time would have been side-splitting. These were grown men and women, supposedly Christians, acting more like children playing some sort of ludicrous cops-and-robbers game.

Kay and I deliberately chose to be away from Nashville during the dramatic days when the Executive Committee met and fired Dan and Al. I found the whole thing distasteful. I believed the conservatives had taken the bait and were dancing to the moderates' orchestrated tune. By hiring armed guards to patrol the hallways of the building the conservatives allowed the moderates to use their vast publicity machine to make the conservatives look mean and abusive. The moderates squeezed every bit of media attention and sympathy they could muster out of the debacle.

Returning to Nashville several days after the firings, we found a much-sobered and frightened Baptistdom. The conservatives had fulfilled on the moderates' worst fears.

* * * * * * *

Unfortunately what this set off would have a highly personal consequence. The worst drama in my life was about to unfold. The two top editors at Baptist Press had been fired. The third had exited the organization just in the nick of time to miss the upheaval. Now three top vacancies existed in the organization.

I had always determined that if ever approached about any of the jobs, I would slam the phone on the person's ear or, if done in person, order the individual out of my office or home. By the time Harold Bennett, president of the Executive Committee, which supervises Baptist Press, and himself a moderate, invited me to his office for a chat, I had strategically developed a different plan. I concluded if I said *no* immediately, I would look as though I was playing a game of "hard-to-get" and would only keep the gossips chattering long after a new director of Baptist Press had been selected. They would wonder if I was biding my time for yet another chance to head BP.

I knew I needed a plan to terminate the matter once and for all.

My first act was to draw up a list of 10 people whose opinions I valued and ask them what I should do. The list included Ken Chafin, my former pastor; Pat Pattillo, my former boss at Southern Seminary; Glenn Hilburn, my former professor at Baylor, and Ed Briggs, religion editor of the *Richmond Times-Dispatch* and an Episcopalian. I included Ed because I considered him a friend and also because when I had left Houston, Ed had asked me about the possibility of succeeding me at the *Houston Chronicle*. I had offered to be a reference for Ed.

Every one of the 10 admonished me, without mincing words, that I would be a fool to take the BP job. Nine of the 10 were courteous and somewhat pastoral, although a few couldn't resist the usual "working-for-the-conservatives" jibe. Most lauded my professional credentials and said they regretted the day I left secular newspapering.

Ed, however, surprised me by turning on me as Baptistdom's moderates had been doing. He accused me of being a part of the greater plot to overthrow the BP leadership. He was accusatory and downright rude. I was stunned, since in our last conversation I had been kind to him and had freely promised the good references. From Ed's reaction, I knew then that the moderate rumor mill and anger had seeped even outside of the Convention and were poisoning my good name and reputation.

Earlier, with my name misspelled, the *Nashville Banner* had run a front-page story that attested, "Some Southern Baptists speculate that Pressler has his eye on newly hired SBC Christian Life Commission associate director Lewis Moore as Shackleford's replacement as head of the press. Moore, an ordained Southern Baptist minister, is a former religion editor for the *Houston Chronicle*."

All this confirmed for me just how serious the situation was, that I couldn't take it lightly, and that I had to find a way out that would be permanent. Though once again in my heart I wanted to pack up my family and leave Nashville in the dead of night, these 10 conversations confirmed that disappearing would ruin my career—and probably my life.

I concluded that rather than run for cover, I needed a master plan that would extinguish the Baptist Press matter once and for all.

* * * * * * * *

I decided that, instead of just maneuvering behind the scenes, I would be better off if the Executive Committee actually officially turned me down. That, I knew, would end the speculation and gossip. It would also prove the "shoe-in" rumors to be exactly what they were—groundless lies—and leave me free to pursue my life without the constant stress and anxiety living in this era of Baptist life was causing me and my family.

The Executive Committee named a group to interview prospective candidates for the top job at Baptist Press. The interviews were held in a posh hotel on Nashville's east side near Opryland.

After the interview, Harold Bennett invited me to his office on the SBC Building's seventh floor. He told me the committee had given him a list of three men from whom he was free to choose a new director of Baptist Press. I was one of the three.

I knew Harold as a fellow churchmember at First Baptist, Nashville. I had always found him to be a genial chap who seemed perfectly suited for the ponderous, bureaucratic role as head of the SBC Executive Committee. Though labeled as a moderate, Harold struck me more as the type of person who would have preferred a quiet, uneventful reign at the helm and who was probably deeply ticked that the Conservative Resurgence, with all of its raucous upheaval, occurred on his watch.

My family and I also had prayed for the Bennett family because of a sad situation that occurred when a granddaughter was born anencephalic—basically without a brain. The infant was supposed to have died at birth but instead lingered for several months. Because we once had lost a child, we, like many others at First Baptist, Nashville and in Baptistdom, became gravely sympathetic with the Bennett family's trauma.

Now face-to-face in his office, Harold first wanted to know whether I thought I could manage the scope and the magnitude of the SBC press room, given the strong opposition to me from among the moderates, including many state Baptist editors.

"Yes," I answered.

Then I threw out the bombshell.

For me to take the job, I explained, I would need for the Executive Committee to enact what I termed a "sunshine law" that I would write for the Executive Committee to adopt.

I told Harold I also wanted the boards of trustees of all of the SBC agencies and entities of the Convention to ratify this "sunshine law." I told him I would meet with each of the boards of trustees to explain my idea and why it needed to be adopted and enacted.

Harold looked stupefied. "What is a *sunshine law*?"

I described a statement that would say all meetings in the SBC would be open to the public and that journalists, both secular and denominational, would be allowed to report on all meetings of the SBC without restrictions. All SBC business would be out in the "sunshine."

Harold shook his head, "That's not going to work"

"Why?" I asked.

"You know why," he countered.

Indeed, I did *know why*. But I also believed the situation could—and should—be changed.

Since arriving in Nashville I had witnessed firsthand the troubling aspects of secret and closed meetings that were far more pervasive in Baptistdom than I as a secular newspaper reporter had realized. The reigning moderates had developed an elaborate set of rules for reporters covering the meetings of the trustee boards of each of the agencies and entities. These were summarized in the words *background rules*. Basically, reporters were allowed to sit in on committee meetings and to report in broad, sweeping generalizations without direct quotations. I believed these rules to be an unhealthy compromise and wondered why denominational journalists acquiesced to them.

These rules, however, did not apply to "forums"—caucuses that are private dinner meetings between the agency heads and their entire boards of trustees. These were totally off-limits to reporters and anybody else.

I had observed how when the Christian Life Commission's trustees arrived in Nashville for a meeting, they went out to dinner *en masse* with the Christian Life Commission's executive, Richard Land. Staff, spouses, and others were explicitly excluded. From listening to Richard and trustees talk afterward, clearly serious business matters were discussed. Richard maintained that these meetings did not violate any rules because the SBC has no "open meetings" laws like secular governments do and because no official business was ever conducted—in other words, no votes were ever taken. He considered these little "get-togethers" somehow above and beyond what they obviously were: secret meetings.

I had learned that most other SBC trustee boards were accustomed to the same top-secret, closed-door meetings.

Harold knew about these meetings, too. He knew about the "background rules," since the Executive Committee had adopted them.

He didn't believe anything could be done to change the situation.

I declared again that this was the condition under which I would accept the job.

Harold changed the subject and ventured other questions about how I would manage.

Since I had written a weekly column in the *Houston Chronicle* for nearly 14 years, he wanted to know whether I would expect to write a weekly opinion column for Baptist Press.

I nodded. I told him I believed Southern Baptists needed someone to interpret events in the Convention through an objective and balanced perspective.

He inquired about how much "right-of-review" he, as

CEO, would have over my columns.

None, I stipulated. I would take full responsibility for what I had written, as I always had.

Harold indicated he didn't think the column was a good idea.

After a few more questions, I could tell I had made the right choice by agreeing to be interviewed by the Executive Committee. Harold knew he could not afford to nominate me for the Baptist Press leadership. He needed a safe Baptistdom bureaucrat, not someone as independent as I. By demanding the "sunshine law" and indicating my desire to write an independent column, he and I both knew my nomination would not succeed.

Deep inside, my heart leaped. I knew that soon I would be free of this horrible burden that had overshadowed everything I had done since arriving in Nashville more than two years earlier.

The gossips would have to eat their words. The slanderers would have to find a new target. I could reclaim my life.

* * * * * * * *

My guarded euphoria was almost short-lived. A few days after I met with Harold, Richard Land showed up at my house one evening with a surprising announcement. His conservative cronies had concluded that I was not electable at that time. (*Duh!*) Things were just too hot, he divulged. He tried to blame the moderates, but I knew his conservative brethren were horrified to learn (which I was sure they already had) of my "sunshine-law" proposal. Speaking for whoever these nameless, faceless people were, Richard recommended I withdraw my name and wait for the next Baptist Press director to fall flat on his face, as he knew he would, so I could be nominated and elected then.

Knowing I had purposely tried to set the stage for my own defeat and that the time had arrived to permanently defang the issue of me and Baptist Press, I told Richard to inform his friends I would not withdraw. Regardless of the outcome, I would let my name go forward, I announced. I thanked Richard because I knew he was concerned about me, but I also knew I had to see this to its conclusion.

Given the stance I had taken with Harold, I knew I could not be chosen. Harold knew my nomination wasn't going to work. Richard knew it wasn't going to fly. Richard's buddies knew I wasn't the right candidate for the job.

Still, Baptistdom's gossip churned on.

* * * * * * *

A few weeks later, the Executive Committee chose Herb Hollinger, editor of the state Baptist newspaper in California, to head Baptist Press. I was among the first to congratulate him. I was suffused with joy! No also-ran had ever been so glad to be bypassed.

I was a bird out of a cage. I could say, with that great American, Martin Luther King Jr., "Free at last. Free at last. Thank God Almighty, I'm free at last."

After Herb was nominated, Greg Warner of the breakaway Associated Baptist Press, formed after the firings at Baptist Press (but with neither Dan nor Al as employees) called to interview me about the outcome. During that phone conversation Greg commented, "I never really thought you wanted the job." A-plus to Greg for his reporting skills! At least one moderate had sized up the situation correctly!

I never had one twinge of regret for my decision to make those demands of Harold nor wished the outcome had been one iota different than it was.

People say that "The Big Flush" occurs in the U.S. during the halftime of the annual Super Bowl. TV viewers who exercise superhuman control over their bladders for two spellbinding quarters of the world's most-watched football game are known to flee their couches and sprint to their respective toilets *en masse* in homes throughout America. Folks who keep statistics on this sort of mindless trivia have documented the precise, vast number of gallons of water that are used when toilets everywhere make this massive, simultaneous flush.

But I contend that I heard the real Big Flush occur on March 1, 1991, the day the Executive Committee bestowed the BP job on poor Herb. Once and for all, it flushed out of the SBC plumbing the toxic rumor that was poisoning my life and was holding me back from finally planting myself in the at-last fertile Nashville denominational soil.

In other religious bodies I saw truth triumph as well. When Central Church of Christ in Houston saw that its nursing home was about to drag it down and into bankruptcy, Minister Dan Anders and the congregation opted for truth rather than expediency, convenience, or subterfuge.

While many persons and churches would have headed to their lawyers seeking legal protection, the mother Church of Christ in the Houston area opted to try to pay every last dime that was owed, even when that meant selling its pews and allowing a developer to purchase its near-downtown building to turn it into condos.

When the sad story ended, the Churches of Christ gave me an award of appreciation for my coverage; actually, the church deserved the award for its integrity and truth-telling.

When the Dalai Lama of Tibet, the Buddhist spiritual

leader of that Himalayan country, accepted the reality that the Chinese were taking over his country in the 1960s, he faced two choices: compromise with the Chinese and save himself and preserve at least some of his wealth and comforts or flee to India and use his platform there to tell the world the truth about China's cruelty toward the people and traditions of his mountain kingdom.

When I once interviewed him over lunch at the home of Dominique deMenil in Houston, I knew I was talking to a truth-teller in person. Today, he has won international acclaim as a person of peace and truth.

The Bible says, *"You will know the truth, and the truth shall set you free"* (John 8:32). After the Baptist Press saga ended, the truth truly had set me free—free to move on, free to forgive those who had spitefully used me (Matt. 5:44).

It had set the talebearers free as well. They no longer had to be shackled by the savage chains of assumptions, misinformation, half-truths, hearsay, and misperceptions. Those gossip-mongers themselves could be released to walk in truth's light. Ideally they also would be free to know conviction for the errors of their ways, to be accountable for them, to vow to be more circumspect next time, and to even seek forgiveness, if the Holy Spirit prompted.

That latter matter was between them and God. All I knew was that I could proceed with a clear conscience. I had been a witness to the truth.

Truth always wins.

* * * * * * * *

Herb Hollinger eventually retired early after what his friends described as some pretty miserable years at the helm of

Baptist Press. I had watched Herb from afar and prayed for him. I always thanked God that he, not I, was in that hot, desolate seat.

By the time Herb stepped aside, I was living in Richmond, VA—well-ensconced in a plum media job that everyone knew I had no intention of leaving. With the BP vacancy this time, thankfully my name never was mentioned.

Chapter 21

The Alma Mater Matter

Truth No. 21: The first shall be last.

The lone moderate who was not too lily-livered to broach the Baptist Press issue squarely with me afterward was none other than CEO Harold Bennett. Several months after the issue had been settled, I encountered Harold in the SBC Building's parking garage.

"I want you to know how much I appreciate your attitude," he offered. "You've been in every way a true Christian gentleman. I and many others have taken note of that."

I responded with a simple, "Thank you."

Everyone else simply ran for cover. Most people who had been accusatory now acted as though the matter had never involved me. No overt apologies were ever forthcoming from a single soul.

One important thing did change, however. Kay's job prospects brightened considerably.

After we arrived in Nashville, Kay had been unable to find much-needed employment. At first we attributed this to our newness in the community. After the Baptist Press rumors unmasked Baptistdom's mean-spirited dark side, we wondered—with just cause—whether she was being deliberately blackballed. No one at the then-Baptist Sunday School Board—Southern Baptists' mammoth publishing house overseeing books and publications galore—seemed willing to give a second look to a Pulitzer-Prize nominee with nearly 20 years of big-city newspaper and wire-service experience and with three books under her belt.

The Nashville Banner hired her as a freelance reporter but seemed unable to find a full-time position.

After the issue of Baptist Press had been put to rest, our friend, Wayne Jenkins, made repeated efforts to try and open doors for Kay at the Baptist Sunday School Board. So did Larry Yarborough, a First Baptist, Nashville friend, who worked in human resources at the BSSB.

A magazine editor's spot opened in one of the denominational publications. Its subject of home and family life matched perfectly with the topics Kay had covered for years as a feature writer at the *Chronicle*.

Earlier Kay had visited with the hiring supervisor, a friend from Baylor days. This supervisor gushed glowingly about how much he'd like to have someone with Kay's outstanding qualifications. He all but assured her that the next magazine opening on his staff would be hers.

Kay interviewed for the family publication editor's post and was almost sure she had the job. But after some time passed with no notification, she called to check. "Oh, we've decided to go in another direction," our Baylor colleague, the supervisor, shrugged to her nonchalantly, as though the earlier, reassuring talks had never occurred. No further explanation was forthcoming. *Score another one* for Baylor and its unwillingness to care for its own!

A bit later, a curriculum magazine's editorship sprang open in another area. The department recruited her as an interim editor while candidates were sought. For several months Kay stepped in and produced quality magazines that received high praise. But when a permanent editor was hired, Kay was bypassed again. She hit similar deadends after she completed several other successful contract assignments.

By that point our suspicions were on red alert. A clear case of discrimination on the basis of my conservative connections was becoming highly apparent.

* * * * * * *

About that time, the leadership at the BSSB changed. As its president, Lloyd Elder, left, Texas pastor Jimmy Draper, former SBC president, was hired to replace him. That set loose a dramatic shift in the culture and attitudes not only at the BSSB but also in Baptistdom in general.

We were now positioned to be eyewitnesses to one of the most significant and important transitions in the nation's largest non-Catholic denomination. The giant, highly influential SBC publishing arm was about to change remarkably for the better.

Before Jimmy's arrival in Nashville, the BSSB was a sleepy, tradition-bound, minister-of-education-driven institution. Many rank-and-file Southern Baptists knew of the BSSB's image as the dumping ground for nice-guy church staff members who couldn't cut it in either the local church or in secular business. Some products took years to generate; many were dull and irrelevant.

Jimmy's brilliant success at steering the BSSB's nearly 2,000-strong workforce into an entirely new direction without setting loose gale-force anger against him is one of the SBC miracle stories during the 1990s. He mostly let teams of employees look for ways to make the BSSB more efficient, effective, vital, and cutting-edge. As these teams worked, the groups targeted the systems and people who perpetuated the BSSB mediocrity. He looked to associates such as John Kramp, a pastor with an MBA and a keen business acumen, to grasp the core of what ailed the BSSB and to make it more corporate and competitive.

As the "let's-take-forever-to-do-nothing" crowd exited and a whole new breed of business-oriented and trained professionals took over, Kay found herself in a better place during the transition.

After Jimmy Draper took office, Kay and I approached him with our concerns about Kay's employment difficulties. Jimmy was horrified and said his antennae would be out. He said he couldn't imagine why someone with Kay's amazing credentials wouldn't be snapped up quickly in a BSSB editor position.

Simultaneously our BP nightmare ended. People became more open-minded and stopped regarding us as though we were lepers.

Ultimately the Lord opened the floodgates of heaven for Kay and well compensated her for the indignities she suffered during her first 2 1/2 years of BSSB establishment insults.

In 1992 the Board suddenly set up a special, high-profile unit to fast-track some books on personal-issues topics and to get them into print quickly. It needed someone who could circumvent the slow-as-molasses timeframe and do a fast publication turnaround.

Kay's credentials as a deadline-oriented reporter pushed her application to the top. First hired as an editor, she was almost instantly promoted when her supervising manager resigned. Within months she became one of the BSSB's senior editors—the first female "design editor" of non-seminary background in BSSB history. From the bottom of the heap Kay almost instantly held one of the highest-visibility positions anyone could have had at BSSB then. She also was one of the highest-paid female employees on the entire BSSB payroll.

The products she supervised were the LIFE Support Series,

a curriculum designed to help churches minister to alcoholics, sexual-abuse survivors, codependents, sex addicts, smokers, and people with depression, eating disorders, and weight-control issues. It yielded Bible studies for divorce- and grief-recovery and for people with painful pasts and difficult family situations.

Kay could hardly believe that she was at the helm of a church-related product with so much potential for practical life change. The workbooks were wild successes and helped bring Southern Baptist churches out of the Dark Ages in dealing with such sensitive, critical topics.

The LIFE Support books were the first to be produced under a brand-new BSSB publishing imprint called *LifeWay*. In 1998, when the SBC decided to rename the Sunday School Board with a moniker that more reflected its broad scope of services, it chose the name *LifeWay*. Jimmy Draper explained that the name was chosen partly because the fledgling *LifeWay* imprint (which by then included her products plus others) in its brief history had become a symbol of excellence. Kay felt gratified when she saw that the unit she supervised had made such a strategic contribution that the entire, massive corporation would take on the name first put on the map by her scrappy, hard-working editorial team.

Kay's employment brought in the added income we needed to boost our flagging personal finances that were still bruised after the Texas economic recession. God had truly prepared a table before us in the presence of our enemies (Ps. 23:5). He sustained us through a deep valley and in the process had grown us immeasurably.

* * * * * * *

Though I tried my best to accustom myself to the limited culture of Nashville's Baptistdom, I went into a fever of excitement the day Richard Land approached me about joining the ongoing Southern Baptist-Roman Catholic Dialogue Team. A leftover relic from the Moderate era, the Dialogue Team presented the new conservative leadership with some unusual challenges. To kill it abruptly would draw unwanted negative headlines. To let it continue unbridled could potentially damage their relationship with their anti-Catholic conservative constituency back home. I never was quite sure why I received the appointment except that I worked for Richard Land, which made me more palatable to the conservatives in the pews. To me it was clearly an answer to my prayers for the kind of diversity I craved.

As a newspaper reporter, I had kept up with the SBC-RC Dialogue Team and wrote about it over the years. Nothing could have put me into overdrive more than when I was named to a five-year term. Now at least once a year for a three-day weekend (usually in a Catholic monastery somewhere but once at our offices in Nashville), I would spend quality time dialoguing with peers in the U.S. Roman Catholic Church. Because of my deep familiarity with the subject, my Catholic counterparts on the team enjoyed visiting my office for in-depth, unofficial briefings on my perspective of Roman Catholic leadership but, more importantly, on my take on current Southern Baptist life.

I'm not sure our Team developed or said anything particularly profound. At the end of our five-year term, we were unceremoniously dropped—fired—*en masse* and replaced by the top tier of conservative leadership including Paige Patterson and Al Mohler, who turned the Dialogue confrontational. To me, the very fact that our Team even existed and was able to meet annually during those tumultuous years was significant enough.

Amazingly, just after I was appointed to the Southern Baptist-Roman Catholic Dialogue Team, Kay was appointed as the only woman on the Southern Baptist-Church of Christ Dialogue Team. Since these were the only two official "dialogues" under way in the SBC at that time, that meant two of the 12 Southern Baptists participating on official dialogue teams lived in our home. Although Kay had been reared a Southern Baptist, she was extraordinarily familiar with Churches of Christ theology and traditions because her dad and his family had all been a part of this religious body. Thus, she had a natural affinity for the dialogue itself.

At Christmastime I still hear from one of the team members, Catholic Pastor Frank Ruff. This fellowship was a wonderful way to help bridge the gap for me from some of the things I liked best about newspapering and to make Nashville's monoculture more palatable.

* * * * * * * *

God also used my interest in race relations that stemmed from Baylor days and that first story about the trailblazing black professor to impact Southern Baptists in my current assignment. I was delighted when some new products I supervised for the Christian Life Commission, including a brochure and a short film promoting better relations between white and black Americans, won several national media awards.

When these products were lauded by the Baptist Communications Association and the Religious Communications Council, I felt the Lord's confirmation that he could continue to use me in this task that He had given me in Nashville.

* * * * * * * *

Unfortunately as our life in Nashville was beginning to flourish, our wonderful pastor and friend Charles Page fell victim to Baptistdom's anger. To us, he preached solid, heartfelt sermons and was a splendid shepherd of the flock, but to the moderates at First Baptist, Nashville, Charles was a secret agent in the enemy force outside the walls. Decent and magnanimous, Charles refused to sanction or to join with the BSSB and other Baptistdom employees in their constant harangue against the Conservative Resurgence. (At that point Charles seldom spoke out publicly in support of the conservatives, though years later he would.)

Kay and I were sad when Charles' former congregation, First Baptist Church of Charlotte, NC, asked him to return to that pulpit and he accepted. Charles could hardly be blamed. Who would want to continue to face angry scowls and then receive ugly, anonymous letters while a hugely intimidating parade of whining Baptistdom bureaucrats marched into your office and demanded that you take up their cause?

Many of Charles' antagonists assumed that because of our friendship with the Pages, we would move our church membership elsewhere, too. We decided to stick around and see what would happen next. I've seen God pull some real zingers in situations in which Christians fail to act Christlike. And in running off Charles Page, Baptistdom had made a colossal blunder. God surely would not allow such grievous sin toward a good man to go unpunished. I just wondered how He would hold this church accountable for such an unconscionable act.

The church's Pastor Search Committee soon produced a new pastor candidate—Dan Francis, a graduate of my alma mater, Southern Seminary. No three-figure IQ was necessary to see that the church was looking for basically *anyone* with moderate credentials who would be different from Charles. Kay and I thought that Dan was a fine person and a substantive preacher. But listening to his testimony only one time convinced us that the search committee had stumbled badly.

The problem was that the church misperceived itself. And in so doing it badly misperceived Dan. The church and Dan never were a good match. This truly was a marriage made for the divorce courts.

Dan had become a Christian after some rough teen years that culminated in his witnessing the shooting death of his older brother, who was somewhat like a father figure to Dan. To his credit, Dan was transparent about his waywardness and his dramatic conversion. I grew to admire him for this honesty.

However, Kay and I just couldn't imagine how someone with his background—despite his polished appearance—would ever fit in emotionally with the blue-blood, correctness-oriented FBC Nashville/Baptistdom crowd.

Dan's honeymoon with the church was passionate; the congregation practically canonized its new pastor, largely because he was *anybody* but his predecessor. But predictably, before long, the bubble began to burst.

Baptistdom workers accustomed to maneuvering behind the scenes and guiding the church from their hip pockets were soon fuming that Dan wasn't listening to them. A great sense of apartness began to build. *He's no better than Charles Page*, they said under their breaths. Unfortunately some of our best friends at the church were among Dan's earliest critics.

Dan genuinely wanted to reach out to non-Christians—the very people that Baptistdom wanted to convince other churches that they should try to win to Christ. He could clearly identify with hard-core unbelievers outside the church because he, unlike most of the First Baptist, Nashville congregation, had once been one of them.

He started an unprecedented seekers church in First Baptist's fellowship hall in the basement below the gorgeous, stained-glass sanctuary. The "contemporary worship service" grew and grew and grew. The people who attended included some jeans-and-sandals-wearing new Christians—nothing like the buttoned-up bluebloods upstairs. And also unlike the upstairs Baptists they genuinely loved their pastor because he could relate.

Soon Dan and the contemporary worship service were gone. First Baptist Church, Nashville had suffered a major split of epic proportions! I believe the St. Peter's Basilica of Baptist life had known God's wrath for its earlier harm to an innocent pastor.

* * * * * * *

Its reluctance to embrace a seeker service is not atypical of the type of tradition-bound response that occurs in many "First" churches. Despite the denomination and the town, churches that have *First* in front of their names often are synonymous with resisting new ways.

In our 38 years of marriage Kay and I have now been members of five "First Baptist" churches in a variety of cities; in most cases we'd found great caches of hideboundness and lethargy that were impossible to shake. Oftentimes, the "First" may be the "Last" in terms of trying new ministries or embracing new ideas.

In one of our early Sundays as members of our current church, Sunnyvale First Baptist Church in the Dallas area, the pastor announced the number of decisions for Christ that had been made in the previous night's weekly service for ex-offenders.

Ex-offenders? Kay and I pinched ourselves and later commented to each other, "Are we sure we're in the right place?" In all our years we had never heard of a First Baptist Church, in its congregational worship, openly rejoice over the announced decisions of convicted felons. That kind of clientele typically doesn't cross paths with a "First Baptist" ministry. (No wonder, then, that African-American inmates are easily swayed to become Muslims, as we discussed earlier.)

We saw this in other denominations as well. When we arrived in Garland in 2001 and began promoting a marriage-enrichment program that Kay and I enjoyed as a side ministry, we tried to make an appointment with the pastor of First Methodist Church in our neighborhood. The secretary couldn't imagine why this church would be interested in such an outreach and why someone whose program hadn't been filtered through the Methodist conference office was approaching them. The pastor ultimately ended up canceling his appointment.

First Presbyterian Church of Houston was one of those congregations that always puzzled me. Situated in Houston's near-downtown corridor, it never seemed to be able to develop cutting-edge programs or ideas that captured the imaginations of Houstonians and led other churches to follow in its path. Yet the church plodded along with traditional ministries that stayed stable and strong.

This First/Last situation usually occurs because "First" churches are populated by families and individuals tied to the old guard in the community. A town's "First" church probably would be branded within its own denomination as conservative and most likely would not be on the forefront of new programs or reaching out to special-interest groups. To shake such a church loose from its decades-old patterns often requires a major disruption such as a scandalous pastor, a severe membership loss or a financial crisis, or a monumental event such as a fire, hurricane, or earthquake. In Houston this massive contemporizing occurred with Houston's First Baptist after its suburban move from its downtown location and a dynamic young pastor in John Bisagno.

* * * * * * * *

As we approached six years of living in Nashville, our son, Matthew, was graduating from high school and was determined to go to college at Baylor University in Waco—Kay's and my alma mater. As a child, Matthew had attended Baylor Camp for eight straight summers and was intimately familiar with the campus and its people. His bedroom was adorned in the school's green and gold, with Baylor memorabilia everywhere. Each year of our children's lives our family had made an annual fall trek back to Baylor Homecoming, with our kids dressed in specially chosen green-and-gold outfits. From the time Matthew was small, friends and Baylor alums Reg and Caroline Hancock from Houston had generously offered to help underwrite his and Katie's tuition there.

Although Kay and I had experienced some profound personal disappointments with Baylor people since we left Houston and had many ongoing hurts about Baylor alums' responses to us, we held fond memories of our own years at the school where we met. Although we had not forced our choice on our children, from before their births we had secretly hoped they also would grow up to be Baylor Bears and carry on the family tradition. When Matthew received his acceptance letter from Baylor, we were proud parents indeed.

Trouble was, this college choice, though inconsequential for some parents, likely would end up launching me and Kay into a real sticky wicket with our employers. The new conservative leadership was white-hot furious with Baylor—and, in some cases, with ample cause.

Conservatives could document many specific cases in which Baylor students were being given some harmful takes on theology—the same sort of historical critical approach that troubled me about Southern.

Early Conservative Resurgence focus initially led by Baylor alum Jimmy Draper had targeted the Baylor religion department, of which, naturally, I was a product. They were certain that any student entering in this era would embark on a path of serious spiritual depravity. I couldn't help but worry about this myself.

Their ire was multiplied in 1990 when Baylor President Herbert Reynolds, as the height of paranoia over the Conservative Resurgence, removed Baylor from Baptist control. Reynolds acted behind closed doors to rush through Baylor's Board of Trustees a secretly approved charter change which reduced the Texas convention's governance of Baylor and instead set up a mostly self-perpetuating Board of Regents.

Richard Land, my boss at the Christian Life Commission, repeatedly spoke critically against Baylor for its moderate leadings. I had accustomed myself to his barrage of opinions on just about everything, but the Baylor diatribes hit close to home. My Baylor-Southern credentials were a sore point with the conservatives. They had to swallow hard when they remembered these two hated institutions on my résumé. I knew they were already weary of having to explain me away.

But for me to consciously choose to send my children to Baylor, in the wake of the arm-wrestling trouble Baylor was making for the new ruling establishment in SBC life, would look like in-your-face defiance.

The flip side was this: would Herb Reynolds and his associates have a personal vendetta against my son because his dad worked in post-Resurgence Nashville? A Waco newspaper reporter had alerted me that, during a recent interview, Reynolds had disparaged me for my continued employment in Baptistdom. Still remembering the Baylor pie supper, I wondered whether some mean-spirited person would set a trap for Matthew as retribution for me.

This Catch-22 situation was agonizing. Any decision we made seemed shot through with land mines. To deny this privilege to our son who had Baylor Bear paws all over his heart struck deep at my parental conscience.

Kay and I began to pray earnestly that God would show us some way out of this tremendous personal wrenching. In whatever way we chose, both our professional and family lives were sorely at stake. The Bible says in Psalm 77:14, *You are the God who performs miracles*. We needed one.

Chapter 22

World Apart

Truth No. 22: If you clothe yourself in the Language of Zion, you may not be fully dressed.

In my dreams I still envisioned one day becoming an independent, self-employed journalist/publisher. Doing something of this nature would let me be my own boss. My children could attend college wherever they chose; I would not need to concern myself with supervisors' possible retributions. Unfortunately I did not have the wherewiths to start a company from scratch right then. I was only beginning to learn the how-to pragmatics of accomplishing this goal. Kay and I calibrated, however, that we approached a window of time in which we could entertain other employment possibilities apart from Nashville Baptistdom.

Besides the natural break that Matthew's high-school graduation afforded us, our daughter, Katie, had her teen years ahead of her. Relocating now would not be as dreadful for her as it would a few years hence. Kay's dad had succumbed to Alzheimer's and died just before Matthew's senior year. Her mother, 82, had regrouped with her health intact and was still living independently. For the time being, things were stabilized for her in Texas, so we felt the freedom to move where the Lord might lead. We sensed the Lord was about to do *a new thing* (Isa. 43:19) in our lives; we waited for Him to direct us.

About that time I learned that the Foreign Mission Board was seeking a journalist to fill in a one-year vacancy in its

East Africa bureau based in Kenya. I talked at length with Robert O'Brien, who supervised the overseas correspondents, about the possibility of moving to Nairobi to fill in for some missionaries on a year's stint. Our daughter, Katie, then 12, was intrigued with the idea of living overseas temporarily. This relocation would get us off the hot seat for a while as Matthew transitioned to college and would make his attending Baylor highly possible, without my having to deal with the fallout. I, of course, remembered my long-ago calling to missions and wondered whether working as an overseas journalist might be God's way of tapping into that earlier commitment.

As the idea took root in our minds, we started buying maps and books about Kenya and Africa.

Suddenly, this concept took an unusual twist. I received a call from a search committee seeking a new vice president for communications for the Foreign Mission Board. The vice president would manage that organization's massive media office, the largest of any Christian institution or denomination in the country. I knew about the opening but had concluded that I would be snubbed because of the Baptist Press fiasco. This was a high-profile job. I figured the moderates who pitched such a hissy fit about my being at Baptist Press would throw an equally ridiculous temper tantrum about my going to Richmond. I was just not up for more Southern Baptist political infighting. I'd had enough of that in the Nashville Baptist milieu. Africa seemed like a much better place to be.

God apparently had other plans. In early August 1994 I picked up my phone in my Christian Life Commission office and heard Jerry Rankin, the Foreign Mission Board's new president, on the other end. He invited me to be one of five people to be interviewed by a staff-trustee committee looking for the new vice president. The interview was scheduled in Atlanta the week after we were to deliver Matthew to Baylor to begin his freshman year there.

Since I had my eyes on Nairobi, I figured talking with this group would be a great way to learn more about the Foreign Mission Board. I could not imagine that I would be chosen for the position. I did only the minimal preparation for the interview.

Just before the interview with the staff-trustee committee, Robert O'Brien called to tell me that he had looked up the rules and that the Foreign Mission Board could not appoint me to Nairobi because Katie would be 13 before we could complete the appointment process. He said the Board had a firm policy about not appointing missionaries with teen-age children. I thought that was an awfully strange rule. *Why could we be appointed when she was 12 years and 10 months but not when she was 13 years and two months?* That would not be the last time I would puzzle over some of the Foreign Mission Board's odd policies. But the Kenya possibility, at least, was jettisoned.

Several days after the Atlanta meeting, Jerry Rankin called to tell me exactly what I had presumed—that I was not chosen for the vice president's job. He said, however, that he was impressed by my interview and wanted to talk with me further. He said the second-in-command position in the office also was open and that he intended to talk with the new vice president about hiring me for that role. Jerry would be in Nashville the next Sunday evening and would take Kay and me to dinner at a downtown restaurant.

Our interview with Jerry was pleasant. I was intrigued by the fact that Jerry's two children were Baylor graduates, so he was not the least bit concerned that I had a son there. Hearing Jerry's vision for reaching the world for Christ was exhilarating. He described the job in the Communications Office with such enthusiasm that Kay and I left the restaurant believing

God already was speaking to us about moving to Richmond, VA, where the FMB was headquartered.

A few weeks later, Jerry was back in Nashville on business. He invited Kay and me to his hotel room to meet David Button, the soon-to-be new communications vice president, and his wife, Denice. The meeting was cordial. David had owned several radio stations around the country and lived in upstate New York, where he not only owned a local radio station but also was mayor of the city where he lived. David was also a trustee for the SBC Executive Committee.

The more David and Jerry talked, the more I could see our talents and gifts meshing well. David signaled that he wanted me on board as the associate vice president.

Kay and I noticed immediately that Jerry seemed to be the one in charge, not only with the vision for the Foreign Mission Board but also for how David and I would do our jobs. Jerry conducted the rest of the negotiations about our move to Richmond. Even though he would be my new boss, David was seldom the one later contacting me about the move; I usually heard only through Jerry.

One strange episode occurring during that period gave my first major glimpse into Jerry's administrative style. He initially quoted a salary which would have meant about a $20,000 raise from what I was earning at the Christian Life Commission. That was not an overwhelming amount but was sufficient for us to make the move. The raise was to be about half of Kay's salary at the Baptist Sunday School Board at that time. We believed we could move to Richmond and adjust to my salary alone if Kay determined that she wanted to return to freelance writing and editing. Kay believed that if she moved, some of her projects on which she had worked as LIFE Support design editor could continue on a contract basis.

We planned our budget based on the proposed increase in

my salary and the possible loss of Kay's considerable income.

When we arrived in Richmond for the Board of Trustees meeting at which David and I were to be introduced, Jerry pulled me aside and began apologizing for a mistake he had made. The error: my salary would be $5,000 less than I was making in Nashville, not an increase of $20,000. However, he said he was sure everything would be OK, since God's will clearly was for us to move.

Kay and I were stunned. Surely this was not as it appeared—an aberrant bait-and-switch game! We hoped that what we encountered was simply an honest mistake. After all, we were dealing with the top level of Southern Baptists' largest and most trusted agency.

We were so captivated by the new position in Richmond and had such a strong sense that God was orchestrating this move that we swallowed hard and then told Jerry that the mistake about the money would not deter us from moving to Richmond to accept the position.

We arrived in Richmond the end of November 1994 to begin my new job. Within a few days I became aware of another meeting in Jerry's office that had involved David Button and his wife, Denice. During that meeting Jerry unveiled David's salary. David later disclosed that his wife left the meeting in tears. The same sort of switcheroo apparently had been pulled on the Buttons, but Jerry said he was sure God wanted them there. I had a difficult time figuring out how Jerry could make such puzzling mistakes as offering people salaries that later were found not to be applicable.

By December 1, Kay and I had already quit our jobs in Nashville, sold our home, and had moved our family to Richmond. Matthew was now at Baylor; the FMB seemed to be a world apart from some of the shenanigans that had occurred in Nashville Baptistdom and not as hyped up with conservative concerns about such matters, so this was a true benefit of living away from the denomination's headquarters in a somewhat insular situation. We believed that with this FMB appointment our prayers of concern about Baylor were answered.

The Buttons, on the other hand, were still in the process of selling their home, their radio station, and making the full move to Richmond. David brought one son with him to an apartment in Richmond, but Denice stayed behind in New York with other children to oversee the sales and move. Five years later the Buttons still owned their home in New York and had only finally found a buyer for their radio station. Though they made regular visits to Richmond, Denice and the Button family members never moved totally and completely to Richmond.

I saw no discord in the Button home that would account for the unusual living arrangements. I attributed the situation totally to the odd way Jerry had dealt with David's and my salaries as well as other administrative matters.

By spring 1995 I became aware of additional tension that was building between Jerry and David. One afternoon late Jerry summoned me to his office for a brief chat. He shared, "David has never had a boss. I'm going to have to teach him what having a boss means." (David apparently had always been a highly successful entrepreneur.) Jerry then went on to advise me to be very careful in my interactions with David and to stay out of the way of any conflicts that occurred between the two of them. He also told me not to mention anything about our conversation to David. Thus, the curtain of how the SBC's largest, wealthiest, and most respected agency operated at the top began to be pulled back even further.

I left the meeting shaking my head and wondering what was going to happen.

On the drawing board was a book that the IMB was supposed to produce about Lottie Moon, the legendary 19th-century missionary to China for whom the annual Southern Baptist Lottie Moon Christmas Offering was named. That offering raises a sizable portion of the Foreign Mission Board's (now International Mission Board's) annual budget. David was supposed to help Jerry write the book and manage the marketing surrounding it, while I was to be the nuts-and-bolts editor and shepherd the book to publication.

Jerry and David soon seemed to disagree over many, many things involving the book. The ensuing tension was very uncomfortable. I observed that Jerry did not like to be edited and wasn't fond of suggestions or feedback. When he got an idea in his head, nothing seemed to be able to alter his plan. All this, however, was couched in the "Language of Zion"—terms that invoke God's will, talk of "spiritual warfare", and other spiritual expressions. I never doubted Jerry's sincerity in using such terminology to explain his desires, but I often wondered whether he truly could differentiate between hearing God's voice speaking to him and his own inner desires/feelings/thoughts. In the dealings between the two men, I also observed David could be very persistent, too. These two men reminded me of the proverbial Unmovable Object and the Unstoppable Force on a collision course. *Which is going to win?* I wondered.

Simultaneously, the editor of *Commission* magazine, the Foreign Mission Board's flagship publication, decided to retire. Jerry told me to look for a new editor but that meantime, I was to be the acting editor. Since my teen-age years I had read *Commission* magazine; I was thrilled at the assignment. However, I never got to function fully as acting editor. Jerry and David had conflicting ideas about what needed to occur with the magazine. Often both went to staff and lobbied for whatever they wanted without ever informing or consulting me. I felt caught in the crossfire between the two men, so I concentrated on finding a new editor quickly. I chose FMB staffer Mary Jane Welch as the editor because I perceived that she was professional and emotionally equipped to deal with a lot of interference from superiors.

Soon Jerry made an announcement that solidified the situation. He told trustees that he had realized that as president one of his primary roles was that of being the organization's "chief public-relations officer". He sounded to me and to others as though he was saying that he saw himself as doing David's job as well as mine besides his own.

Thus, the stage was set for a new kind of tension and heavy ballast that would permeate our lives for the rest of the 1990s.

Now the guy who had "never had a boss" had to deal with a boss who not only was determined to be the boss but who also saw himself as performing his underlings' roles. Learning to swim amid the tension these undercurrents created was per-haps my greatest career challenge ever—not unlike the typical pitfalls that middle managers face in the secular world.

One of Jerry's credos was that he wanted to "flatten the organization." I thought that sounded noble and idealistic until I realized that this was a president whose style was that of micromanagement—again, not unlike some top bosses in the business world. Jerry wanted to have a heavy influence on even the smallest details of the organization.

By 1997 I was already wearying of the constant battles in the executive offices at the Foreign Mission Board. These bat-tles were different than anything I had ever seen before—once again, a world apart—and I thought I had seen everything pre-viously. I was also very worried that I would become caught in the squeeze between the two warring parties immediately above me in rank.

278

At the same time, I loved my job—at least what it was designed to be. Ever since my high-school days, I have held international missionaries in high esteem. I admire their ability to live in a world and a culture far different from their own. I admire their ability to master another language. I admire their commitment to God, which propels them to take risks and lead lives far different than the average Christian does. I find missionaries—both male and female—fascinating people though living a world away from U.S. life—figuratively and literally.

I especially liked the world scope of the now-International Mission Board. In my job I traveled frequently overseas to Africa, South America, Asia, and other places. I was working to expand the Overseas Correspondent System to include videographers and photographers—it previously had been only for writers—and to base the overseas correspondents in a truly worldwide pattern. I enjoyed managing the large staff and especially enjoyed seeing how missionaries were pushing back the darkness in areas of spiritual blight all over the world.

I also found traits to admire and appreciate about both David and Jerry. Despite their bickering, I learned much from both men—things I don't believe I could have learned in any other setting. From David I learned what living as an entrepreneur truly means. David was in so many ways the consummate entrepreneur. He understood the fine art of small-business management and could flex his schedule and priorities easily to accommodate the moment—key elements for any successful small businessperson. From Jerry I learned what is required to be a truly successful church bureaucrat. Jerry was a consummate one. The FMB presidency was a job that no average missionary brought in from the field could tackle; it required someone with the special administrative shrewdness that Jerry possessed. While publicly disdaining church bureaucracy, he knew the fine art of committees, structures, and organization and had an uncanny ability to achieve long-term goals through other people. God's name was always involved, of course.

Baptists were not the only church leaders I heard invoke God's name, only later to find that the Language of Zion (pietistic talk) never left them "fully dressed." When I first arrived in Houston, the *Chronicle*'s religion section carried weekly columns by two local religious leaders—a rabbi and the pastor of First United Methodist Church of Houston, Charles L. Allen.

In my first meeting with Allen, I told him I received numerous complaints from other local clergy who believed the *Chronicle* was unfairly giving his church free publicity in running his column. He grew highly defensive and told me how he was more important than was any other local clergyman, because of the popularity of his books and his pulpit, from which he spread God's Word.

He then intimated to me that he was God's anointed to carry out this column-writing function. He threatened that if I ever tried to cancel his column, he would go over my head and get me fired.

Eventually the *Chronicle* management and I opted jointly to cancel both clergy columns. I was grateful to Dr. Allen for early on letting me in on his political style, so that when the time eventually arrived to make a change, I had all my bases covered. I pulled this off without much community backlash, which led me to believe that he had less support for his column than he intimated.

When Bishop Finis A. Crutchfield arrived as the new head of the Houston-based Texas Methodist Conference, he immediately told his staff members in the Methodist Building that they were not to talk to newspaper reporters without his permission. Naturally, several of my best sources in the building dutifully called to tell me about the strange mandate.

When I called to interview the bishop, I received vague excuses why he never seemed to be available. These were always presented in holy language—that he was out about the Lord's work, or something that sounded like a platitude.

Eventually the bishop took a different tack and agreed to interviews; he always ended them by heaping enormous praise on my work. This about-face puzzled me as much as did his initial behavior.

Years later when Crutchfield died of AIDS and his double-lifestyle was revealed, I saw that his reputation left him "dis-robed" before the entire community. I saw clearly why he tried to manipulate me and the other media around him.

* * * * * * * *

In terms of my own two bosses, I determined that I could learn from both men and not fall victim to their conflict. That never was an easy task.

David was impromptu, energetic, boisterous, and fearless about trying things new and different. Jerry, on the other hand, was organized, structured, strategic, headstrong, visionary, a master at scalpel-sharp rejoinders, and the type of leader who did not easily bring himself to say, "I made a mistake," mean it, and change.

That last characteristic turned out to be a detriment to Jerry, at least with his supervising board.

Leaders, like the rest of us, make mistakes. Church leaders often find admitting their foibles more difficult than do secular leaders, even though they preach a "we're-all-sinners-saved-by-grace" theology. After a lifetime of observing top religious leaders in various denominations, I believe the most successful are both self-focused and prone to make others the fall guys rather than to admit in certain instances their own personal shortcomings.

Elected by a strong majority of FMB trustees, Jerry at first seemed to deal well with trustees who voted against him. When I first met Jerry, I was truly impressed with his spirit of reconciliation with those who publicly opposed him. This honeymoon was short-lived and ended abruptly over what to many seemed like unnecessary and unimportant issues. Some of the more conservative trustees worried that the FMB's home office in Richmond was overly influenced by Virginia Baptists' more moderate theological positions on just about everything. To their credit, I must quickly say Virginia Baptist moderates are more honest, forthright, and transparent than are Texas Baptist moderates or moderate Baptists in other states about where they stand and what they believe.

For instance, when our family was looking for a new church home in Richmond, we visited a church one Sunday morning and opted not to return because a Sunday-school teacher in the church's youth department taught that Jesus was not the only way to heaven. We appreciated the person's honesty, but we didn't want our teen exposed to such theology. A basic tenet in our beliefs is that Jesus is *the way, the truth, and the life* (John 14:6) and that no entry to heaven exists apart from Him. Regrettably, our experience at that church was what we found too often among Virginia Baptists.

Nevertheless, Jerry masterfully put an end to the "Move-the-Board-out-of-Virginia" effort by leading the trustees to set up a committee to study the matter. Jerry then maneuvered two strong moderates (Carl Johnson and Don Kammerdiener) on his top staff onto the committee. They produced a report showing how disruptive and expensive the Board's making such a move would be. Trustees, who flinched at the costs, concurred with the findings; the matter was laid to rest.

Shortly after that Jerry launched a massive overhaul of the FMB's office on Monument Avenue in Richmond and then later a major renovation and expansion of its Missionary Learning Center in Rockville, VA.

What trustees thought was going to be an expenditure of a few-million dollars eventually turned into a total cost somewhere around $40 million—far more than the originally estimated cost of selling the Board's property in Virginia and relocating to Texas, Oklahoma, or another more conservative state.

As the cost was nearing $10 million, some trustees began questioning why they were being asked to appropriate funds piecemeal and wanted a full accounting of how much had already been spent on the renovations and what the full anticipated cost was going to be. Questions eventually arose over nearly $1 million in renovation contracts that had been signed by the administration without trustee authorization.

Once the issue bubbled to the surface, trustee anger flared dramatically. The honeymoon was over. Staff wondered whether this could result in a new president for the FMB.

One day while the cauldron churned, I was walking down the hall near Jerry's office. Suddenly I encountered Carl Johnson, the FMB's highly respected vice president for finance. A skilled businessman as well as church bureaucrat, Carl was somebody I admired greatly. An eloquent and polished Virginia gentleman in every sense of the words, he had a remarkable command of FMB finances, history, and polity.

On that morning Carl pulled me into a nearby conference room. Ashen and visibly distressed, he began querying me about how he could retire early and quickly from the FMB without attracting ugly, negative publicity. We discussed various ways this could be presented, but I kept saying, "But I don't understand why you would want to do this." I reminded Carl that while many conservative trustees perceived him as a moderate, his masterful skills as a businessperson had earned him much respect within the SBC and among trustees. I reminded him that trustees, who generally held moderates in low esteem, were high on him personally.

I left our encounter dazed by what had been said. Only later did I piece things together and begin to wonder whether Carl thought he might be blamed for what one legally minded trustee called a "misappropriation of funds." I wondered, though I was never absolutely certain, whether Carl suspected he might be put in a position of being the sacrificial lamb whose departure would get Jerry off the hook with his board.

Would Jerry really allow one of his vice presidents to be sacrificed in this manner? My perspective on this probably was because I was accustomed to the *Chronicle*'s Don Pickels, an Episcopalian, whom I knew would rather be fired himself than have one of his reporters' reputations soiled in a political intrigue. Nevertheless, the ill will caused by the renovations and their ever-escalating costs caused convulsions among a strong minority of the trustees. Their trust violated, they began to question everything Jerry did. Instead of responding with openness and transparency, Jerry turned to the age-old political tactic of circling the wagons and hunkering down for a fight. Trustees who questioned him were seen as challengers to his authority and as threats to peace. Such an attitude only made things worse.

Because Jerry kept a firm grip on news coverage emerging from the IMB and because Southern Baptist media generally like Jerry, most Southern Baptists never knew about the inception of the early turmoil surrounding Jerry's presidency.

Later, when Paige Patterson began to question Jerry's leadership, moderates and some conservatives attributed to Paige some kind of evil motive. They never acknowledged when or how the issue really began.

I firmly believe had Jerry offered a genuine, heartfelt apology, moved to tender his resignation, and refused to let his staff take any hits, trustees would have forgiven him, insisted that he remain in office, and pulled together to support his presidency. Instead his stubborn resistance gave way to almost a decade of internecine warfare that still flares up today.

While this was one side of Jerry's presidency, some stellar accomplishments occurred and emerged from his leadership.

When I was at the *Houston Chronicle* and had traveled in 1985 to the Soviet Union as the only Christian in a group of American Jews, I was amazed how many Jewish and Christian organizations were at work in that country, but I was equally appalled how little Southern Baptists were doing there. The Foreign Mission Board as well as the Southern Baptist Convention had literally abandoned Christians in the Soviet Union as well as China. This seemed strange to me, since the SBC was so anti-communist. During the late 1980s when Christians could more safely work in that area, Southern Baptists did begin, so to speak, "to put a toe in the water" in the Soviet Union. But the real push in that region began after the Soviet Union ceased to exist in 1991, when being there was easier and far less hazardous. The Foreign Mission Board and Jerry Rankin instigated that push.

Once again God allowed me to be an eyewitness to a major religious development—the refocusing of Southern Baptist evangelism on about a third of the world that Baptists had ignored far too long.

I was gaining much from learning about missions and missionaries. But I also kept a sharp eye on what my ultimate future in this missions organization would be.

Chapter 23

When the Wind Blows

Truth No. 23: Fingers licked and in the wind, church bureaucracies (like political organizations) go the direction in which the public outcry is the least. Bible principles are not always the guiding force.

On the surface, the International Mission Board (which in 1997 changed its name from the FMB) appears to be one of the most spiritual, most conservative, and most evangelistic business operations on the face of the earth. After all, the organization's stated purpose is to send out as many men and women as possible as missionaries to convert the pagan-atheistic-Muslim-Hindu-Buddhist-Jewish-Roman Catholic world to the Baptist view of Christianity.

Yet from the day I arrived in Richmond, I found the place a puzzling enigma. In some instances the principled mission board seemed to operate on the basis of which way the wind blew rather than asking that popular question—"WWJD?" (What would Jesus do?).

People on the IMB staff know missions inside, outside, and backward. They talk the language. They know the material and espouse the cause eloquently. And well they should. Southern Baptists give the IMB through the Lottie Moon Christmas Offering and the Cooperative Program around $300 million annually to do its job. Also the IMB has about $300 million in liquid assets and about another half-billion dollars in real estate situated in countries around the world. (This real estate consists of office buildings, houses, and apartments, most of which are used by Southern Baptist missionaries. But in some cases, these are investment properties used to generate income for the IMB.) The IMB is the best-funded and largest mission board in the United States and possibly the whole world.

This convert-the-world-to-Christ attitude mixed with great wealth creates some interesting situations.

Significant hunks of money are used each year to buy thousands of airplane tickets and to rent tens of thousands of hotel rooms for missionaries and staff to crisscross the world on IMB business. The IMB thinks nothing of flying in dozens, sometimes hundreds, of staff and missionaries for special meetings and events held all over the world. I was always amazed how many staff members needed to attend, at IMB expense, the annual Southern Baptist Convention or get-togethers with Woman's Missionary Union in Birmingham, AL, or joint sessions with the North American Mission Board in Atlanta, GA.

Because my office had staff traveling overseas for as many as six to eight weeks at one time, I soon faced a most perplex-ing situation that, before I moved to Richmond, I could not have imagined. This pertained to a practice of male and female staff members (reporters, photographers, videographers, etc.) traveling in groups of two on some of these extended trips overseas.

At first I didn't connect the dots. Then missionaries began mentioning to me how odd they felt having to entertain a man and a woman—not married to each other—from my office vis-iting them on the mission field for extended periods of time. One day the wife of one of my male employees told me she was greatly discomfited over the fact that her husband traveled overseas for lengthy time blocks—anywhere from three to six weeks—with female staff members in my office. The wife said she trusted her husband but thought the IMB ought to be more sensitive to the fact that people are people, men are men, women are women, and that problems sometimes do arise when people flirt with the lure of fallen humanity.

Kay and I had seen heartbreaking situations in Nashville's Baptistdom in which males and females traveling together as unmarried duos on official Convention business ultimately had adulterous liaisons and divorces. I was concerned that such a scandal could develop in my office from this odious practice.

One day I raised the issue in staff meeting. Almost as one monolith my directors rose up in opposition to my even breathing a cautionary word about the subject. I dropped the matter for the time being.

Some time later, when I met with Jerry Rankin, Don Kammerdiener, and Avery Willis (Vice President for Overseas Operations) to discuss the overhaul and expansion of the Overseas Correspondent System, I was surprised to hear Don address the subject forthright. He said over time numerous missionaries had raised the mixed-gender travel issue with the administration. He said the Communications Office was the only entity at the IMB in which males and females traveled together in pairs (one male and one female) on extended trips overseas. Jerry and Avery joined Don in expressing dismay that the policy was continuing.

They said the time had arrived to get tough. As a condition for approving my plan to overhaul and expand the Overseas Correspondents System, they directed that I must institute a policy eliminating male and female staff members from traveling together overseas in groups of two. I agreed to their plan, since I already believed the situation was fertile ground for serious problems to develop.

When I reported this conversation to them, my department directors went ballistic. Instead of supporting the policy, several directors launched an all-out campaign to reverse the new policy. They questioned it at every turn. They set up scenarios to prompt my having to approve exceptions to the policy.

Much to my surprise, Jerry, Don, and Avery ducked the issue in public. They let me take the heat publicly and offered little support privately. They also failed to clue in David Button, my immediate supervisor who had not been in the meeting when the ultimatum was handed down. David heard the angry outcry in my office and at first questioned me for creating the new policy. After I explained that Jerry, Don, and Avery had demanded it as a precondition for approving the revitalized Overseas Correspondents System, he backed off but didn't publicly support me in the situation.

Again I was reminded that Baptist bureaucracies operate much like political organizations. Fingers licked and in the wind, they go the direction in which the public outcry is the least. In such circumstances Bible principles are not always the guiding force.

* * * * * * * *

A similar situation involved the religious affiliations of IMB staff members.

Publicly the IMB stands for converting anyone—Roman Catholics, Episcopalians, United Methodists, and the like— who don't adhere to "Baptistic" doctrines. Some in the organization are particularly loath to acknowledge that Roman Catholics, for instance, could possibly be Christians and bound for heaven.

But when the issue of staff hiring arose, the IMB seemed to go in a different direction. Whereas in Nashville's Baptistdom I seldom encountered a non-Southern Baptist working there, in Richmond's version of Baptistdom I found just the opposite.

My first week at the IMB, the librarian in our office requested a meeting. She said she wanted to be sure that I knew that she was an Episcopalian. She said she had always tried not to let that be a factor in her work at the IMB. She even invited Kay and me to join her and her husband for an evening at their local Episcopal church. Throughout my tenure at the IMB I truly admired this staffer's honesty and integrity. She was upfront, honest, and the model of professional decorum. But I did find the fact that she was a long-term IMB veteran rather odd, given the official SBC attitude of suspicion about the Episcopal Church and its liberal leanings.

The librarian said I would be surprised how many of my staff members were not affiliated with the SBC. Professionally discreet, she did not point fingers. However, I deduced just after our conversation that the main curator for the IMB was a Roman Catholic. I thought truly novel the fact that the person charged with collecting historic data and objects associated with Lottie Moon, the patron saint of Southern Baptist missions, and other SBC international missionary efforts was herself a card-carrying Roman Catholic.

I already knew that I faced a problem with a sizable number in my office being affiliated with Southern Baptist churches associated with the breakaway Cooperative Baptist Fellowship. Now I was left wondering how many—and who— were the non-Southern Baptists.

Within weeks I was thrown into an impossible dilemma on this very subject. Just after my arrival at the IMB, the longtime editor of *The Commission* magazine, the IMB's award-winning publication, announced his retirement. I set about looking for a replacement for him. I didn't take long to spot what I thought was the obvious solution.

At the top of my list was a man who was the graphic designer for the magazine. He seemed to already run the publication anyway and truly was the "brains" behind the outfit. I decided I would "make the covert overt" rather than to bring in a new editor who might engage in a power struggle with this designer.

Just before I went to Jerry, Don, and David with my recommendation, the designer asked for a meeting. In it, he followed the librarian's choreography. He said he just wanted to be sure that I knew he was not a Southern Baptist but that he was a United Methodist. Again, I was stunned. I had been within a few hours of nominating this designer for one of the key public posts at the IMB. With this new information in hand, I was certain that nominating a United Methodist to be the editor of one of Southern Baptists' flagship publications would not fly, particularly with the IMB's trustees. Had I realized then what I know now—what a great job the IMB management does at keeping its trustees in the dark about such matters—I would not have worried. Instead I could envision being roasted by astute trustees who believed only a Southern Baptist should head the IMB's flagship publication.

Over the years, I learned about other non-Southern Baptists in key positions in my office: a graphic designer who was a member of a Disciples of Christ congregation and a department manager who was a member of an independent Baptist church, as well as several others.

The biggest surprise of all was the Unitarian-Universalist fellow who was one of my senior graphic designers. After I had been on the staff of the IMB for nearly four years, I learned totally by accident that this man was a vocal and dedicated Unitarian-Universalist and was, in fact, quite antagonistic toward Southern Baptists.

I later learned that all of my directors were aware of the

Unitarian-Universalist on the staff. Each claimed that he/she thought another director had already informed me about the situation. To each of them, it was no big deal: the man was a good artist; his religious beliefs were his own private business.

I had no personal dislike for any of the non-Southern Baptists. In fact, I personally was fond of all of them. I just found the dichotomy between life in Nashville's Baptistdom and Richmond's Baptistdom to be truly amazing. Nashville's Baptistdom hardly seemed to know that other denominations existed beyond the SBC's borders. On the other hand, Richmond's Baptistdom seemed to go in an entirely different direction—embracing whoever was thought to do a job best without any regard to religious affiliation or belief.

I never discovered any Jews, Muslims, Hindus, or Buddhists on the IMB staff, though I would not be able to swear under oath that none worked there.

The IMB staff's rationale for this unusual twist was that no qualified Southern Baptists had ever applied for those jobs, so they went to people of other denominational affiliations. I was amazed that Richmond's bureaucrats couldn't find capable Southern Baptists to fill those jobs. After all, the SBC claims to be the largest Protestant denomination (nearly 16-million strong) in the United States.

I found the staff's attitude interesting, however, when I did interview (and eventually hire) a tried-and-true-blue SBC conservative from Southeastern Baptist Theological Seminary. Though this man truly was a gifted graphic designer, several staff members initially opposed my hiring the Southeastern grad. They claimed the fellow with the impeccable Baptist credentials was not the same calibre of artist as the Unitarian-Universalist or the United Methodist. (The Southern Baptist later proved to be the best artist on the staff.)

When I mentioned to Don Kammerdiener and Jerry Rankin

my surprise at the religious affiliation of some of my staff, they once again sidestepped the issue. Don's response was a noncommittal, "Well, I'm glad I can tell the trustees they were hired before I became executive vice president." Jerry said he hoped I would be smart enough to get rid of the non-Southern Baptists without tipping my hand to anyone that the real reason for their dismissal was their denominational affiliation (a matter that might have been tested in court). For the record, when I left the IMB in 2001, all of the non-Southern Baptists were still on the staff!

* * * * * * * *

The wind direction again was tested over one of my department's prized products—sets of spiffy, full-color leaflets that promote missions as they are inserted into the Sunday bulletins in Southern Baptist churches. The upgrade and wider distribution of bulletin inserts such as these had been one of my greatest successes at the Christian Life Commission, as we promoted race relations, sanctity of human life, and other themes. Jerry wanted the IMB to generate similar products promoting international missions. Again, God blessed our efforts far beyond our greatest desires. I was amazed at how many copies of these leaflets we printed and distributed.

The North American Mission Board (NAMB), which focuses on home missions while the IMB focuses on overseas missions, wanted to partner with the IMB in the popular bulletin-insert program. The home board wanted its programs to be promoted on the same leaflet as ours were.

In no uncertain terms Jerry told me that he did not want this to happen. He directed me to oppose any NAMB efforts to partner. About 50 IMB staffers were soon to fly to Atlanta for a multi-day meeting with the NAMB staff. Jerry told me that if the subject cropped up at this conference, to insist that we were unalterably opposed to it.

I did as Jerry directed. In the context of the Atlanta meeting, this was not a popular position to take. I could hardly believe my ears when, seeing the winds blowing a different direction, Jerry later and without proper explanation changed course and started talking cooperation on our prized project. I ended up looking like the lone naysayer, with Jerry looking like the olive-branch-bearing dove who swooped in to resolve the debate.

I knew that the Bible speaks to equivocating. In Ephesians 4:14 the Bible speaks of people who are *tossed back and forth by the waves, and blown here and there by every wind.* In 1 Kings 18:21, when Elijah was on Mt. Carmel, he *went before the people and said, "How long will you waver between two opinions?"*

The Baptist missions organization wasn't the only place in which I was aware of church leaders who seemed to take a read on popular appeal before they made a decision.

One of my all-time favorite books is Charles Merrill Smith's *How to Be a Bishop without Being Religious.* A Christian bestseller in the 1960s, the book was a spoof on Methodist elections of bishops based more on images created by clothes (dark colors and loosely fitting), cars (small with dark colors and very non-sporty and traditional), and wives (neither shapely nor beautiful) than on faith in God and spiritual gifts. Smith paints the picture of clergy leadership more prone to testing the wind direction than on commitment and dedication to theological principles.

When I worked at the Christian Life Commission, my colleagues who had spent much time around W.A. Criswell described the legendary Dallas pastor, though he had strong theological beliefs, as commonly setting up others to do uncomfortable tasks, such as staff dismissals or carrying out controversial matters with monied church members. He was by far not the only one who operated in that way. Much wavering *between two opinions* went on.

* * * * * * * *

These puzzling developments did not detract from the awe I continued to feel at being an eyewitness to history over and over again in my job at the IMB. In 1999 I traveled to China, to learn more about the cutting edge of missions today— "secret" Southern Baptist workers operating throughout that economically expanding country. I went to study the unregistered house churches promoted by them. These churches trouble the communist government.

This practice is a result of China's refusal to allow missionaries to operate legally within its borders. Missions organizations send their workers as business people, doctors, teachers, tourists, and other legal professionals—what missions organizations call their "platforms." While some people believe this is deceptive, missions organizations argue that they are pursuing a higher good that overlooks the spin they put on this practice.

While in China, I visited not only with some of these "secret" workers but also attended worship services of some house churches. I saw for myself firsthand how all this fascinating, clandestine system operates. While this may be one of the biggest and most important religion stories in the world today and is widely known in Evangelical church circles, few secular newspaper reporters are even aware of its existence and the extent of the practice throughout not only China but also the Middle East and other places where missionaries are not welcome.

* * * * * * *

As awesome as trips such as this were, and as thrilled as I was to be a witness to the truth of God's work in the world, I continued to wonder whether my job situation in Richmond was one that I wanted to be a part of for the rest of my professional life.

The time had arrived that I needed to be my own boss. I wasn't sure how I would manage that, but I believed God knew my need. I shouldn't have been surprised at how He showed up.

Chapter 24

Better Than Sacrifice

Truth No. 24: For an institution that's supposed to promote family values, the church sometimes creates major impediments to family ties.

A call from Kay's widowed mother while I was in Dallas for an IMB meeting in 1998 set in motion a multi-layered, many-staged process that showed us how God was revealing where He wanted us to serve Him next.

Kay's mother, by then 87, wanted me to have lunch with her. I could tell she had something major on her mind.

Mable was pondering what to do with the family home in Garland when she no longer could live alone and needed to move to a retirement community. She wondered whether she should sell it, since we now lived in faraway Virginia.

I didn't have to call Kay back in Richmond to ask how I should answer.

From our early marriage, I heard Kay's lore about how her parents built her growing-up home, which sat on a huge tract in what was now the Historic Downtown Garland District. Determined that this dwelling would withstand the shrink-swell of North Texas soil, her dad had the foundation dug to 11- to 16-feet underground, down to solid bedrock. (I used this example in my eulogy at J.D.'s funeral, as I compared his faith in Jesus to the bedrock on which he built his home.)

Kay also described the workers her father hired—how he inspected their work daily and sometimes personally ripped out boards that were faultily nailed. He had hand-picked every stone for its great, curved fireplace, which for more than 20 Christmases served as the hearth where Santa delivered presents for our children.

I told Mable that Kay and I had always hoped we could live there in retirement and couldn't abide the thought of this very special residence being sold. That was all the green light Mable needed. She announced plans to call her attorney and deed to us the house on Garland's 11th Street. Although at that moment she wasn't ready to move out, the house now would be our responsibility. She could relocate to a retirement center when the time arose and could believe that the memory-rich family home was in loving hands.

This event served as a wake-up call to us that our loved ones back in Texas were not getting any younger. Kay's mom was moving toward 90. Her Aunt Frances, her mother's older sister who had no children of her own, had already reached the 90 milestone. Uncle Buford, her dad's surviving brother who also was childless, was approaching 100. My widowed mother was nearing the 90-and-above category, too. Although she now lived in the Tulsa area near my sister and we now were not directly responsible for her care, I knew that her time on this Earth was growing shorter. God had blessed these four remarkable family members with long lives and had blessed us through them, but common sense reminded us that they would not be around forever. Suddenly we began viewing the world with a different set of glasses.

The Lord had kept our loved ones safe while we made necessary transitions to Nashville and then farther east to Richmond, but we were convicted that we needed to do our part. A new call to ministry for us was taking shape.

This posed a dilemma, since those who worked where I did were regularly in the position of ENCOURAGING people to

298

leave family members and forsake all to serve on overseas mission fields. They adhered to the verse, *"If anyone comes to me and does not hate* [give lesser priority to] *father and mother, wife and children, brothers and sisters–yes, even life itself–such a person cannot be my disciple"* (Luke 14:26). To prepare to serve cross-culturally, missionaries are trained to somewhat steel themselves to family needs back home. Having an elderly parent would not always be seen as a valid reason to leave the field or sometimes even take a leave of absence. I could only imagine the fever pitch that would be raised around the IMB if I began vocalizing about this heightened sense of responsibility to our Elderly Four who lived elsewhere. I wondered whether it would fall on deaf, insensitive ears.

But as we mulled over this, the Lord seemed to draw us to another passage of Scripture. As we read it, we felt as though God had placed a giant red arrow above 1 Timothy 5:4: *But if a widow has children or grandchildren, these should learn first of all to put their religion into practice by caring for their own family and so repaying their parents and grandparents, for this is pleasing to God.*

I reread this and camped on the *for this is pleasing to God* portion. How often do people browbeat themselves as they look for ways to bring God pleasure? They think by singing in the choir, teaching Sunday school, volunteering for Meals on Wheels, or even serving on a foreign field, they can bring a smile to God's face.

Yet this Scripture couldn't be more specific: we please God by caring for our family members. We obey what the Bible says to do.

We were on mission.

* * * * * * *

Putting feet to that mission was another matter altogether. *If we were to move back to Garland and use this as a caregiving base for our loved ones, where would we live?* Kay's mother was still not ready for a retirement center. She was still maintaining herself without much trouble in her home on 11th Street. Even though her house now belonged to us, we wouldn't boot her out.

On our next trip back to Garland for a holiday, I walked her 11th-Street neighborhood. I was shocked to find that one beautiful, old, large, historic home was boarded up and in foreclosure. Several others were in extreme disrepair. Kay and I worried about where the neighborhood would be in a few years. Would we ever even be able to fulfill our eventual dream and live in Kay's storied, growing-up house when we were in retirement? Things were in more of a state of decay than I had realized.

I began to inquire about the historic home in foreclosure. On a lark I made a low-bid offer to the mortgage holder. To my utter amazement I was the winning bidder. Thus was born what we lovingly called the "11th Street Restoration Project." Within a year we owned two other homes on the street. Over the years we have purchased others on 11th Street and in the Historic Downtown Garland District. We either held them for rentals or renovated them and then sold to carefully selected people who seemed to love the old neighborhood and wanted to be a serious part of its future.

The ease with which those real-estate transactions occurred convinced us God clearly was pointing us back to Texas and to Garland. *But how could we make the transition careerwise while we now were in our mid-50s? What kind of jobs could we hold? With our ages working against us, could we find employment in our professions?*

The popular chorus, "God can make a way when there

seems to be no way," echoed through both of our minds.

I looked up the *Houston Chronicle*'s retirement plan and realized I could begin drawing my pension, though somewhat reduced, starting on my 55th birthday. Thus May 2001 became our target date. Dealing with the sometimes inexplicable behavior at the IMB now seemed tolerable, since I could see the sun setting on our lives in Virginia just two years away.

A paid-for home, nearby rental properties (funded with equity from our home in Virginia), and a small but steady annuity provided the basic foundation for what we needed.

Still, we knew we must find some kind of meaningful work to do and also another source of income. We asked God for direction. We believed we really could obey God's call back to Texas only if we could find the final missing piece to the puzzle unfolding before us.

* * * * * * *

In August 1998 I became convinced that God was pointing us toward owning our own book-publishing company. Though our backgrounds had been in newspapers and denominational media offices, Kay and I had each written, co-authored, edited, or been involved in some way with the publication of dozens upon dozens of books. We found much fulfillment in that line of work.

My years in Nashville and then in Richmond had uniquely prepared me for managing this kind of business. I had learned how to manage complex budgets and staffs, how to juggle multiple publishing projects simultaneously, and perhaps most importantly had developed a clear focus on new publishing technologies and trends.

But own our own book-publishing company? That seemed

like a pipe dream. We had never been successful full-time entrepreneurs before. *How would it work? And could it work? Could we really make a living at it?* we asked ourselves warily.

I began discreetly making inquiries about how one goes about purchasing a book-publishing company or starting one from scratch. Unsolicited and much to my surprise, within a few days from the start of my quest an invitation arrived in my IMB mailbox inviting me to speak at a special dinner sponsored by Midwestern Baptist Theological Seminary in Kansas City, MO. This dinner was to honor my old friend, book publisher Jim Hefley. Knowing that Jim and his wife, Marti, had started Hannibal Books 13 years before seemed like the perfect open door for uncovering how to do this as well. I could hardly wait the four weeks until the dinner in Kansas City. I had a keen sense that God somehow was up to something.

Jim had started Hannibal Books as a reaction to the bigotry he encountered among Christian publishers who disdained him for seemingly siding with the conservatives in the Resurgence. Despite writing nearly 50 books published by just about every major and minor Christian book company in the country, Jim had been rejected by every major publisher for what eventually would become his most famous work, *The Truth in Crisis* six-volume series.

Jim decided to borrow the money against his home in Hannibal, MO, to found Hannibal Books so he could publish Volume 1 of *The Truth in Crisis* series. Surprisingly he asked me to write the foreword to that historic book, which today is a textbook in at least three of the six Southern Baptist seminaries. At the time of its publication, however, the book was banned in Baptist Book Stores (now LifeWay Stores); Convention moderates tried to suppress it. Moderates condemned the volume for its failure both to chastise the conservatives and to glorify the moderates. As I stated in the foreword, I would have written the series differently than he had, but I thought Jim did a fabulous job of trying to provide balanced reporting in an era when almost all Baptist state newspaper editors and most secular religion writers and editors were biased in favor of the moderates.

Jim went on to publish through Hannibal Books the remaining five volumes in the series. He also acquired for the company the publication rights to several of his other, better-known works, including the *Way Back* series and *Arabs, Christian and Jews,* a landmark call from an Evangelical Christian leader for support for a Palestinian state parallel to the Jewish state of Israel.

Just as he had Hannibal Books up and taking off like a cruise missile, Jim began to suffer the symptoms of Parkinson's Disease. Not long after his diagnosis, our histories were now about to intersect again.

* * * * * * * *

I arrived in Kansas City about noon before the dinner honoring Jim. Once at the hotel I called Jim and invited him to coffee in the hotel restaurant. In my briefcase was the manuscript for Kay's latest book (a novel, *When the Heart Soars Free*). In my mind were a million questions about how one goes about launching a book-publishing company.

Jim could hardly concentrate on our conversation. He seemed much older than at our last time together just a few years earlier. "I don't have the energy to take on this book," he said about *When the Heart Soars Free.* That struck me as a very strange comment. My questions about starting my own book-publishing company seemed to fly right over his head.

Mystified, I returned to my hotel room, called Kay, and told her this didn't look like it would be a very fruitful trip.

Returning to the hotel lobby in time to leave for the banquet, I encountered Jim and Marti just as Midwestern Seminary President Mark Coppenger arrived to chauffeur them to the dinner. On the spur of the moment, Mark issued an invitation for me to join them for the ride. I did and sat in the backseat with Marti, while Mark rode in the front and tried to engage Jim in a conversation.

I leaned over to Marti and asked, "Is something wrong with Jim?"

"You don't know?" she whispered with a puzzled look. "He's been diagnosed with Parkinson's; it's already impacting his mind."

After I voiced my concern, a long silence followed. Finally I said to Marti, "What does this mean for Hannibal Books?"

"I don't know," she replied sadly. "None of our [three] girls wants the company. I've got to spend the next years taking care of Jim."

Another beat of silence followed, as did some words that burst from my lips before I knew it.

"Then would you sell it to me?" I blurted.

Her reply, "Make me an offer," to this day rings in my ears.

I remember very little about the banquet or what I said in my talk that night. With excitement welling up inside me as the evening droned on, I could hardly wait to return to the hotel to talk privately on the phone with Kay.

That night in late September 1998 would change our lives forever and set us on a new course—a direction I now firmly believe God was leading us toward ever since our last days at the *Houston Chronicle* some 15 years earlier.

First, of course, were many, many pragmatic steps. I had

not a clue about how one went about making an offer for and purchasing an existing company. Neither did the Hefleys have any idea how to "sell" Hannibal Books to Louis and Kay Moore.

Returning to Richmond, I raced to the nearest Barnes & Noble and bought an armload of books on starting or buying a business. I next called our family attorney in Garland, who said he would have to research the matter further.

Eight months later—in May 1999—I flew to Hannibal, MO, with the paperwork and check in my briefcase. Jim and Marti seemed pleased that the company was passing into hands of friends who would work to further develop their dreams and hopes for Hannibal Books.

* * * * * * * *

By May 1999 Kay and I had carefully crafted our exit plan from the SBC bureaucracy. The plan called for my final day to occur on my 55th birthday—on May 11, 2001. Between May 1999 and May 2001—a very long two years—our plan called for about 25 steps that would need to occur, including selling our home in Richmond, moving Hannibal Books into offices in Garland, applying for my *Chronicle* retirement, securing independent health insurance, and all the other mundane and not-so-mundane tasks that would be involved in such a gigantic transition in our lives. Without a firm belief that God was guiding us each step of the way, we no doubt never would have been able to make it through the revolution under way in our lives.

I credit David Button with unwittingly showing me how everything might work. David had done an amazing job of running his radio station in New York (including remaining for a while as mayor of the upstate New York town where he lived) while being fully employed in the executive wing of the IMB in Richmond. Without ever saying what I had in mind, from the minute in August 1998 (nearly three years before I actually left the IMB) that the plan began forming in my head I started observing David's fascinating juggling act. I discreetly queried him about what running one's own business was like.

As Kay and I took over ownership of Hannibal Books, our "11th Street Restoration Project" seemed to take wings. Whenever possible, I flew back to Dallas to oversee renovations under way on Kay's parents' home (now ours) and two new acquisitions on the street. I watched in amazement as neighbors began to take notice and start to improve their own properties to bring about new life on the historic street.

* * * * * * * *

About five months after we purchased Hannibal Books and made a major step up in the 11th Street Restoration Project, the situation at the IMB suddenly shifted.

Jerry Rankin announced to trustees that he was splitting David's office. My staff and I would report directly to the president. Next Jerry summoned me to his office, told me that David would be leaving his duties, and stated that Jerry would name me as "special assistant to the president." I would lose my staff but would remain in the president's office doing writing and editing assignments for Jerry. He would reassign my staff back to David's old office, with a new vice president in charge.

As I left Jerry, I realized that, as I had feared, it would appear to many that I was trapped in the scapegoat role as the turmoil between Jerry and David reached its final crescendo. I believed that the drama now ensuing looked for all the world as though David and I could not work together, when in truth the conflict all along had been between my two superiors.

As Kay and I analyzed the happenings, we reaffirmed to each other our strong belief that God had prepared the Garland scenario for us and placed Hannibal Books precisely in our laps at just the right moment. *If God had done all this for us, could He not also be at work in this drama now unfolding before our eyes at my workplace*, we wondered? We reassessed our plan and determined that I would wait to resign to as close to my 55th birthday as possible, so we would have the *Chronicle* pension undergirding us. Although our first response was to fight this administrative decision at the IMB, we decided to "bend" with the wind until that time.

On January 1, 2000, I became special assistant to the president of the IMB, as Jerry had instructed. A few days earlier David and Jerry parted company for the final time as employer and employee. Jerry had not succeeded in his plan to teach David his definition of "what it's like to have a boss." In June Kay and I sold our home in Richmond and moved into an apartment to prepare for our ultimate exit. In August Kay and Hannibal Books moved to Garland to begin unfurling our plan. Katie was headed back to Texas anyway, as she had just graduated from high school in Richmond and was about to start her freshman year at Baylor, two hours to the south. The historic Garland home that we bought in foreclosure had now been thoroughly renovated as a place for us to live—just down the street from Kay's mother so we could help her as she struggled to continue independent living past age 90. For the next nine months I quietly commuted from Richmond to Garland almost every weekend and spent weekday evenings in Richmond on the phone or on email with Kay to work out details of the transition of our lives from denominational servants to independent business owners. At no point did I ever regret the direction our lives were moving.

I bided my time until April 2001, when I submitted my resignation letter, effective on my May birthday. When I stated my reasons—that we were returning to Texas to care for elderly relatives—some reactions predictably were ones of "How could you?" The idea of leaving international missions for a ministry to family members was not especially popular. I am sure that whispers of *defector* and *turncoat* were heard in the halls of the IMB.

Nevertheless, Kay and I believed 1 Samuel 15:22: "*To obey is better than sacrifice, and to heed is better than the fat of rams.*" We simply were being obedient to what God called us to do. Although we didn't know the total outline of the future, we trusted that He would honor that obedience and would provide for us.

Numerous times in my life I've seen certain religious leaders determine to trust God, even when what they did looked to corporate leaders like pure stupidity. When they obeyed God, He always worked things out for them.

In my *Chronicle* days, I read Pat Robertson's *Shout It from the Housetops* and then interviewed him about his calling to become a TV evangelist. At the time he was little known, had no significant financial backing or TV ministry, and looked to all the world like some kind of deluded dreamer. Over the years I tracked with much interest how Pat's ministry grew and *The 700 Club* eventually became all that the dreamer had said it could be.

Angelo Roncalli was 77 when he was elected to head the Roman Catholic Church as Pope John XXIII. He was supposed merely to be a caretaker pope and to fill the office until a much younger man could succeed him. When he announced plans to open the windows at the Vatican and let fresh air into the church by calling Vatican Council II, many Catholics and non-Catholics alike scoffed at such nonsense. Though he did not live long enough to see the great council end, what he set in motion during his five years as pope changed not only the Roman Catholic world but also the Orthodox and Protestant worlds dramatically.

Our dear, trusted friend Ken Chafin in 1984 resigned as pastor of South Main in Houston to move to Louisville to join the Southern Seminary faculty. He did so following God's leading at a time in which everything indicated the conservatives were on the verge of taking over the seminary and terminating all of the moderates employed there. What seemed so questionable then put Ken in a prime spot to later accept the pastorate of Walnut Street Baptist Church in Louisville, which enabled him to minister to the deeply hurting moderate seminary community. He eventually retired from Walnut Street and returned to minister at South Main, where "the prophet before his time" was greeted with the vast respect that had eluded him during his previous years in the pulpit there.

Over the decades, I've also seen numerous clergy of many denominational stripes, who to their families' detriments, have become overly involved in their professions. Despite their adjuring others to put family first, they sometimes acted as though they were exempt personally from this teaching. I believe this is what frequently happens when a pastor, church-staff member, or missionary suddenly shocks the church with a divorce, affair, or scandal.

I interviewed Walker Railey, former pastor of First United Methodist Church of Dallas, once before the scandal emerged over the attempted murder of his wife, Peggy, and his liaison with Lucy Papillion, a United Methodist bishop's daughter. In 1993 *The Dallas Morning News* reported that a San Antonio jury acquitted Railey of strangling his wife to near-death, but a civil court eventually held him liable for the attack after he failed to contest a lawsuit filed on her behalf.

Reading the news stories and courtroom testimony quickly pointed to the same old problem—profession above family— plaguing the clergy.

The same situation may have been at play in the recent sensational murder trial of Matthew Winkler, a Selmer, TN, Church of Christ minister whose wife, Mary, shot and killed him in the family home. The Fox network reported that when apprehended she said, "He had really been on me lately criticizing me for things—the way I walk, I eat, everything. It was just building up to a point. I was tired of it. I guess I got to a point and snapped." Mary was convicted of voluntary manslaughter and given only a short jail sentence.

Taking time to care for our families is important. With the short shrift that some in the church give families, I'm not surprised at my earlier observation about once finding so many former Southern Baptists turned Mormons. People ally themselves with churches where their families are supported.

Kay and I were convicted and were taking action.

* * * * * * * *

As I left the IMB president's office that day in April 2001 after I turned in my resignation, I had great sense of relief that my emancipation from church bureaucracy was occurring. In my career I had seen the best and the worst the church had to offer and in each case had been a witness to the truth. I could say, as Job did, that when tested I had *come forth as gold* (Job 23:10).

Now I could continue to bear witness to God's work in the world on my own (as led by His) terms.

Chapter 25

Reborn Again!

Truth No. 25: Ultimately the pigs on the Animal Farm take on the odor of the humans who precede them.

One of the first potential authors to approach us after Kay and I bought Hannibal Books was retired missionary Jean Phillips, who knew about us from IMB contacts. Jean and her husband, Gene, had a chilling story. They had been abducted and threatened with death as they were on a short-term, post-retirement missionary assignment in southern Africa. Her manuscript, *Rescue*, was about God's powerful hand that had delivered them again and again—in dealing with a son's drug problems, another son's mental illness, and various challenges on the field besides their scrape with death.

Outside of Kay's novel, *Rescue* was the first book we published as new owners of Hannibal. Jean's phenomenal success with *Rescue* caused word to get out in the missions community—both in Southern Baptist and other circles, such as the Wycliffe group. Soon we were besieged with people who wanted us to help them share their missions experiences.

Our absolute best-selling books were the three-volume Jungle series (*It's a Jungle Out There, Life Is a Jungle*, and *Jungle Calls*) about a Wycliffe missionary kid who grew up in remote Peru and who related some humorous yet sobering tales of his life in the Amazon. Just as I was in Missouri signing the contract to buy Hannibal from the Hefleys, a fax announced that a major Homeschooling material distributor had chosen to carry the Jungle books. Over the next six months the Jungle books with their missions emphases sold thousands upon thousands of copies. These important sales represented a major cash infusion as we started off on our own. We saw it as God's sign that He would bless our enterprise undertaken in obedience to Him.

At a publisher's meeting a leading Christian publishing executive who knew we had taken over Hannibal from the Hefleys advised us, "Dump all those missions titles. They don't sell." He said our missions books would drag us down if we kept them among our inventory. He suggested we focus on more popular topics.

The meteoric sales of the Jungle books plus Jean's early success with her riveting *Rescue* convinced us not to listen to this well-meaning but off-base exec. Instead we rapidly saw missions books as a major niche market for us, since LifeWay was hardly giving missions manuscripts a nod and the Woman's Missionary Union publishing house (which previously emphasized such topics) had largely gone in another direction.

Ultimately the ubiquitous slogan, "Our mission is missions" would be on our signage, catalogs, and website.

This interest cropped up in some of the most unlikely places. Jean Phillips is a very conservative Southern Baptist. Yet much to our amazement *Rescue* was chosen by the United Methodist Board of Global Missions, one of the more liberal-leaning missions groups in the U.S., for its coveted "missions reading list." Just after that Jean and her book were featured in a primely placed story (not just a book review) in the *New York Times*.

None of this would have happened had I not experienced those years at the International Mission Board. Of course I also continued to remember my calling as a teen-ager at Falls

Creek and my early consecration of my life to missions. God's waste management department is still the best place to work.

* * * * * * * *

My new life in Garland at the Hannibal helm combined the best of all the worlds I had experienced throughout the previous 30 years. The first half had been spent working as a newspaper journalist. The second half had been spent working in communications in the Southern Baptist bureaucracy in a variety of settings and cities. From each I had gained much. Each contributed to my ability to do my current job as a Christian book publisher.

From the *Houston Chronicle* I had learned the width and breadth of the community of faith. I had learned how to discern cutting-edge issues and how to ferret out information about those issues as well as about the people speaking out on them. (By the way, the *Chronicle* ultimately was bought by the Hearst Corporation, which, as I long ago predicted, brought new management and eventually a sizeable housecleaning.)

The *Plano Star Courier* gave me management and business training that I never could have obtained elsewhere in such a short period of time.

The year-and-a-half of freelance/self-employment during the Texas Economic Depression in the late 1980s taught me how much I value freedom to be my own boss. Perhaps nothing whetted my appetite for the day when I could be independent again more than did the satisfaction of that brief period.

My job at the Christian Life Commission trained me remarkably well for my role today in owning and operating my own Christian-oriented book-publishing business/ministry. Without those skills learned managing the CLC's publishing and distribution, I doubt that I could perform my current role as a Christian publisher so effectively.

From the IMB I gained a wider perspective on the world. Whereas Nashville shrank my world, Richmond expanded it. I gained a greater appreciation for the world's diversity and its vast array of cultures. I managed a large office of more than 80 people and learned the costs and talents necessary to guide a large group of people in creative work.

More than anything else, life in Baptistdom taught us how much we value our own freedom to express our own faith and talents under God. We emerged from Nashville and Richmond more firm than ever about holding to essential Baptist doctrines including that of the "priesthood of the believer" who is accountable to God and not to individuals wearing their own definitions of clerical collars.

* * * * * * * *

So here we were—reborn again!—in Garland, TX, with all of these experiences behind us. It was an opportunity to truly *taste and see that the Lord is good* (Ps. 34:8).

We arrived in Garland needing to care for four elderly relatives all in their 90th year and above. Two mothers. One childless aunt. And one childless uncle (not related to the childless aunt.) We have had the great privilege of running to grocery stores, doctors' offices, hair appointments, Sunday-school class parties, friends' funerals, and vast numbers of assorted other errands to help our elder charges have a greater quality of life in their last months. We had numerous bedside talks to get family history and trivia recorded while we still had time. We've learned more about eldercare, including the issues of nursing homes, dying, death, hospice, funerals, estates, medical powers of attorney, DNR instructions, etc., than we ever dreamed possible. Each of the four lived and three have died with his/her own formula, issues, and style. (Fodder for another book!) Through it all we've been blessed by what these loved ones have shown us, what they've given us, and the wonderful memories they've left behind. Thank God we had gotten home before dark!

Because we were obedient, God truly showed us He was pleased, as the verse in 1 Timothy noted. We have not known wealth in our new setting, but God has blessed beyond our wildest imaginings. He has grown and expanded our business commensurate with what we could manage given our knowledge and responsibilities at that particular time. He was never late; at the right moment He was there moving us on to the next step in the process.

He even expanded my horizons by honoring my commitment to preserving the Historic Downtown Garland District. Because my business and home both are in the downtown area, I was given a seat on the City of Garland Plan Commission, where I can watch out for the interests of people in my district. I traded denominational politics for secular politics at the local level. A citizen of the Chickasaw Nation, I also enjoy being involved in tribal activities and decision-making. My years in Nashville and Richmond Baptistdom, as well as watching other denominations over the years, taught me well.

* * * * * * *

God still had new lessons for us. One was about His incredible sense of humor.

Just as we had decided that our story would end happily without ever seeing anything further of life under the Big Tent of Religious Life in America, a funny thing happened one day on my way to the gym.

As I was leaving for my morning fitness workout, I read in Baptist Press that David Button had been appointed a trustee at the International Mission Board. That meant he now would be a boss of his former bosses! My imagination was captured with the dynamics that might ensue with David sitting in the audience as a voting board member with Jerry onstage looking out at his one-time nemesis. I had always wondered what one would do in serving as a trustee on a denominational board.

About four hours later the phone rang. On the other end was the chairman of the nominating committee for trustees for all Southern Baptist agencies and institutions. He said one of the IMB trustees from Texas had just resigned and left a two-year unexpired term that needed to be filled immediately. He said he had polled other Texans on the IMB trustee board, including my friend, Fort Worth pastor Bob Pearle, for a nominee. My name immediately had risen to the top. Would I accept the nomination? he asked. I was blown away.

Only three years previously Kay and I had shaken the dust from our feet and said goodbye to the innerworkings of Southern Baptist bureaucratic life. *Surely God will not approve of my taking this assignment,* I thought as I soul-searched.

After prayer, however, I had the unmistakable feeling that God was telling me that by accepting this appointment I could yet gain a final set of insights that I had not received in any of my previous jobs or involvements. As a trustee I would be beholden to no one except to Him.

With Hannibal Books having such an ongoing interest in Southern Baptist missionaries and helping them tell their stories, the trustee role seemed as though it would be an ideal way to stay current about missions.

Hardly believing I was hearing my own voice, I called back the committee chairman and told him *yes*.

* * * * * * * *

So in July 2004 I began traveling every other month to some city in the U.S. (including Richmond, our former home) to join other trustees in managing the business of the International Mission Board, my immediate past employer. Each meeting I shared with other trustees the latest book Hannibal had published by an IMB missionary. At every meeting David Button and I usually found ourselves cordially sitting beside each other and collaborating on business matters being discussed. All this from two people who, in the end of our IMB tenures just four years beforehand, seemed unfairly and erroneously painted as bitter enemies!

I was assigned to the committee that oversees the approval of new missionary candidates. In our meetings we heard reports about a special study under way involving the baptism of and charismatic leanings of some candidates. I recalled how Jerry's election as president in 1993 had been clouded with rumors of his own charismatic inclinations. This was a primary reason that 14 trustees, a minority, voted against him. I remembered how he told me privately that the whole issue was a big misunderstanding. He said it sprang from his once being in a meeting in which someone spoke in tongues (glossolalia) and where Jerry got up and "translated" for the person. He seemed to be embarrassed by the whole episode and pledged to never do that again. With his stoic demeanor, Jerry didn't fit with any image I'd seen in Pentecostal or charismatic churches that I had covered for the *Houston Chronicle*. After a dramatic episode in which he fired one Pentecostal-leaning missionary, I figured he had instructed his staff dealing with missionary appointments to quash any candidate who even looked the least bit Pentecostal.

Still, I could see a curious pattern emerging among some candidates for missionary appointment. During our meetings, a fellow trustee would point out that a certain candidate was a member of a church with known charismatic leanings. Another trustee would point out that a candidate had been a Southern Baptist only a brief time after a long history in a Pentecostal denomination. (In one particular case I wondered how a candidate could experience a lifetime of speaking in unknown tongues and not believing in the Trinity and then after only a brief stint in a Southern Baptist church accept appointment as a Southern Baptist missionary in a faraway country. I wondered whether the person in the new assignment would be making United Pentecostal or Southern Baptist converts.)

I had no idea that this undercurrent was shaping up into the makings of a major schism among the conservative ranks and that once again—even during my temporary, fill-in term—I would be on the front row of yet another major religious event in the making!

* * * * * * * *

After serving on the trustee committee that oversees screening and appointment of IMB missionaries, I moved on to the trustees' Administrative Committee. Then, wonder of wonders, I was selected to serve on that body's subcommittee, which is supposed to conduct the IMB president's annual performance review! As a former employee who only four years beforehand had worked totally at Jerry's behest, this was an astonishing development, to say the least!

The process I observed left me, in a strange way, feeling immensely empathetic for my former boss.

Previously the president's annual performance review had been a matter of rumor and conjecture, since its contents were never made public—often not even to trustees. Once I had the facts in hand, I became very bothered by the way the review had been administered in the past. It appeared to be extremely mercurial, sloppy, and unprofessional. A strong leader such as Jerry needs very clear and precise boundaries and guidelines; otherwise, such a leader could tend to overstep his authority and end up trying to manage his managers (as was the case in the old moderate regime).

Instead, what I saw was an odd system whereby the rules and goals seemed to fluctuate yearly depending on the personalities and political leanings of who had been on the performance-review subcommittee. The president of any organization such as the IMB needs an evenhanded professional system in place to guide trustees in their annual review of the official's job performance.

Under the current arrangement, a pro-Jerry trustee could twist the system to produce a glowing report one year, but the next year a trustee not fond of Jerry could steer the process in the opposite direction and produce a negative review.

I told my fellow subcommittee members that this confusing, mercurial system was tremendously unfair to Jerry, who, like the rest of us, is a Christian who strives to do right but has human foibles. Without clear guidance, he had no firm accountability. This left him in a very vulnerable position. Therefore, I argued, without success, that the trustees needed to hire a non-Southern Baptist management firm to set up clear performance guidelines for the president—guidelines that would exist regardless of who served in the office.

Both pro-Jerry and anti-Jerry trustees seemed to prefer the

sloppy political system that often produced the ongoing stale-mate that existed on the Board over how to properly supervise the president.

Thus I witnessed something I might never have learned otherwise. I wondered whether many denominational bureau-cratic shenanigans could be prevented by a trustee board with unflinching backbone and good professional advice from somewhere. I saw that the buck truly stopped one notch further back than with the administrator. I wondered whether a tough, non-political evaluation system for denominational execs, bishops, and even popes could benefit the cause of Christ.

* * * * * * * *

Although I didn't like the upshot of this Administrative Committee decision, at the same time I felt comfortable with the guidelines on "private prayer language" and "baptism" that the Overseas Personnel Committee had adopted while I had served there. I was somewhat surprised that neither statement passed by more than a 60-percent majority. I had expected the margin to be much higher. Since the votes were taken by a show of hands, I also was surprised by which trustees voted against the matters. Almost to a one they were trustees who seemed to support Jerry Rankin unequivocally. I was unaware at the time of the vote that Jerry privately had objected to both measures. Those on the Board aligned with him appeared to know, somehow, some way, where he stood and decided to stand with him. However, the votes for the two guidelines were solid, so I presumed the case was closed.

After moving on to my new committee assignment, I let the issues of private-prayer language and baptism fade into the back of my mind.

Much to my surprise a few months later, the issues rose in a firestorm stirred up by Wade Burleson, a new trustee from Oklahoma who told me he is a descendant of first Baylor President Rufus C. Burleson. After I moved on from Overseas Personnel, Wade had been appointed to the OP committee. In a very confusing set of circumstances, Wade appeared before the whole trustee board. He objected to the two measures and claimed his efforts to bring them back to the committee floor had been rebuffed. The intensity of his remarks and the drama that ensued puzzled me.

Since the matter had been settled so recently and so firmly by the committee, I wondered what was driving Wade's blatherings. Not long beforehand Wade had shared with me that I was the only trustee who had treated him decently during his brief time on the board already. I wondered why, if he was concerned about not winning friends and influencing people, was he now engaged in a public spectacle destined to foment trouble, make enemies, and burn bridges?

Later I was amazed to read on a Baylor University website about Wade's crusade to overturn these two measures.

Why, oh why, is he doing this? I asked myself over and over as I observed the debate widening and exploding.

At another IMB board session, the second volley was fired in the battle to dislodge the new policies on private prayer language and baptism. I sat with my jaw dropped as low as it would go as Jerry Rankin, in a closed-door meeting, told trustees that he prays in a private prayer language during his personal prayer times. After revealing that bombshell, he asked that the new policy be rescinded and accused trustee leaders of ignoring his earlier opposition to the policy.

Since I never had previously heard him state his opinions on these subjects nor ever had seen an inkling of Pentecostalism from him, I couldn't imagine why he laid that card on the table, especially in a closed-door session attended by more than 100 people. Surely he knew the rumor would—as it did—spread far and wide about what he had just said and done. *How can anyone possibly hope to keep such a matter quiet given the content of the message and the large size of the audience?* I wondered. I would have much preferred that Jerry make the comments in a public session open to the press so that rumors and innuendos and half-truths would not have emerged about what happened, as they did.

As the dogfight developed, I read news stories by moderate SBC denominational journalists who did not have the issue straight, including the vote-count taken by the IMB board on the matters. I was astounded how the denominational media played a role in confusing the debate.

Much to my surprise I learned that the practice of and tolerance for speaking in unknown tongues in private—once the activity of Pentecostals from whom Southern Baptist moderates as well as conservatives distanced themselves—was far more prevalent in the SBC than I had ever dreamed. Daily SBC pastors, missionaries, and laypeople wrote to IMB trustees testifying to their support for the practice of tongues in private. Whereas during the heyday of the moderates, a Southern Baptist pastor would have been reluctant to make such a revelation to his best friend, now the head of the largest and most prestigious SBC agency not only was stating his own personal practice of glossolalia but was asking his trustees to rescind a policy about it. And a vocal group of SBC pastors, missionaries, trustees, and laypeople were supporting him! The matter was, of course, confused by Jerry's launching his counteroffensive in closed-door sessions instead of out in the open and by his often contradictory statements in public.

As over the weeks and months the issue began to grow from a minor discussion in a trustee committee meeting to a full-blown denominational debate, I realized that yet once again I was somehow an eyewitness to a major, momentous event spiking in a major Christian denomination. Now I was observing from the inside what as a reporter I had only covered from the outside. My trustee stint had given me one final glimpse as an eyewitness of what really goes on behind the scenes in a major U.S. church body. Without this, I always would have had a slightly incomplete picture.

With my two-year, fill-in trustee term ending in 2006, I declined to accept re-nomination for a full four-year term. By that point our publishing company was growing by leaps and bounds. I knew I could do more for the missions cause through my missions-oriented company than I could on a trustee board.

* * * * * * * *

Earlier I mentioned my *Houston Chronicle* column in which I likened the Conservative Resurgence in the SBC to the revolution trumpeted by the pigs in George Orwell's classic *Animal Farm*, itself a satire on Soviet communism. In that story, the farm animals rose up against their human masters and overthrew them on a platform which pointed out the evil the humans had committed. Slowly at first, then eventually pall-mall, the animals—led by the pigs—became every bit as bad, if not worse, than the humans they had overthrown. Orwell struck a bull's eye on Stalin, Marx, and Lenin. In my column, however, I wondered out loud if the moralistically high road of the Conservative Resurgence would eventually falter, crash, and burn, with the new SBC leadership falling into the same self-perpetuating patterns and bureaucratic behavior as the moderates they replaced.

During my years inside the SBC bureaucracy I saw clearly

the answer to my question about whether the Conservative Resurgence would end up like the pigs in *Animal Farm*. I saw conservatives lose their ideals about reducing the size and scope of the bureaucracy, about eliminating the bureaucracy's lavish expenditures, and about making the local church the true "headquarters" of the denomination. Once in power these conservatives found the large staffs, exciting expense accounts, and the controlling executive style of the denomination too tempting a prize to give up. I saw conservatives who once disdained the moderates' love affair with statistics instead fall in love with and try to manipulate these numbers themselves. I saw conservatives who once lamented moderate control of the press and lack of transparency in the denomination turn and advocate more press control and more secretiveness than the moderates ever could have dreamed.

Instead of triumphing in their victory over the moderates, I saw conservatives begin to turn on each other, just as the pigs in the barnyard had. With this latest battle on tongues, which now seemed destined to continue for years, the conservatives' infighting would deplete energy that could have been spent on far more important matters.

Regrettably, the early ideals of the Conservative Resurgence have not happened. Yes, on paper the SBC espouses a more conservative theology. And yes, the Republicans have replaced the Southern Democrats in the seats of power in the denomination. Yet in so many ways, the denomination is exactly what it was when the moderates reigned supreme. Union cards and networks are still the order of the day. Names, faces, and in a few cases places have changed, but the "good-ole-boy" network still works just as it did three decades ago. Who you know and where you went to school (and when) are as crucial today as in yesteryear.

Sadly, the similarity between Orwell's *Animal Farm* is

more appropriate today than ever. The Baptist pigs have taken on the odor and style of the humans they sought to replace in the halls of power within the denomination.

The current generation that fought the war for the Conservative Resurgence now is either retiring and fading into the sunset or simply dying off. Most of the current denominational leaders have forgotten or have chosen to ignore how they got into their current posts. None would ever have been selected for denominational leadership by the previous moderate regime. Had early leaders such as Paul Pressler and Paige Patterson not led the charge, members of the current Convention leadership would still be pastors, evangelists, or missionaries looking in from the outside of the denomination. Yet a sizable number of denominational execs who rose to power because of this duo recoils at the mention of Pressler's and Patterson's names.

Like the moderates before them, the conservatives have for the most part failed to train and equip a new generation of younger, effective leaders to follow after them in their footsteps. Though Jimmy Draper and some other leaders tried to help younger pastors forge a movement to gain a voice and influence in the Convention, it quickly became questionable when some of the young leaders grabbed onto such issues as glossolalia and consumption of alcoholic beverages. I wonder whether any in the next generation of conservatives have any idea how the foot-soldiers of the past worked to lead the Convention in its current direction.

* * * * * * * *

Over the years I've seen other popular religious movements go astray as well.

After the conservatives' triumph in the Lutheran Church-Missouri Synod, the pendulum began to swing somewhat back to the middle after Jacob A.O. Preus, Robert Preus, and their followers moved into retirement and eventually died. The early euphoria of the Missouri Synod moderates faded into oblivion; the few stragglers left eventually merged into other Lutheran bodies.

When I was a Baylor student, ecumenism was the hottest topic in the church in the United States at that time. This, of course, coincided with the dramatic openings to Orthodox and Protestants created by Vatican Council II. The thinking at that time centered on actual organic re-union of Christendom. COCU, which stood for Consultation on Church Union, was the symbol of this era.

COCU emerged after 1960 from a sermon preached by Eugene Carson Blake, a leading Presbyterian official at that time. Exciting, controversial, and new, COCU was like a shining lightbulb that glows brightly and then suddenly goes out. Today, the current generation, except for a few theological scholars in some mainline denominational seminaries, wouldn't recognize the initials COCU from things posted on YouTube. Marvelously idealistic, the whole idea of COCU fell apart when confronted with the reality of entrenched church bureaucracies and structures. COCU ceased to exist in 2002, long after it had dropped off the public's radar screen.

That same type of euphoria propelled the World Council of Churches and the National Council of Churches into the forefront in the 1960s and 1970s. Though these entities existed further back than COCU, the ecumenical heyday of those years caused these structures to flower and grow. As opposition developed and the same realities that silenced COCU rose up and created strong barriers to church union, the words *downsizing* and *restructuring* entered both the WCC and NCC vocabularies. In the press room at the last large General Assembly of the National Council of Churches in Dallas in the late 1970s, many of us wondered whether the NCC even had a future. It did, of course, but a much more limited one, as it became more like the entrenched church bureaucracies it once sought to replace. Today it is mostly the mouthpiece for liberal social-theological agendas.

* * * * * * * *

I emerged from my last IMB trustee meeting in 2006 shaking my head and wondering, "Whither Southern Baptists?" With the 30th anniversary of the Conservative Resurgence approaching in 2009, I wondered what truly lay ahead for this body of believers that helped shape religious history in the 20th century in such an auspicious way.

But as I stepped aside from my trustee role that had afforded me a last, parting glimpse into the bowels of one denomination's bureaucracy, I knew that future would not be up to me.

Now, as a non-trustee, I no longer would be helping create it.

And, since I no longer was a working journalist, I no longer would be personally recording it.

As a publisher of Christian books, however, I now would be helping others preserve that future—whichever way the wind blew it.

Through books that live on through the generations, I would continue to be a witness to the truth—still through the awesome, matchless power of the printed word.

Chapter 26

Sing On!

Truth No. 26: Failing to cast one's lot with the church is risky, since it's the only institution that the gates of hell won't prevail against.

In my more than four decades of observing religious life, I truly have experienced, as Charles Dickens once assessed human events, the best of times and the worst of times.[1]

I have seen church people lie, deceive, abdicate responsibility, obsess on ego trips, demonstrate untrustworthiness, commit adultery, turn a blind eye to wrong, be poor stewards of money, act spineless, and dishonor God in multitudes of ways.

I have seen them violate every one of the Ten Commandments, act boorish and selfish, be prejudiced, broadcast secular value systems, and in general behave worse than the heathen people they tried to reach.

I have seen hypocrisy, mean-spiritedness, jealousy, wrath, inconsiderateness, spitefulness, hate, chicanery, and profound dysfunction.

Just name some sin or some act the Bible eschews, and I could pair that vice up with some church leader or member I have known.

All that is on one hand.

On the other hand—in the "best of times" part—I have experienced church people so servant-hearted and so demonstrative of Godlike virtues that my eyes moisten at the remembrance of them.

For example, when Hurricanes Katrina and Rita devastated the Gulf Coast during 2006, one news story quoted a city official of a town that was practically annihilated by the storm. The official said, "Southern Baptists were everywhere. Everywhere I looked, I saw Southern Baptists." He was talking about the caravan after caravan of Baptist relief workers who rapidly descended on devastated areas and brought in food, clothing, baby formula and diapers, and materials to begin the rebuilding process.

From my office window in downtown Garland I daily watch coolers containing food trays for the Meals on Wheels program being delivered to the local Presbyterian church. I then see countless volunteers who give up their free time daily to carry these meals to shut-ins. From our personal eldercare experience I know the huge ministry that this daily sustenance provides. These volunteers truly give the cup of cold water in Jesus' name.

I think of the overseas missionaries I visited *in situ*—some living in thatched huts with dirt floors, some adjusting their lives to having electricity for only one hour a day, some having to spend hours visiting market after market just to forage enough food for that day's meal for their families.

Within the brief nearly seven years I was employed at the International Mission Board I knew even a handful who made the ultimate sacrifice—giving their very lives—so that others might know of God's love.

They gave up cushy lifestyles in the U.S. and the privilege of worshiping around like-minded folks and being nearby while their grandchildren grew up so that they might be lighthouses to people overseas.

For each of these circumstances I've mentioned are thousands of others in which believers act like Jesus would have them do—selflessly ministering, giving of themselves, making lives brighter, pushing back the darkness, sacrificially shepherding their flocks, putting feet to the gospel.

Despite all these good works, these examples I've just cited are not the reason why I believe we can never give up on the church.

These do not represent the reason why, when Kay and I find ourselves having moved to a new town, we get dressed on the first Sunday morning we are in our new city and begin the pilgrimage of finding a local church with which we can affiliate.

This we have done faithfully during our almost 39 years of marriage, even though (as we've related) our first choice of churches ended up not always being the best for our needs. Even in making our most recent move, back to Garland, the church we were sure would be a perfect match for us ultimately wasn't. Although the people where we first joined were perfectly lovely and kind to us, the church didn't have ministries that matched our typical areas of service. After prayer, we knew we must move on and find a church home better suited to us, even if that meant driving some distance to attend elsewhere. We would do that again if the need arose. Throughout the years we've learned to be good consumers in our church situations just as we would be at the grocery or the department store. We never want to let the grass grow under our feet much until we've linked up with a local church body.

Some people who read this book and have followed my trail of incident after incident in which church people dealt crushing blows may wag their heads and say, "Why would you still bother? If religious people will treat you this way, forget 'em. Why waste your time?"

That's a really good question—one I even ask myself occasionally—but never longer than for the blink of an eye.

Thankfully my faith in God supercedes and goes far beyond the actions of individuals, be they clergy or laypeople.

I'm grateful that I learned early on that my faith is in God, not religious leaders. People will always be people, regardless whether they wear the regalia of high church officials or just the street clothes of ordinary blue- or white-collar workers.

God is much bigger and far more important and powerful than the egos, personalities, and political machinations of mortal humans, including all the religious leaders who've ever lived.

The Bible says, *Some trust in chariots and some in horses, but we trust in the name of the Lord our God. They are brought to their knees and fall, but we rise up and stand firm* (Ps. 20:7-8).

The name of the Lord our God is the only thing fully worthy of our trust, after all.

The church also is worthy of our devotion for another reason. It is the only institution the Bible mentions which Jesus says the gates of hell won't hold up against.

He makes this statement to Peter when He says, *"and upon this rock I will build my church; and the gates of hell shall not prevail against it "*(Matt. 16:18 KJV).

He doesn't say that the gates of hell won't prevail against the local bank or the department store or a 401K or the Super Bowl or a college education. He doesn't say that the gates of hell won't prevail against the Peace Corps or the Red Cross or Habitat for Humanity.

But He does say that His church, for which He died—which He bought with His blood—will prevail even against the mightiest of the devil's schemes. Personally I don't want to thumb my nose at an institution in which Jesus puts this much stock and makes this statement so exclusively about.

About the church, lyricist Samuel J. Stone wrote these words (in the hymn *The Church's One Foundation*) that paraphrase Matthew 16:18:

From heaven He came and sought her
To be His Holy Bride;
With His own blood He bought her,
And for her life He died.[2]

God did not found the church on an imperfect human being. The apostle Peter, who is referenced in the first part of the verse, made serious blunders before and after Jesus said these words to Him. That church wasn't founded on "Rocky" (the rough translation of Peter's name), because he was just as mortal as some of the church leaders I've described in these pages. Instead, the type of faith exhibited by Peter, sinner though he was, in his individual confession of Christ as Lord forms the bedrock on which the church is built.

As with Peter, today's church is not built on the blunders of the finite, fallen mortals who attempt to superintend the church on earth. If we let what poet Robert Burns called "man's inhumanity to man"[3] cloud our view of the church, we are not following Christ's example. Jesus, fully knowing Peter's sinfulness, still fully chose to use this mere mortal's confession of faith as the foundation on which He founded the church on earth.

The church will endure to Christ's return; the gates of hell—even death itself—cannot crush that community of God which He founded. No opposition, no oppression, no assault of any time can overcome that faithful remnant of His people.

To me that sounds pretty powerful. Personally I don't want to take the risk of not being on the side of that community of faith. In Hebrews 10:25 the Bible says believers are to be about *not giving up meeting together, as some are in the habit of doing, but encouraging one another.* This springs from the context of the local church.

Despite its faults, its frailties, and its manifestations of its humanity, I would not be a witness of the truth if I did not state that I still cast my lot with the church. It is worthy of our devotion, our allegiance, our alliance, and our love.

After 40 years of watching the church at work, I sing with the songwriter Daniel S. Warner:

'Tis not in the church of Jesus
That people yet live in sin;
But in the dark creeds they're joining,
And vainly are trusting in.

God's church is alone triumphant,
In holiness all complete;
And all the dark pow'rs of Satan
She tramples beneath her feet.

Thank God for a church triumphant,
All pure in this world below!
For the kingdom that Jesus founded
Does triumph o'er every foe.[4]

Church triumphant, sing on!

[1]Charles Dickens, *A Tale of Two Cities* (New York: Penguin/Signet, 1960), 13.
[2]"Man Was Made to Mourn," Robert Burns. *The Poems and Songs of Robert Burns, Harvard Classics, Vol. 6* (New York: P.F. Collier & Son, 1909-14), 54.
[3]"The Church's One Foundation," Samuel J. Stone, 1866, public domain.
[4]"The Church Triumphant," Daniel S. Warner, 1893, public domain.

Where Are They Now?

A favorite quote of mine says, "There are many pious people who believe themselves to be saints who are not, and many people who believe themselves to be impious who are."[1] My previous chapters have listed numerous individuals who fall into both of these categories. In many cases the previous pages have updated the current status of characters I've mentioned. For those whose status I left hanging, this compilation updates the life situations of major players in *Witness to the Truth*.

Charles L. Allen—Although he never realized his dream of becoming a United Methodist bishop, Allen's congregation, First United Methodist in Houston, became by his retirement in 1983 noted for being the largest integrated congregation in Methodism. By 1995 Allen had written or edited more than 50 books which sold more than 8-million copies. After his retirement he became a counselor to a Houston corporation. He died in 2005.

John R. Bisagno—Retired as pastor of Houston's First Baptist Church in 2000 after 30 years of celebrated ministry in the pulpit there. As his successor HFBC called student ministry leader Gregg Matte, a youthful pastor with musical gifts, just as Bisagno had been when he took the helm.

Wade Burleson—Resigned as a trustee of the International Mission Board in January 2008 after the IMB declined to accept as an apology a statement he made attempting to explain his actions. Baptist media reported that the trustee board cited numerous violations of its code of conduct and was concerned that he, on his blog, criticized board actions and spoke out of turn about private information.

David Button—Lives with his wife, Denice, in upstate New York, where he serves as town supervisor in his community. His term of office representing New York as a trustee of the International Mission Board, where he continues to oversee those who once managed him, began in 2004 and continues to the present.

Kenneth Chafin—Served as seminary professor and pastor of Walnut Street Baptist Church in Louisville before he returned to Houston for his final years. At last back at his beloved South Main, he taught a widely popular Sunday-school class that reached out to formerly churched individuals. Before his death to leukemia in 2001, he told others that these final years back at the "church I'll never forget" were his very best.

John R. Claypool—Retired in 2000 as an Episcopal priest, a few years shy of being in a position to be the first Southern Baptist pastor to become a bishop in the Episcopal Church. On his death in 2005 of multiple myeloma, his writings in the area of grief work, especially his *Tracks of a Fellow Struggler* about the passing of his daughter, Laura Lue, were considered classics by people of all faiths.

Jimmy Draper—Retired back to Texas in 2006 after completing 15 years as a lionized, mightily respected captain of the LifeWay transition into relevancy. Probably no individual other than the brilliant yet thoroughly pastoral Draper could have herded the hostile, 2,000-plus establishment mob he encountered into the kind of cooperation and *esprit de corps* that would have immensely direct, personal benefits for the average Baptist in the pew.

Jim and Marti Hefley—These mentors and founders of Hannibal Books died within two months of each other in 2004, after Marti developed cancer as she cared for Jim in his final months. Jim's *The Truth in Crisis* series, originally snubbed by other publishers, and his *Way Back* series about his growing-up days in the Ozarks continue to be among Hannibal Books' bestsellers.

Glenn Hilburn—Retired in 2003 after more than 40 years in the Baylor University religion-department faculty, including 15 years as chair of the department. Today lives in the Waco area and prefers to avoid discussing anything about the Baptist controversy. We were grateful that his Baylor tenure extended long enough that he could greet both of our children as Baylor students and see Katie inducted into the BU Phi Beta Kappa chapter, which he helped obtain for the campus, and Omicron Delta Kappa, the leadership fraternity of which he served as national president.

Richard Land—Became the *go-to* spokesperson for the Religious Right on social and ethical issues. Never one to back away from controversy, his self-assured, knowledgeable, confident mien has propelled him into the forefront of the national media, appearing on *Larry King Live* and a host of other talk shows and other program. The Christian Life Commission, now known as the Ethics and Religious Liberty Commission, has evolved into something akin to a Republican-oriented lobby group that speaks both to Southern Baptists as well as the nation's politicians.

David McHam—Well past retirement age, he continues to teach journalism at the University of Houston. After his Baylor tenure he also enjoyed a long stint in the journalism department at Southern Methodist University before he moved to UH. The sun never sets on a McHam journalism alum, as his tremendously skilled J-school graduates span the globe in media positions they hold.

Matthew Moore—After four exceptional years as a Baylor University student, he was asked to stay on as a Baylor employee in the campus TV station and later in BU-sponsored public TV and supervised interns in the communications department. Ultimately a roommate and personal friend with a son of Baylor President Robert Sloan. After our fear of reprisals from the former BU administration, Matthew's friendship with the Sloan family put out for him (and us) a permanent welcome mat at the new Baylor president's home. Matthew now is vice president of a Phoenix, AZ, advertising agency.

John L. Morkovsky—Retired head of the Roman Catholic Diocese of Galveston-Houston died of a stroke in 1990. He led the diocese from June 1963 until his retirement in 1985. He lived for 16 years after a beating and robbery at his Houston home left him blind in one eye. He would be deeply pleased to know that his Houston-based diocese in 2004 was elevated to an archdiocese, with his future successor, Daniel DiNardo, named a cardinal.

Charles Page—Died in 2005 of multiple myeloma. After leaving First Baptist, Nashville, he returned for 14 marvelously fruitful years as pastor of his former church, 3,500-member First Baptist, Charlotte, NC, where he was considered one of the Carolinas' most prominent preachers. Members of his former Nashville church, who belatedly recognized his immense contributions to their lives, greatly mourned his passing.

Paige Patterson—After serving as president of the Southern Baptist Convention and of Southeastern Baptist Theological Seminary, Paige assumed the presidency of Southern Baptists' largest seminary, Southwestern in Fort Worth, where he quickly shaped faculty, curriculum, and mission in his conservative mold. The originally inconsequential Criswell College, which he once led, is now one of conservative Baptists' most highly esteemed learning institutions, with its graduates filling some major pulpits throughout the country, holding a high percentage of positions on trustee boards, and taking on some of the political roles Baylor grads formerly held.

Wesley M. "Pat" Pattillo—My former boss and mentor at Southern Seminary ultimately left the employ of Southern Baptists and since 2001 has been affiliated with the National Council of Churches. After he left Southern, he held several positions including vice-president for university relations at Baptist-owned Samford University in Birmingham, AL.

Don Pickels—Permanently exited newspapering with his early retirement from the *Houston Chronicle* and lived in San Antonio until his death from cancer in 1998. A starry heavenly crown no doubt awaited this Episcopal layman for his consistent Christian example in a highly secular profession.

Paul Pressler—This former jurist continues an active legal practice in Houston despite advancing well into his retirement years. He serves on boards of numerous Christian organizations and continues to maintain an interest in the Southern Baptist Convention, although he no longer involves himself in its day-to-day operation. His autobiography, *A Hill on Which to Die*, which gives his side of the Conservative Resurgence, at last was published in 1999 by Broadman & Holman, the denominational publishing house.

Jerry Rankin—After 15 years at the helm of the International Mission Board, he continues in the presidency though now past the typical retirement age. Off-and-on skirmishes with his trustee board, which have characterized his years in the job, continue. Southern Baptists' international mission force of field personnel has grown from about 3,500 when he took office to almost 5,400 today.

Adrian Rogers—This "prince of preachers" from Tennessee who was the inaugural SBC president of the Conservative Resurgence died of cancer in November 2005. After a 2005 Union University reception honoring him during his last Southern Baptist Convention ever to attend, Adrian lingered behind to sit with me and reminisce in what was one of his last private audiences before his downward health slide began. He never forgot the role my *Chronicle* stories played in lending validity to the infant resurgence movement and continued, with a grateful heart and eyes aglow with contentment, that evening to walk down memory lane with me until his wife, Joyce, at last pried him away to retire for the evening. Only five months later, he was dead.

Robert B. Sloan Jr.—In one of the most direct, dramatic acts of God's personal provision we've ever experienced (Isaiah 49:25), Robert assumed the Baylor helm on Herbert H. Reynolds' retirement just after our son, Matthew, became a Baylor student. That meant that both Matthew and our daughter, Katie, passed safely through Baylor under the direct superintendency of Sloan's more conservative direction and, despite our fears, had no cause to worry about reprisal because of their father's employment. Now president of Houston Baptist University after resigning at Baylor under fire, Robert's Baylor 2012 plan remains BU's manifesto despite severe personal criticism he sustained over it.

Katie Moore Welch—Graduated from Baylor University a semester early, *summa cum laude*, Phi Beta Kappa, with every BU academic honor she could glean and with her field of study unsuccessfully begging her to remain there for graduate work. The saddest day of her life was saying goodbye to her richly fulfilling Baylor years. Both of our children, already solidly grounded in their faith, emerged from Baylor with their spiritual lives vastly deepened and matured, in part due to Robert Sloan's Baylor 2012 emphases. Katie is completing her Ph.D. at the University of Texas at Arlington and is publisher of CrossHouse Publishing.

[1]Tony Hendra, *Father Joe* (New York: Random House, 2004), 4.

Photo Album

Pictured at about the time Oklahoma pastor Hugh Bumpas telephoned seminary president Duke McCall.

Lariat newsroom, spring 1968. From left, Kay Wheeler, Louis Moore, and Mike Kennedy, later a *Los Angeles Times* staffer

Staff of *The Baylor Lariat*, spring 1968. Louis is second row, second from left. Kay is second row, far right. Editors Tommy Kennedy and Ed Kelton are on the front row. Lariat sponsor David McHam is back row, right.

Interviewing Dr. Vivienne Mayes, Baylor's first black professor, for a *Baylor Lariat* story.

Editor, *The Baylor Lariat*, 1968-1969

A Baylor student journalist's dream—to be among the faces on the *Lariat* photo wall of editors. Tommy Miller, photographed with Kay as a lab student, is pictured at top left.

At Baylor Press, reviewing the next day's *Lariat* on the linotype machine.

Winning the Religious Public
Relations Council award in 1975 for
the *Chronicle*'s religion section

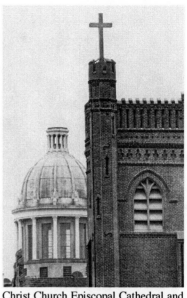

Christ Church Episcopal Cathedral and
the Harris County Civil Courts
Building in downtown Houston. These
nearby structures each housed princi-
pals in divergent major religious
movements that would shake the
nation.

Celebrating the release of *When You
Both Go to Work*, 1982. Matthew is 6,
Katie is 6 months.

Named one of Baylor's Men of Distinction
by Omicron Delta Kappa, 1982

341

Receiving Houston's Jewish Anti-Defamation League award, 1985

In Red Square, Moscow, 1985, covering story about plight of Soviet *refusniks*

With Vice President and Mrs. George H.W. Bush at a New Year's worship service at St. Martin's Episcopal Church, Houston, 1984.

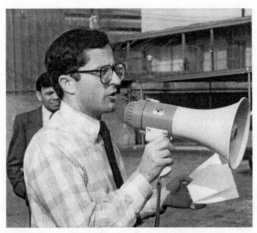

Conducting tour of a Houston mosque, 1985

Outside Houston's Hindu temple, 1985

Houston Chronicle
Section 6
Saturday. Nov. 10, 1984

**LOUIS
MOORE**
Religion Editor

Theologies come, theologies go

G OD NEVER changes, but Christian theologies that try to explain God come and go.
   Remember the God-Is-Dead theology popular in the 1960s? You seldom hear about it today, except in some history of theology class in seminary. This controversial theory came and went so fast that most people hardly had time to grasp the theological meaning behind the wild headlines.
   Late last century the search for the historical Jesus was another popular theology that crashed. In 1906, Albert Schweitzer published his classic, Quest for the Historical Jesus, and ended the theological discussion by pointing out that there is no way to

One of many Louis Moore columns that greeted readers of the Saturday-morning religion section

343

Representatives of the Church of Jesus Christ of Latter-day Saints (Mormon) visit the Plano Star Courier newsroom to film a documentary on how to work with the news media, 1987

Appreciation plaque presented by Collin County Community College for being the founding sponsor of the *Quad-C Chronicle* student newspaper for and teaching journalism there, 1988-89

Above, with Richard Land outside the American Embassy in Moscow in 1990. At right, Richard and Louis visit with the pope of the Republic of Georgia. Pictured with tour guide.

344

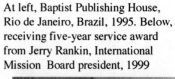

At left, Baptist Publishing House, Rio de Janeiro, Brazil, 1995. Below, receiving five-year service award from Jerry Rankin, International Mission Board president, 1999

Hannibal Books' display at Christian Booksellers Association trade show, Denver, 2006. Louis and Kay with Katie.

The Moore family, 2008. From left are son Matthew with his wife, Marcie, and their daughter, Caroline; Kay and Louis; and daughter Katie with her husband, Casey Welch

Index

Adams, Jim 90
Allen, Charles 53-54, 280, 334
Anders, Dan 254
Athenagoras, Patriarch 88
Bagby, J. Thomas 110-112
Bakker, Jim 18, 94, 155
Bakker, Tammy 18, 155
Bates, Carl 138-140
Benedict XVI, Pope 105
Bennett, Harold 245, 249-252, 257
Berg, Lee 227-228
Bisagno, John 73, 75, 268, 334
Blake, Eugene Carson 326
Bradley, Martin & Ruth 232
Bradshaw, John 110-111
Bramlette, Howard 233-234, 245
Baugh, John 206-208
Briggs, Ed 103, 247-248
Briggs, Ken 103
Bumpas, Hugh 36-37, 39, 54
Burleson, Wade 321, 334
Button, David 274-279, 281, 291,
    305-307, 316-317, 334
Button, Denice 274-276, 334
Bush, Barbara 111-112
Bush, George H.W. 111-112
Callaway, Joseph 58-59, 70
Carter, Jimmy 29, 131-133, 140, 222
Carter, Rosalynn 131
Cauthen, Baker James 42
Chafin, Kenneth 155-156, 158-160,
    181, 183-188, 192, 247, 309, 335
Chandler, Russ 103
Cheavens, Dave 31, 38-39
Chen, Bob 205
Claypool, John R. 156-157, 335
Clifton John 34-35, 38, 46
Clements, Bill 220
Cobb, Dan 89, 159, 176-177, 204, 223
Cohen, Marty 81
Collier, Everett 165

Coppenger, Mark 304
Cornell, George 98
Criswell, W.A. 62, 93, 125-127, 133,
    145, 149, 168, 294
Crump, Virginia 51
Crutchfield, Finis A. 280-281
Culver, Virginia 103
Dalai Lama of Tibet 254
Davis, Karen 245-246
Dawson J.M. 31
deMenil, Dominique 255
Dilday, Russell 40, 187-188
DiNardo, Daniel 336
DiOrio, Ralph A. 157
Dooley, Tom 24-25
Draper, James 186, 260-261, 269,
    325, 335
Druin, Toby 178
Dunn, James 180
Drinan, Robert 122
Dykeman, Alice 5
Elder, Lloyd 259
Ferguson, Milton 188
Fields, W.C. 138-139, 158-161, 172,
    177, 242
Ford, Gerald 132
Francis, Dan 264-266
Franks, Zarko 69, 81
Friedman, Dick 117-118
Galloway, Paul 144
Garrison, Candace Mossler 136
Gorbachev, Mikhail 18, 29
Gore, Al 222
Graham, Billy 43-44, 86, 94, 121,
    170, 180
Gregory, Joel 133, 145
Haaland, Gary 95
Hancock, Reg and Caroline 215, 268
Harrell, Roy 32
Heckmann, Carl 91-93
Heckmann, Mrs. Carl 89-90

Heckmann, Mark 90-91
Hefley, Jim & Marti 302-305, 311-312, 335
Herring, Reuben 229
Hilburn, Glenn 42-43, 115, 222, 247, 335
Hinckley, Gordon 209
Hines, John 69, 113-114
Holbrooke, Bob 146-147, 164
Hollinger, Herb 253-255
Honeycutt, Roy 59, 187-88
Hornaday, Joe 57
Howard, W.F. 32
Huckabee, Mike 133
Hull, William E. 59-60
Hunt, Alma 42
Hyer, Marge 103
Iakovos, Archbishop 88
Jenkins, Carolyn 231
Jenkins, Wayne 231, 258
John XXIII, Pope 308
John Paul I, Pope 45, 117-118
John Paul II, Pope 14, 103, 116-122, 126-127, 130, 132, 133, 136, 154, 161
Johnson, Carl 281-282
Johnson, Lyndon B. 26, 51
Jones, Jesse 209
Kammerdiener, Don 281, 287-288, 290-292
Kennedy, John F. 71
Kennedy, Tommy 33
King, Martin Luther 47, 58, 252
Kinsolving, Lester 68-70, 95-96, 99, 104
Knox, Marv 242
Kramp, John 258-259
Kuhlman, Kathryn 155
Land, Rebekah 219, 221, 227
Land, Richard 144, 188, 214-215, 218-220, 225, 227, 250-251, 261, 268, 335
Langley, Grace 74, 225
Langley, Ralph 74, 149, 225
Larsen, Roy 101

Law, Janice 69-72, 75, 97, 101, 106, 116
LeBurkein, Michael 53
Lee, Howard Sr. & Sarah. 206, 208
Lewis, Larry 146
Loftis, Jack 195
Luther, Martin 60
Martin, Dan 242-246, 253
Mason, Debra 4
Mayes, Vivienne 48
MacArthur, Gen. Douglas 26
Mathis, Marie 34-35
McCall, Abner V. 38, 39
McCall, Duke 37-38, 61
McCarthy, John 117
McClune, Nancy 212
McDonald, Dorothy 217
McDonald, Roger 218
McHam, David 31, 33, 38, 45-47, 51, 65, 67-69, 72, 80, 200, 205, 336, 340
McGehee, Pittman 113
Miller, Tommy 4, 31, 171, 200
Mohler, Al 262
Mong, Bob 215
Moon, Lottie 277, 286, 290
Moore, Caroline Grace 7, 345
Moore, Grace 7, 170, 172
Moore, Marcie 7, 345
Moore, Matthew 7, 101, 112, 172, 187, 193, 268, 270-272, 275, 336, 338, 341, 345
Morkovsky, John 116, 128, 336
Mossler, Candace, Jacques 136
Moyers, Bill 53
Nall, Janet 80
Neumann, Tom 84
Nixon, Richard 94, 100
Newton, Jim 70-71, 138, 242
Oades, Bill & Peggy 212
Oates, Wayne 62-63, 125
O'Brien, Robert 147, 242, 272-273
Odle, Joe 62
O'Hair, Jon 125-126

O'Hair, Madalyn Murray 125-126
O'Hair, Richard 126
O'Hair, Robin 125-126
Orwell, George 166, 173, 323-324
Osteen, Joel 133
Osteen, John & Dodie 133
Oyler, Frances 7, 298
Page, Charles 230, 264-265, 336
Page, Sandra 230
Papillion, Lucy 309
Parmley, Helen 103-104, 120, 159, 183, 215
Patterson, Dorothy 171, 174, 178
Patterson, Paige 40, 148-150, 164-166, 171, 174-176, 181-186, 188, 190, 262, 284, 325, 337
Patterson, T.A. 150
Pattillo, Wesley M. "Pat" 52-53, 61, 64, 65, 72, 242, 247, 337
Paul VI, Pope 117
Pearle, Bob 316
Pederson, Tony 14, 198, 212
Phillips, Gene 311-312
Phillips, Jean 312
Piccard, Jeannette 173
Pickels, Don 67-72, 118, 162, 200, 284, 337
Powell, Bill 147, 164
Powers, Melvin Lane 136
Pressler, Nancy 15, 174, 177-178
Pressler, Paul III 15, 114, 137-138, 148-150, 158, 164-166, 168, 171-178, 181-186, 188, 190, 206-208, 219-220, 230, 236, 239-240, 243, 248, 325, 337
Pressler, Paul IV 177-178, 185
Pressley, Dewey 207-208
Preus, Jacob A.O., 41, 90-91, 95, 326
Preus, Robert 41, 326
Railey, Peggy, Walker 309
Rankin, Jerry 272-279, 281-285, 288-289, 291-294, 305, 307, 316-322, 337
Ratzinger, Joseph 105
Reed, Bill 99-101

Reynolds, Herbert 269-270, 338
Riley, Michael 206, 214, 222
Rios, Carlos Antonio 119-122
Robertson, Pat 308
Robison, James 133, 167, 169
Rogers, Adrian 142, 145, 147, 164, 168, 171-172, 174-176, 178, 181-183
Rogers, Joyce 178, 338
Roncalli, Angelo 308
Roosevelt, Franklin D. 28
Rosenblatt, George 95
Rowland, Tamara 79
Ruff, Frank 263
Schachtel, Hyman Judah 53
Seale, Mary Ann 212
Seals, Woodrow 142
Seelig, John Earl 52-53
Shackleford, Al 72, 242-244, 246, 248, 253
Shaw, David 104, 107
Sherman, Bill 181, 183, 185, 188
Sherman, Cecil 181, 183, 185, 187-188
Sloan, Robert 104-105, 336
Smith, Bailey 60, 158-172, 183-186, 242
Smith, Charles Merrell 294
Songer, Harold 57
Sullivan, James L. 42, 229
Summers, Ray 38-39
Templeton, John M. 102
Terry, Bob 65
Tietjen, Robert 90
Townes, E.E. 165
Turner, Bill 187, 192
Valentine, Foy 227
Vardaman, Jerry 62
Warner, Greg 253
Welch, Casey 7
Welch, Katie Moore 7, 161, 187, 193, 205, 268, 271-273, 307, 338
Welch, Mary Jane 278
Westbrook, John 45

Wheeler, H. Buford 7, 298, 307
Wheeler, J.D. 205, 271, 297, 306
Wheeler, Mable 7, 129, 297-298
White, Mark 84
White, Willie 48-49
Williams, Cecil 61
Williams, John 199, 204, 209-211
Willis, Avery 94, 288
Wilson, Milburn 4
Winkler, Mary, Matthew 310
Wojtela, Karol 118, 129
Wood, James E. 48
Yarborough, Larry 258
Young, Ed Sr. 207
Zollars, Betty 81-82, 86

Study Guide for Student Journalists

Witness to the Truth easily can be used as a springboard for discussion in a journalism-classroom setting. These discussion questions relate to the true story told in the previous chapters.

1. Was the newspaper correct in giving the reporter the green light to break the embargo on the Bailey Smith speech and release it before the religious group's annual meeting? Why or why not?

2. Was the reporter correct in assessing that being a newspaper reporter is a "young-person's profession"? Is this assessment true in today's practice? What can a reporter do to practically prepare himself/herself for the day in which younger, more recently trained journalists are entering the field as competitive factors?

3. What can a newspaper journalist do to prepare for the inevitable situation of transition such as buyouts or changes in management that impact the rank-and-file employee?

4. What are the inherent dangers of transitioning from the role of objective reporter to media person working inside a group he or she once covered?

5. What are some of the challenges that face a reporter covering a major event that is occurring within an institution with which he/she has personal connection? What steps can a reporter take to be sure he/she can remain objective in such a situation? How does a reporter brace for personal repercussions in such a situation?

6. Was the reporter correct in stopping the news source from revealing his own identity in an effort to remove the reporter from personal reprisal in the midst of the embargoed-speech story?

7. What are some of the personal challenges in which a reporter, having transitioned into a media role within an organization, finds himself/herself when spotting news stories while working inside an organization but not always being able to tip the news media to them?

8. The author touched on some serious impacts that the Texas Economic Recession of the 1980s had on the newspaper business in Texas. What are some ways that media is impacted by changing financial times now?

9. If a reporter found himself/herself in a situation as did the author— blackballed in front of professional colleagues before ever filling a job— what criteria should the reporter use to determine whether to continue to accept the assignment?

10. What role should a reporter's personal faith have in impacting his or her judgment on covering religious and ethical matters?

To order additional copies
of *Witness to the Truth*
contact:

Hannibal Books
PO Box 461592
Garland, Texas 75046-1592
Call: 1-800-747-0738
hannibalbooks@earthlink.net
visit: *www.hannibalbooks.com*

Printed in the United States
116525LV00001B/52-66/P